Barron's Review Course Series

Let's Review:

English

4th Edition

Carol Chaitkin, M.S.
Former Director of American Studies
Lycée Français de New York
New York, New York

Former English Department Head
Great Neck North High School
Great Neck, New York

BARRON'S

Acknowledgments

Page 89: "Pitcher" from *The Orb Weaver* by Robert Francis © 1960, Wesleyan University Press. By permission of University Press of New England.

Page 92: "Old Photograph of the Future" from *New and Selected Poems 1923–1985* by Robert Penn Warren © 1985. Reprinted by permission of Random House, Inc.

Page 94: "Child on Top of a Greenhouse" from *The Collected Poems of Theodore Roethke* by Theodore Roethke © 1946 by Editorial Publications, Inc. Used by permission of Doubleday, a division of Bantam Doubleday Dell Publishing Group, Inc.

Page 94: "The Sleeping Giant" from *Old and New Poems* © 1990 by Donald Hall. Reprinted by permission of Ticknor & Fields/Houghton Mifflin Company. All rights reserved.

Page 97: "Juke Box Love Song" from *Montage of a Dream Deferred* by Langston Hughes. Reprinted by permission of Harold Ober Associates Incorporated © 1951 by Langston Hughes. Renewed 1979 by George Houston Bass.

Page 99: "As You Say (Not Without Sadness), Poets Don't See, They Feel" from *Selected Poems* © 1964, 1985 Karl Shapiro by arrangement with Wieser & Wieser, Inc. New York.

Page 103: "The Bean Eaters" from *Blacks* by Gwendolyn Brooks © 1991, Third World Press, Chicago.

All inquiries should be addressed to:
Barron's Educational Series, Inc.
250 Wireless Boulevard
Hauppauge, NY 11788
www.barronseduc.com

ISBN-13: 978-0-7641-4208-6
ISBN-10: 0-7641-4208-9

Library of Congress Catalog Card Number: 2009045517

Library of Congress Cataloging-in-Publication Data

Library of Congress Cataloging-in-Publication Data

Chaitkin, Carol.
  Let's review : English / Carol Chaitkin. – 4th ed.
    p. cm. – (Barron's review course series)
  Includes bibliographical references and index.
  ISBN-13: 978-0-7641-4208-6 (alk. paper)
  ISBN-10: 0-7641-4208-9 (alk. paper)
  1. English language–Examinations–Study guides. I. Title.
  LB1631.5.C52 2010
  808'.042076--dc22

                          2009045517

PRINTED IN THE UNITED STATES OF AMERICA
9 8 7 6 5 4 3 2 1

TABLE OF CONTENTS

PREFACE TO THE FOURTH EDITION

Let's Review: English is designed as a handbook for high school English courses and as a review book to prepare students for the New York State Examination in Comprehensive English. *Let's Review* also offers students and teachers a detailed outline of the Regents Learning Standards for English Language Arts.

Because the Regents exam in English is not a test of a specific curriculum but an assessment of skills in reading, listening, literary analysis, and composition, *Let's Review* offers a comprehensive guide to essential language, literature, critical reading, and writing skills all high school students should seek to demonstrate as they prepare for college and the workplace.

HOW CAN THIS BOOK HELP ME?

First, *Let's Review* gives you a comprehensive review of the concepts, language, and skills you need to do well—and enjoy!—your high school or college courses in literature and composition. You will find everything from tips on how to study vocabulary to suggestions for writing about poetry, from tips on how to listen well to a helpful review of literary elements and techniques. There is a detailed index to help you find whatever you need. Second, *Let's Review* is specifically designed to help you prepare for the Regents exam. You will find a chapter for each part of the exam, with actual texts, questions, and answers from past Regents exams, and model essays and analysis.

QUESTIONS AND ANSWERS ABOUT THE COMPREHENSIVE EXAMINATION IN ENGLISH

What does the exam look like?

The exam is administered in **two sessions consisting of two parts** ("tasks") each, and **each includes an essay response**. The first three parts require you to listen to or read extended passages of informational text or literature, answer multiple-choice questions on those passages, and write an essay for a particular purpose and audience. For the fourth part you must write an essay of critical analysis and evaluation of two works of literature you have read. All written responses require effective use of language and standard written English.

How and when is the exam given?

The English Regents exam is completed over two days of three-hour sessions each, with two tasks per session. It is offered in January, June, and August of each year.

Why is the exam six hours long?

Each of the four tasks on the English Regents exam is designed to take most students about one hour to complete. The additional time gives you the opportunity to do your best work.

Why is doing well on this exam important to me?

Passing the English Regents exam is a requirement for a high school diploma in New York State.

WAYS TO USE *LET'S REVIEW: ENGLISH*

As a handbook for literature study in high school and college courses, see especially:

Chapter 3—Reading Prose
Chapter 4—Reading Poetry
Chapter 5—Writing About Literature: A General Review

As a handbook for writing, see especially:

Chapter 2—Reading and Writing for Information and Understanding
Chapter 5—Writing About Literature: A General Review
Chapter 7—Writing on Examinations
Chapter 8—Grammar and Usage for the Careful Writer
Chapter 9—Punctuation: Guidelines and Reminders

As a guide to listening, reading, and language skills, see especially:

Chapter 1—Listening and Writing for Information and Understanding
Chapter 2—Reading and Writing for Information and Understanding
Chapter 3—Reading Prose
Chapter 10—Vocabulary
Chapter 11—Spelling

As a review text for the English Regents exam, see especially:

Chapter 1—Listening and Writing for Information and Understanding: Session One, Part A of the Exam
Chapter 2—Reading and Writing for Information and Understanding: Session One, Part B of the Exam
Chapter 6—Writing About Literature on the Regents Examination: Session Two, Parts A and B of the Exam
Appendices A–E—The New York State English Language Arts Learning Standards
Appendix F—Scoring Rubrics
Regents Examinations

Chapter 1

LISTENING AND WRITING FOR INFORMATION AND UNDERSTANDING

People told stories long before they wrote them down. Although much of the oral tradition has been replaced by print and electronic media, students still learn a great deal simply by listening: to lectures, discussions, instructions—and to one another. Much of what we know has been acquired by listening.

HOW TO LISTEN WELL

As author and teacher William H. Armstrong points out, "While listening is the easiest and quickest . . . way to learn . . . it is the hardest of all the learning processes to master." Listening well requires a concentration and a discipline that allow you to "hold your mind on the track of the speaker." Here are some tips on how to do that:

How to Listen Well

If you are listening to a speech or a reading from a memoir, keep the following questions in mind:
What is this piece about? What is the main idea or purpose?
What does the author say? believe? recall? value? assert?
What does the author mean? imply? suggest? agree with? disagree with?
How are language and imagery used?
To what conclusions or inferences is the reader led?
What experience is meant to be shared and understood?
If you are listening to a lecture or a passage from a text, ask yourself:
What is the subject? What do I already know about this subject?
What main idea or theme is being developed? What phrases or terms signal the main thought?
What is the purpose? to inform? persuade? celebrate? guide? show a process? introduce a new or unfamiliar subject?

These questions summarize much of what is meant by comprehension. They summarize what we are meant to understand and appreciate. Keep them in mind as you listen to any kind of presentation, and use them as reminders of what to include when you take notes. You should also review them as you prepare for the listening and reading comprehension parts of the Regents exam.

The first part of the New York State Regents Comprehensive Examination in English is designed to assess skills in listening and writing for information and understanding. You are expected to analyze and interpret a passage by noting salient information and by drawing inferences. *Noting salient information* means noting the key ideas, the most significant points; *drawing inferences* means forming conclusions and general understandings to which the text leads.

In addition to answering six multiple-choice questions on key ideas, you must also be able to compose an extended written response that conveys, to a given audience for a given purpose, the information and understanding you have gained. The selected passages may come from speeches and memoirs, lectures, or texts on the arts, history, or social sciences. They are often passages with distinctive voices, which are meant to be heard.

LISTENING PASSAGES AND QUESTIONS FOR REVIEW

Below are two examples of listening passages from past Regents exams. Each is followed by multiple-choice questions and analysis. Use these questions to help you understand what is meant by the terms *salient information* and *drawing inferences*; note also the questions about vocabulary and literary elements or techniques. Sample listening and writing tasks from recent Regents exams follow these examples.

If possible, have someone read the passages to you while you take notes; then, compare your notes with the ideas and information featured in the questions.

Listening Passage A

The following is adapted from "Writing for Monkeys, Martians, and Children," by Sandy Asher.

As a child, I sensed there was something I desperately needed from books. As a writer for young readers, I've tried to figure out what that something was. It turned out to be a combination of three things: companionship, a sense of control, and magic.

First, companionship. Life can be a lonely journey, and adolescence the loneliest stretch of all. Books, novels, and stories are one way to reach out to one another without losing face, a way of saying, "We are all in this alone together." A story that reminds us of this can be the best friend a teenager has. The characters in that story understand—and they won't let you down.

A sense of control is the second thing we crave from books. Life is chaotic. Adults pretend to be in control, yet we're not. The minute we think we've got it all together, someone shoots down a plane full of innocent people, a child disappears without a trace, or we find out the last three things we ate, drank, or breathed cause cancer. Children and adults would go stark raving mad if they had to deal with life exactly as it comes. It's too hard, too fast, too overwhelming, and far too complex. Since the days of the cave dwellers, we've listened to and told stories as a way of making life hold still long enough for us to make sense of it, to decide where we fit in and what to do. Fiction is not a luxury. It is an absolute, sanity-preserving necessity.

Companionship, a sense of control, and finally, there's magic, the third ingredient in stories. Magic, the illusion of traveling outside oneself and into another life in another world, beyond the limits of probability and into the excitement of possibility. As a child, when I read a good book, I climbed inside and lived there and hated it when the time came to climb back out.

The magic doesn't really take place between the covers of a book; it actually takes place in the mind of the reader. It's our ability to imagine the impossible that makes the trick work. That's why we love great magicians and writers, not because they fool us, but because they remind us that the most wonderful, most unlimited, most miraculous thing of all is our own mind.

Magic, companionship, a sense of control. The wonder of ourselves, of each other, and of life—this is the true subject matter of all novels. The best children's literature speaks not only to children but to the human condition. Writing for children simply means writing for human beings in the beginning, when you can still take part in creation, before habit, cynicism, and despair have set in, and while there is still hope and energy, a willingness to learn, and a healthy sense of humor. These qualities I find irresistible in the young people I write about and for, qualities I want to hang onto and to cultivate in myself. So I write for children, not just for their sakes—but for my own.

MULTIPLE-CHOICE QUESTIONS

1 With which statement about adolescents would the speaker most likely agree?
   1 They should write books in order to understand themselves.
   2 They need to understand that life is often lonely.
   3 They see fiction as useless in their lives.
   4 They believe they are in control.

2 According to the speaker, some teenagers enjoy reading because
   1 books provide a sense of friendship
   2 books show that adults are not in control
   3 teenagers like to read about themselves
   4 teenagers can learn about the past

3 Air disasters and the disappearance of children are cited as evidence of
   1 loneliness in America
   2 the insanity of terrorists
   3 information we can obtain from reading
   4 our lack of control over events

4 The speaker implies that insanity is a threat because our lives are
   1 complex
   2 dreamlike
   3 lonely
   4 meaningless

5 According to the speaker, why do we love magic?
   1 We love to be entertained.
   2 We are mystified by it.
   3 It reminds us of our possibilities.
   4 It makes us feel less alone.

6 The speaker says we love great writers because they
1 answer our questions about life
2 make the impossible probable
3 show us the magic inside us
4 are able to fool us

7 According to the speaker, what is the true subject matter of novels?
1 an adult sense of control
2 the wonder of ourselves and of life
3 miraculous occurrences
4 ideas that appeal to children

8 According to the speaker, what does the best children's literature do?
1 It encourages children to write.
2 It creates the illusion of magic.
3 It projects hope for the future.
4 It represents the human condition.

9 The speaker implies that she benefits from writing children's books because she
1 retains and cultivates her youthful outlook
2 enjoys performing magic
3 feels rewarded in getting to know young people
4 likes sharing her knowledge and experiences

10 The speaker's purpose in writing this speech most likely is to
1 persuade us to read more books
2 explain her childhood addiction to reading
3 explain why she writes children's books
4 show how books can be our friends

LOOKING AT THE QUESTIONS: PASSAGE A

Note the key terms.

1 With which statement . . . would the *speaker most likely agree*?
(The answer should restate a point made by the speaker.)
2 "They need to understand that life is often lonely." The second paragraph is about the power of books to enable us to "reach out to one another . . . [to say] '[w]e are all in this alone together.' " It is easy to eliminate the other answers because none reflects a point made by the speaker.

2 *According to the speaker,* some teenagers enjoy reading because
(The answer requires recall of what the speaker actually said.)
1 "books provide a sense of friendship" The speaker states, "A story . . . can be the best friend a teenager has . . . . The characters . . . won't let you

down." Students should be cautioned that, while each of the other statements may in fact be true, none is specifically made in this passage.

3   Air disasters . . . are *cited as evidence of*
(The answer requires understanding *how specific details support* the speaker's point.)
4 "our lack of control over events" The second point the speaker develops is the theme, "Life is chaotic. Adults pretend to be in control." Again, students must be cautioned not to select answers that are generally true statements—or that express ideas they agree with—but rather to select answers that are supported by the passage itself.

4   The speaker *implies* that insanity is a threat because our lives are
(The answer requires stating explicitly what is suggested by the passage.)
1 "complex" This is a relatively easy connection to make because, as the speaker asserts, "[Life is] too hard, too fast . . . too complex," and because stories are a way of helping us "make sense of it. . . . Fiction is . . . an absolute, sanity-preserving necessity."

5   *According to the speaker,* why do we love magic?
3 "It reminds us of our possibilities." She says, "We love . . . magicians and writers . . . because they remind us that the . . . most miraculous thing of all is our own mind."

6   *The speaker says* we love great writers because they
3 "show us the magic inside us" This is a reiteration and emphasis of question 5 and its supporting passage. Choice 1, while true, is not the point the speaker is making; choice 2 must be rejected because writers do not make the impossible *probable*. Students must read the choices carefully and avoid selecting an answer simply because it includes a key term from the passage.

7   *According to the speaker,* what is the true subject matter of novels?
2 "the wonder of ourselves and of life" This is nearly a direct quote from the passage.

8   *According to the speaker,* what does the best children's literature do?
4 "It represents the human condition." This too is taken from the passage itself: "The best children's literature speaks . . . to the human condition."

9   *The speaker implies* that she benefits from writing children's books because she
1 "retains and cultivates her youthful outlook" As the passage comes to an end, the speaker *says*, "These qualities I find irresistible in the young people I write . . . for, qualities I want to hang onto and to cultivate in myself."

10 *The speaker's purpose* in writing this speech most likely is to
3 "explain why she writes children's books" Although she does indeed explain her "childhood addiction to reading," and she does show how books can be friends (and she might hope she has persuaded us to read more books), the title of the passage, the introduction, and the main clause in the concluding sentence, "So I write for children," make it clear that this is the overall purpose of the piece.

Comment

This is a good passage to begin a review with because it offers direct and clear organization. The opening paragraph reveals that she "sensed there was something I desperately needed from books" and that "it turned out to be a combination of three things." The listener expects to hear what those three things are, and each section begins with one of the key ideas and an indication of where we are in the discussion—"first, . . . second, . . . and finally."

The listening passages on the Regents exam will be longer and more complex than the passage above, both in language and in structure. *Recall, however, that you are expected to take notes during the reading.*

This second passage is from a speech by former Pittsburgh Steelers' football coach Chuck Noll about successful management techniques. The questions require both recall and interpretation.

Listening Passage B

As head coach, I didn't do very much differently from one year to the next. One thing I learned—and I learned it early—was not to single out a player for blame in public.

I once made the mistake of saying Mel Blount had missed an assignment on a key play. It was written up in the papers, and the fans booed Mel the rest of the season. I made sure I never did that again. When I felt the need to criticize a player, as often as possible I tried to do it in private. I didn't want it in the newspapers and didn't like doing it in front of the other players. I tried to keep that stuff, and anything else negative, behind closed doors.

One thing I stressed in speaking to the team was that nothing would bring us down quicker than complacency. I included myself in that warning. In the National Football League no one's job is secure. If you don't produce, you don't last. It doesn't matter what you accomplished in the past.

I did not believe in having a lot of rules, but we did have some—and the players were expected to obey them. And the rules were the same for everyone: that uniformity is the only way to have harmony. The rules weren't for punishment and weren't for the money we collected in fines. They were to keep everyone on the same page. I've heard about teams on which there are different sets of rules—one for the superstars and another, stricter, set of rules for the other players. That does more harm than good. It drives a wedge between players who have to work together on the field.

One time our star player, Joe Greene, went out for a pizza and missed our curfew by five minutes. I could have looked the other way and said, "Next time you do that, Joe, it will cost you." But it wouldn't have been fair to the players who abided by the curfew. Instead, I said, "That pizza will cost you fifty dollars, Joe."

He paid the fine without protest.

In any business, consistency is important. If one group of workers feels another group is getting special privileges, whether it is longer lunch breaks or better parking spaces, it's bound to cause friction that will interfere with production. As the person on top, you make the rules—so you'd better apply them fairly and wisely.

The bottom line is that if you do a good job picking your people, as we did in the 1970's, you don't need a bunch of rules, because the people are able to handle things. Also, it helps if you have quality leaders on your team to keep everyone in line. We had some excellent leaders, particularly Greene and Jack Lambert, our middle linebacker. Like Greene, Lambert was a leader almost from the first day he arrived at training camp in 1974.

We had a lot of focused individuals on our championship teams, but Lambert was the most demonstrative. He did not tolerate any fooling around, even in practice. If someone made a silly mistake or cracked a joke in the huddle, Lambert jumped right in his face. As a coach, I loved having a player like that.

There's a lot to be said for that kind of leadership within the ranks. That is the Japanese concept of management: not a dictatorship where one man at the top says, "This is how it's going to be," but a system in which all parties at all levels work together.

That was how we operated in Pittsburgh. As head coach, I relied a great deal on my assistant coaches; as a staff, we relied on the leaders within the ball club to keep things together. Everyone shared in the responsibility—so when we won, everyone shared in the team's success.

One of the worst things you can do, either as a coach or a corporate head, is take an idea and try to jam it down the throats of your staff or players. Ideas, even good ones, have to be sold to the team first, then objectively evaluated on the field.

In football—and this distinction applies in business as well—there is the "what to do" and the "how to do it." The first part is the plan, what you have on paper or in your head. The second part is the application: how your idea actually works on the field. Some people would say the first part is the most important because without a plan, you have nothing. I think the second part is most important because that is where your team gets its confidence. A plan isn't worth a thing if the team isn't sold on its merits.

This is where, as a coach or a boss, you have to put your ego aside. In football there is no pride of authorship. Only one thing matters: getting the job done. So if you come up with an idea that you think is brilliant, but when you put it on the field, the players cannot grasp it or they don't have the speed or whatever to make it work, the worst thing you can do is say, "I don't care. This is my idea and we're going to make it work." Well, it won't work, and it also will cost you respect in the eyes of your coaches and players.

Good management involves give-and-take. Your job as head coach is to give the team its best chance to win through preparation. That means coming up with a game plan the players can believe in, not one that creates doubt. We did well as a football team because as coaches, we eliminated—or at least minimized—doubt. As a result, our guys played with a lot of confidence and aggressiveness: they believed in the plan and believed in each other. They believed they were going to win, regardless of the opposition.

MULTIPLE-CHOICE QUESTIONS

1 The speaker implies that allowing star players more privileges than other players is likely to
   1 inspire the other players
   2 discourage team unity
   3 ensure a successful season
   4 embarrass the star players

2 According to the speaker, coaches will need fewer rules if they
   1 hire the right players
   2 establish clear penalties
   3 set appropriate goals
   4 demonstrate the correct procedures

3 The speaker considered Jack Lambert a good leader because Lambert
   1 made important decisions
   2 designed strategies
   3 worked hard
   4 kept everyone focused

4 The statement "In football there is no pride of authorship" means that
   in football no individual should
   1 claim credit for a success
   2 create a plan for the players
   3 feel proud after a game
   4 expect praise for a victory

5 The speaker implies that if the players cannot understand a plan, the
   coach should
   1 retrain the players
   2 eliminate the assistant
   3 replace the manager
   4 abandon the plan

6 What technique does the speaker use to develop the speech?
   1 definitions of sports terms
   2 a chronology of his career
   3 anecdotes about players
   4 a list of his achievements

LOOKING AT THE QUESTIONS: PASSAGE B

Note the key terms

1 **2** *The speaker implies* that allowing star players more privileges . . . is
   likely to "discourage team unity." The first section of the speech offers
   several examples of how and why the speaker acted on the principle
   that "the rules were the same for everyone; that uniformity is the only
   way to have harmony." He also says that, in business, allowing one
   group more privileges than others is "bound to cause friction that will
   interfere with production."

2 **1** *According to the speaker,* coaches will need fewer rules if they "hire
   the right players." The speaker says, "The bottom line is that if you do
   a good job picking your people . . . you don't need a bunch of rules,
   because people are able to handle things."

3 **4** *The speaker considered* Jack Lambert a good leader because Lambert "kept everyone focused." In discussing Lambert, the speaker says, "We had a lot of focused individuals on our championship teams, but Lambert was the most demonstrative. He did not tolerate any fooling around, even in practice . . . I loved having a player like that."

4 **1** *The statement* "In football there is no pride of authorship" *means* that . . . no individual should "claim credit for a success." Just before this statement, the speaker says, ". . . as a coach or a boss, you have to put your ego aside. . . . Only one thing matters: getting the job done."

5 **4** *The speaker implies* that if the players cannot understand a plan, the coach should "abandon the plan." The speaker makes this point indirectly when he says that "the worst thing" a coach or leader can do is insist on a plan that players don't understand or can't execute—". . . it won't work, and it also will cost you respect in the eyes of your coaches and players."

6 **3** *What technique* does the speaker use to develop the speech? "anecdotes about players." The first half of the speech is a series of examples involving particular players: Mel Blount, Joe Greene, and Jack Lambert; he concludes the speech with reference to the players and coaches: "We did well as a football team. . . ."

The two passages and sets of questions above are a good introduction to what is expected in comprehension of the listening passages on the Regents exam. In the next section, you will find additional examples of actual exam passages and tasks, with model student essays.

SESSION ONE, PART A: LISTENING AND WRITING FOR INFORMATION AND UNDERSTANDING

In this first part of the Regents exam you are applying skills that you use daily, in nearly every subject you study. The listening passages on the Regents exam range in length from 750 to 1000 words or more and require ten to fifteen minutes of careful listening. <u>You may take notes at any time during the reading</u>. The author and the source of the passage are identified before it is read, and this helps you anticipate the sense and tone of what you are about to hear. The purpose and audience for the written response will also be indicated and should guide you in taking notes.

Sample Passages, Tasks, Questions, and Essays

SAMPLE TASK I

Overview: For this part of the test, you will listen to a speech about the Dust Bowl, answer some multiple-choice questions, and write a response based on the situation described below. You will hear the speech twice. You may take notes on the next page anytime you wish during the readings.

The Situation: For a school library exhibit recognizing National Environmental Awareness Month, your science class is writing essays about historical events that changed people's attitudes toward the environment. You have decided to write your essay on the Dust Bowl that occurred in the Plains States from 1931 to 1939. In your essay, you will describe the Dust Bowl and explain how that event changed people's attitudes about the environment. In preparation for writing your essay, listen to an excerpt from a television documentary on the Dust Bowl. Then use relevant information from the documentary to write your essay.

Listening Passage

In 1931 there was no better place to be a farmer than the Southern Plains. The rest of the nation was in the grip of the Great Depression, but in wheat country they were reaping a record-breaking crop. Plains farmers had turned untamed prairie into one of the most prosperous regions in the country. Confident of rain, unmindful of wind, they plowed mile after mile of virgin sod. Millions of acres of grassland would feel the plow for the first time. Appearing like giant armored bugs creeping along the horizon, tractors came to the fields in the 1920s.

Whirlwinds had always danced across the fields on hot, dry days. No one took much notice that these swirls of dust were growing thicker, taller, and faster than usual. Then in the summer of 1931, the rains stopped. Wheat withered in the fields, leaving the land naked and vulnerable to the menacing winds.

As dust enveloped the atmosphere, breathing became difficult. The Red Cross issued an urgent call for dust masks, especially for children. Residents grabbed any bits of cloth to cover their faces. Where grain once grew high as a man's shoulder, dazed farmers walked out over their beaten, blown-out fields. It had taken a thousand years to build an inch of topsoil on the Southern Plains. It took only minutes for one good blow to sweep it all away. One hundred million acres of the Southern Plains were turning into a wasteland. A journalist traveling through the region called it the Dust Bowl.

The drought persisted, made worse by some of the hottest summers on record. Windmills provided drinking water from deep wells, but the fields were bone dry. For farmers it was going on three years of planting with little to show for it. The hard times were beginning to take their toll. Outside the Southern Plains, few grasped the full measure of the disaster. In Washington, the Dust Bowl was seen as just another trouble spot in the nationwide crisis of the Depression. The Government began offering relief, and most people had no choice but to suffer the humiliation of relief checks and food handouts. Piece by piece, farmers were losing everything they cherished.

April 14, 1935 was the worst day of them all, the day no Dust Bowler would forget—the day they would call "Black Sunday." As the dark clouds approached, there was an ominous silence. Minutes later, the stillness was shattered by thousands of birds fleeing before the avalanche of dirt. Terrified residents tried to drive through blinding dust. One Kansas farmer, disoriented, drove his car off the road. Searchers found him the next day, suffocated. Living on the Plains was becoming an act of sheer will.

The dust was beginning to make living things sick. Animals were found dead in the fields, their stomachs coated with two inches of dirt. An epidemic raged throughout the Plains. They called it dust pneumonia. In 1935, one-third of the deaths in Ford County, Kansas, resulted from pneumonia. Children were especially vulnerable.

By the end of 1935, with no substantial rainfall in four years, Dust Bowlers watched as their neighbors and friends picked up and headed west in search of farm jobs in California. As people abandoned the Southern Plains, tight-knit rural communities began to unravel. Banks and businesses failed. Schools shut their doors. Churches were boarded up.

As the drought wore on, there were some who claimed that Plains farmers themselves held the key to their own survival. The father of soil conservation, Hugh Bennett, was the leader of a new breed of agricultural experts. He argued that conservation techniques could restore farming to the Southern Plains.

Bennett took his case to lawmakers on Capitol Hill. As he was about to testify, he learned that a great dust storm was heading towards the East Coast. He managed to keep the committee in session until the dark gloom settled on Washington. "This, gentlemen," he announced, "is what I have been talking about." For the first time Easterners smelled, breathed, and tasted the dust blowing off the Southern Plains.

Previously, the Federal Government had regarded the soil as a limitless, indestructible resource. In a major shift, Washington now put its full weight and authority behind soil conservation. Panicked by the flood of penniless refugees heading to the West Coast, a Government report warned, "for its own sake, the nation cannot allow farmers to fail." In 1937, Washington began an aggressive campaign to encourage Dust Bowlers to adopt planting and plowing methods that conserved the soil. Once again farmers ran their tractors from dawn to dark, this time to prevent barren fields from blowing. In 1938, the massive conservation crusade had reduced the amount of blowing soil by 65 percent. But the drought dragged on. The proud settlers of the Plains were becoming dependent on Government work projects for survival.

In the spring of 1939, after the failure of seven wheat crops in eight years, more farmers abandoned their farms and fled, convinced that the Dust Bowl was creating an American Sahara. Six months later, the skies finally opened and nearly a decade of dirt and dust came to an end. With the return of the rain, dry fields soon overflowed with golden wheat.

The harsh years of the Dust Bowl had forced farmers to accept the limits of the land. But with fortunes to be made once more on the Southern Plains, that wisdom would soon be tested. One farmer was hopeful about the future. "People are thinking differently about taking care of the land," he said. "Don't fool yourself," another replied. "You can't convince me we've learned our lesson. It's just not in our blood to play a safe game."

MULTIPLE-CHOICE QUESTIONS

Directions (1–6): Use your notes to answer the following questions about the passage read to you. Select the best suggested answer and write its number in the space provided on the answer sheet. The questions may help you think about ideas and information you might use in your writing. You may return to these questions anytime you wish.

1 The speaker implies that in 1931 the attitude of Southern Plains farmers toward the future was one of
   1 acceptance
   2 curiosity
   3 impatience
   4 optimism

2 According to the speaker, one condition that contributed to the disappearance of topsoil was a lack of
   1 moisture
   2 sunlight
   3 air
   4 heat

3 The speaker implies that when Dust Bowl conditions first appeared, the government's reaction was one of
   1 distrust
   2 fear
   3 indifference
   4 anger

4 The speaker indicates that as a consequence of Hugh Bennett's arguments, farmers began to
   1 install irrigation systems
   2 change planting methods
   3 obtain governmental loans
   4 leave their farms

5 The speaker implies that soil conservation techniques were responsible for an increase in
   1 available moisture
   2 harvested wheat
   3 useable topsoil
   4 Plains settlers

6 According to the speaker, the Dust Bowl taught farmers to view the land as
   1 fragile
   2 friendly
   3 powerless
   4 profitable

LOOKING AT THE QUESTIONS

Note the key terms

1 **4** *The speaker implies* that in 1931 the attitude of Southern Plains farmers toward the future was one of "optimism." The opening of the passage declares that, in contrast to the rest of Depression-era America, "there was no better place to be a farmer than the Southern Plains." Farmers were ". . . confident of rain, unmindful of wind. . . . "

2 **1** *According to the speaker,* [one factor] in the disappearance of top-soil was a lack of "moisture." ". . . in the summer of 1931, the rains stopped." This is followed by an extended description of the drought that persisted for several years.

3 **3** *The speaker implies* that when Dust Bowl conditions first appeared, the government's reaction was one of "indifference." The speaker asserts that outside of the Southern Plains region, "few grasped the full measure of the disaster. In Washington . . . [this] was just another trouble spot. . . . " The passage makes no reference to distrust, fear, or anger from the government.

4 **2** *The speaker indicates that* as a consequence of Hugh Bennett's arguments, farmers began to "change planting methods." The passage points out that by 1937, Washington "began an aggressive campaign [for] planting and plowing methods that conserved the soil. . . . " There is no reference to irrigation systems or government loans. Many farmers left their land because they could not survive, not because of Hugh Bennett's arguments.

5 **3** *The speaker implies* that soil conservation techniques were responsible for an increase in "useable topsoil." The passage points out that the "massive conservation crusade . . . reduced the amount of blowing soil." That is, because less blew away, more remained to be cultivated. Because the drought persisted, however, wheat crops continued to fail and settlers abandoned their farms.

6 **1** *According to the speaker*, the Dust Bowl taught farmers to view the land as "fragile." The passage concludes by pointing out that after the harsh years of the Dust Bowl, farmers were forced to "accept the limits of the land" and to think about "taking care of the land."

> **Your Task:** Write an essay for a school library exhibit recognizing National Environmental Awareness Month in which you describe the Dust Bowl and explain how that event changed people's attitudes about the environment.

16

Guidelines:
Be sure to

- Tell your audience what they need to know about the Dust Bowl and explain how that event changed people's attitudes about the environment
- Use specific, accurate, and relevant information from the speech to support your explanation
- Use a tone and level of language appropriate for a school library exhibit
- Organize your ideas in a logical and coherent manner
- Indicate any words taken directly from the speech by using quotation marks or referring to the source
- Follow the conventions of standard written English

Sample Student Response Essay

Americans have long depended on domestic agriculture to produce essential crops. In the early twentieth century, farmers took advantage of the fertile southern plains to grow wheat in particular. However, the nation's disregard for the health of the land would soon take a toll on the state of agriculture and on the lives of the farmers themselves. In the 1930s, farmers learned the hard way that the environment needs care just as the crops do.

Just before a long period of drought began in 1931, wheat farming in the central plains was at its height. Tractors had recently been introduced and untouched prairie land stretched by the mile. While the rest of the nation struggled with the Depression, to the southern plains wheat farmers the future seemed limitless. Then, in the summer of 1931, the rain stopped. With so much flat, open land plowed and the wheat withered by drought, the rich topsoil was totally unprotected from the relentless wind.

It was a journalist traveling through the area who came up with the phrase "Dust Bowl." He left us with lasting images of the quality of the air. These included the Red Cross distributing dust masks and residents covering their noses and mouths with cloths. As the drought wore on and the summers stayed hot, farmers suffered tremendous losses. The federal government, already overwhelmed by the effects of the Depression, only acted to issue relief checks and food handouts to the farmers. Then came Black Sunday, April 14, 1935. On that day, an avalanche of dust blew through the plains, darkening the skies and temporarily blinding residents. One Kansas farmer drove off the road and suffocated in the polluted air.

Following that event, farmers and their families began to leave in earnest. Banks, businesses, and schools closed. Whole commu-

nities dissolved. Of those who stayed, many grew sick with "dust pneumonia" and other lung diseases. Animals died in great numbers as their stomachs became coated with inches of dust.

At last, the issue of soil conservation was raised. Hugh Bennett, as spokesman for a new group of farming experts, brought his ideas on how to save the Plains to Washington. Luckily, Bennett timed his testimony to last until the effects of a dust storm blowing from the west reached Washington. The federal government was convinced of the need to support a program for soil conservation. Once again, the plowing and planting began in the Southern Plains, this time using methods designed to restore and conserve the topsoil. By 1938, this effort had reduced the amount of soil blown away by 65%. But still there was no rain.

Toward the end of 1939, when the rain finally returned, enough rich soil was there and ready to receive it. Soon the fields overflowed with wheat again, though the human losses were not so easily forgotten.

Did the farmers learn their lesson? Did they learn to accept the limits of the land? One farmer quoted in the documentary was hopeful, saying, "People are thinking differently about taking care of the land." Another was more doubtful when he said, "You can't convince me we've learned our lesson. It's just not in our blood to play it safe." If nothing else, this time in our history at least got people thinking about the need to protect a fragile and limited resource. The experience of the Dust Bowl taught Americans that careless exploitation of the environment may lead to disaster.

Analysis

This essay meets the expectations of the task very well. The writer offers a vivid summary of the period in history known as the Dust Bowl by citing specific and relevant details from the documentary text; the essay also clearly shows how people's attitudes were affected by environmental disaster. [Many students were also likely to recall this period from their study of history and perhaps from their reading of *The Grapes of Wrath*, by John Steinbeck.]

The essay is coherent: There is an introduction that establishes the historical context and, in the last sentence, asserts the broader theme for the task. The body of the essay follows the logic of the passage and remains focused on the topic of learning from the Dust Bowl experience. The writer develops the ideas effectively, using many of the details from the text. The conclusion is especially good because it shows very clearly how this particular historical event "changed people's attitudes toward the environment."

The writer successfully echoes the dramatic tone of the text and uses language that is informative and persuasive. The writer is also skillful in varying sentence structure, notably in the dramatic use of brief assertions within the narrative style: "Then came Black Sunday, April 14, 1935." "Whole communities dissolved." The use of rhetorical questions to begin the concluding paragraph is also very effective. The writer demonstrates control of the conventions with no significant errors. This essay meets the criteria for a high score in all respects.

SAMPLE TASK II

Overview: For this part of the test, you will listen to a speech about the importance of music and art in people's lives, answer some multiple-choice questions, and write a response based on the situation described below. You will hear the speech twice. You may take notes on the next page anytime you wish during the readings.

The Situation: Some schools in your region are considering the possibility of cutting arts education programs from the school curriculum for financial reasons. You have decided to write a letter to the editor of your local newspaper arguing for the importance of an education in the arts. In preparation for writing your letter, listen to poet Samuel Hazo, speaking to a 1997 statewide meeting of music educators. Then use relevant information from the speech to write your letter. (Regents examination, August 2000)

Listening Passage

I begin on a personal note. My son majored in music education at Duquesne University and was graduated with a citation as the most outstanding senior in that field. After graduation he went on to teach in two different high school musical education programs. Then I shared with him a grim period when musical education programs in which he was involved both as a teacher and band director were cut back. The question I asked then and ask now is why, when economies are called for, are the arts the first to be targeted? Instead of striking up the bands in our country, why are we determined to strike them down—and all in the name of prudence and fiscal wisdom?

Let us remember that the word "economics" comes from the Greek word meaning "house management." What kind of good house management is it to deprive a family of that which is central to its cultural life in the name of economics? Above all, why should music be the first to be evicted, for heaven's sake? Why not science, mathematics, hygiene and so on? Personally I'm against

19

any cuts in education across the board, but I have yet to receive an intelligent explanation that justifies penalizing students by depriving them of an artistic education, especially in music. I think I would be somewhat pacified if those who advocate things like the death of music programs would be willing to drop music from their own lives as totally as they would wish it done in schools— no stereo in the home, no opera, no symphonies, no jazz, no music in the car, no CD's, no singing in the shower, no music whatever.

The absurdity of this suggestion answers itself. Unless you are a total troglodyte, a life without music is like a life without oxygen. If it is difficult for a normal adult to imagine a life without music, why is not the cutting out of music programs from the educational curriculum regarded with indignation, shock, and even rage? Is it because the so-called practical programs and technology-related studies are regarded as being ultimately more lucrative? Is it not the responsibility of true educators to resist trendy pressures and enticements and stand up for those values that enhance a student's imaginative and cultural life regardless of what consequences this may have in later life? In other words, does it square with education itself to eliminate what any intelligent educator or administrator would be forced to acknowledge as the heart of education itself, namely, the nurturing of the imagination?

Thomas Jefferson, President of the United States, President and founder of the University of Virginia, framer of the Virginia statutes, author of the Declaration of Independence, was also an inventor, a musician and the author of poetry in English, Latin and Greek. He believed that a total education was rooted in memory, reason and imagination. Translated into a curriculum, this means schooling in history, philosophy and the arts. This is not vocational training. This is not the in-servicing of technicians. This is not short-changing people of those disciplines that mark a liberally educated man or woman, but educating them to be aware that dreaming or imagining the world anew and then realizing those imaginings are what makes living a daily and ongoing drama of creation.

As much as I respect history and right reasoning, I must admit that I am partial to the imagination. Why? Because I believe that everything—repeat *everything*—originates there. I referred earlier to the Declaration of Independence. Where did it originate except in Thomas Jefferson's imagination? Where did Shakespeare's plays originate except in Shakespeare's imagination? We can trace Disney World to one man who years ago imagined a cartoon involving a talking mouse named Mickey, who in time created the whole empire. Where does everything, from the languages we speak or write down to the way we are dressed right now, originate but in the imagination of the many, the few, or you or me? The imagination is the primal source of all that we do. And it is only the arts—dance, painting, poetry, music and so on—that permit the imagination to mature. And yet, amazingly, it is the arts that have been made the undeserved and unexpected enemies of those who believe that saving money by depriving the arts of funding—especially government funding—is simply good bottom-line thinking.

But the bottom line is not everything. There is such a thing as the top line—rarely mentioned but much more important. Without the top line, there would be no bottom line. The top line is concerned with visions, not costs, with what is in the best interest of the young, regardless of the bearable burden it places on their elders. Fathers and mothers who sacrifice for their children would have no argument with this; they would understand its meaning immediately. They know what it is to sacrifice for the good of their children, and they know what the consequences would be if they didn't. Why can we not expect the same spirit from those who are elected and entrusted with the public good? If we educate people "on the cheap," what can we expect but a cheapened adult population in a cheapened society governed by cheapening national policies and attitudes. I, for one, believe that the cheapening of our national values must be reversed. Let those who say that the government should get out of our lives recall the section of the Constitution that stipulates that civic leadership should provide for the common defense, promote the general welfare, and seek the blessings of peace for ourselves and our posterity. I contend that nothing promotes the general welfare and seeks the blessings of peace better than the arts. And of all the arts, music stands alone as the ultimate unifier.

I think it is regrettable that many who believe in the importance of music in the formal education of students often feel compelled to defend it in terms of how it enhances life in other areas. But music needs no justification for its existence other than that existence itself. Does the beautiful need any other justification outside of itself? The hunger for beauty, like the hunger for music and knowledge, is part of our very natures; it touches us. We don't learn because our learning will someday "pay off." We learn because it fulfills us, satisfies our curiosity, delivers us from ignorance. And that's enough.

I believe that educating students with an appreciation for music or, better yet, with the talent and skill to make music is one of the crowns of learning. Like poetry, music puts us in touch with our feelings. Being in touch with one's self, being capable of being alone and enjoying one's company for a time, being moved to feel what one would not otherwise feel—how can any intelligent parent, teacher or, above all, political representative find fault with this? On the contrary, are these not goals that should be abundantly and continually supported?

Contributing to the arts really is contributing to our national wealth. Not doing so is engaging in a conspiracy against our own greatness. And it is this greatness—past and present—that defines American culture at its best. It is what we have to share with one another and the world. What do we do for those who study here or who merely visit our country, but expose them to the national heroes of our past and present who have created our architecture, our poetry and literature, our fine arts, our music?

Excising arts programs from our educational and cultural life is not only shortsighted. It is suicidal. We are literally killing our spiritual selves if we do so.

MULTIPLE-CHOICE QUESTIONS

1 The speaker refers to the derivation of the word "economics" to suggest that cutting arts education programs is an example of
   1 false analogy
   2 poor management
   3 family survival
   4 local control

2 The speaker argues that the purpose of education is to
   1 nurture the imagination
   2 stimulate the economy
   3 preserve tradition
   4 encourage competition

3 The speaker mentions Jefferson, Shakespeare, and Disney to emphasize the
   1 similarity in their backgrounds
   2 differences in their status
   3 impact of their contributions
   4 source of their creativity

4 According to the speaker, an emphasis on "bottom-line thinking" has the effect of
1 strengthening industry
2 focusing education
3 cheapening society
4 reducing unemployment

5 The speaker refers to the Constitution to emphasize that the arts have the potential to promote
1 reason
2 unity
3 security
4 individualism

6 According to the speaker, the United States is defined by its
1 youth
2 visitors
3 heroes
4 art

LOOKING AT THE QUESTIONS

Note the key terms

1 **2** *The speaker refers* to the derivation of the word "economics" *to suggest* that cutting art education . . . is an example of "poor management." The speaker follows the reminder that "economics" means "house management," by saying, "What kind of good house management is it to deprive a family of that which is central to its cultural life in the name of economics." He makes no reference to analogy nor to local control or family survival.

2 **1** *The speaker argues* that the purpose of education is to "nurture the imagination." Following the passage in which the speaker emphasizes the absurdity of life without music and the importance for educators to support "those values that enhance a student's imaginative and cultural life . . . ," he says, ". . . does it square with education itself to eliminate . . . the heart of education itself, namely, the nurturing of the imagination?"

3 **4** *The speaker mentions* Jefferson, Shakespeare, and Disney to *emphasize the* "source of their creativity." In each of the examples— Jefferson, Shakespeare, Disney—the speaker emphasizes the role of imagination as the source of their creativity and great contributions. While the significance of their contributions is implied, the speaker stresses what inspired them, not the impact of those contributions.

23

There is no discussion of similarity in background nor of differences in status.

4   **3** *According to the speaker*, an emphasis on "bottom-line thinking" has the effect of "cheapening society." In the section of the speech in which the speaker explains why "the bottom line is not everything," he says, "If we educate people 'on the cheap,' what can we expect but a cheapened adult population in a cheapened society governed by cheapening national policies and attitudes."

5   **2** *The speaker refers* to the Constitution *to emphasize* that the arts have the potential to promote "unity." The speaker refers to the Constitution to remind his audience that "civic leadership should provide for the <u>common</u> defense, promote the <u>general</u> welfare, and seek the blessings of peace for ourselves and our posterity." He closes that part of the argument with the assertion that, "of all the arts, music stands alone as the ultimate unifier."

6   **4** *According to the speaker*, the United States is defined by its "art." The speaker concludes the speech with an assertion that American culture at its best is our greatness: "It is what we have to share with one another and the world." "Art" representing that culture, is the best answer. He refers to "national heroes," but as those who have created our cultural greatness. He does not refer to youth nor to visitors as those who define us.

The questions can also help you think about ideas and information you might want to use in completing the essay below:

Your Task: Write a letter to the editor of your local newspaper in which you argue for the importance of an education in the arts. Write only the body of the letter.

Guidelines:
Be sure to

- Tell your audience what they need to know to be persuaded of the value of an education in the arts
- Use specific, accurate, and relevant information from the speech to support your argument
- Use a tone and level of language appropriate for a letter to the editor of the local newspaper
- Organize your ideas in a logical and coherent manner

• Indicate any words taken directly from the speech by using quotation marks or referring to the speaker
• Follow the conventions of standard written English

Sample Student Response Essay

The issue of cutting educational art programs in order to meet budget demands has prompted concern throughout the community. Opposition to the cuts has been strong, most notably among students like myself who currently participate in the art programs at the high school. We've performed in the plays, marched in the bands, shown our work at the exhibits, and danced in the recitals. We've experienced the benefits of an education in the arts. We've felt our imaginations being challenged, directed, and inspired, and we know our minds, our lives, and maybe even our souls are the better for it. Can you, our elected officials, tell us what benefit there could possibly be in eliminating these programs? In your attempt to cut costs from the budget, please consider what you are asking future students to sacrifice.

Poet Samuel Hazo stated in a speech given to music teachers: "a life without music is like life without oxygen." Indeed music, as well as any of the arts, nourishes the imagination just as oxygen nourishes life. In these modern times, when it seems practically anything can be made to appear on a computer screen, the power of the imagination may seem obsolete. However, would the computer exist if the imagination had been limited by budget cuts?

Think for a moment of our nation's most valued treasures. Can't we trace almost all of them to the singular brilliance of someone's imagination? Didn't our prized Declaration of Independence begin in the imagination of Thomas Jefferson? This multitalented president was an inventor, a musician, and a writer who wrote poetry in three languages. When young children are asked to make a wish, what do they wish for? A trip to Disney World, of course! Didn't the entire Disney empire begin when a man imagined a cartoon mouse? Without imagination, knowledge is lifeless. Without the study of the arts, how can the imagination thrive?

I strongly urge you, our elected officials, and the community as a whole, to reconsider the proposed budget cuts. Furthermore, as you do so, I ask that you try an experiment. Choose any one day before the budget vote, and on that day exclude any and all music from your life: no radio, no tapes, no CDs, no singing. Experience the emptiness; then, cast your ballot.

Analysis

This letter meets the demands of the task very well: to compose a persuasive essay arguing against proposed cuts in arts education programs. The writer reveals an in-depth analysis of the speech by offering both key details from the speaker's argument and examples of the writer's own experiences in arts programs in school. The writer first establishes the importance of arts in education and then makes a dramatic and skillful plea to elected officials to "consider what you are asking future students to sacrifice." The letter also makes skillful use of the speaker's own rhetorical strategy in suggesting that those who would vote to eliminate these programs consider what life without music would be like.

The strength of the letter is in its focus and coherent argument even though it does not develop all of the ideas suggested in the speech, the threat of cheapening our values, for example. The language is mature, precise, and effective for the task. The writer also makes excellent use of transitions and phrases that address the intended audience directly. Finally, the writer demonstrates skill in varying sentence structure and reveals command of the conventions. This letter meets the criteria for a high score.

The third sample is also from a past Regents exam. In this instance, the text is excerpted from commentary by historian David McCullough for a television documentary on the influenza epidemic of 1918. The questions that follow are meant to assess your understanding of the historical material and its implications. These questions also serve to suggest ideas for the written task, which is to write a position paper arguing that World War I may have contributed to the spread of the epidemic.

SAMPLE TASK III

Overview: For this part of the test, you will listen to an account of the influenza epidemic of 1918, answer some multiple-choice questions, and write a response based on the situation described below. You will hear the account twice. You may take notes on the next page anytime you wish during the readings.

The **Situation:** Your social studies class has been studying World War I and its effects on civilians in America. For a final project, you have decided to prepare a position paper in which you argue that World War I may have contributed to the spread of the influenza epidemic of 1918. In preparation for writing your position paper, listen to this account of the epidemic taken from a PBS broadcast narrated by David McCullough. Then use relevant information from the account to write your position paper.

Listening Passage

In 1918, the United States was a vigorous young nation, leading the world into the modern age. All our fears and anxieties were directed toward Europe, where [World War I] raged; at home, we were safe. . . .

Some say [the influenza epidemic] began in the spring of 1918, when soldiers at Fort Riley, Kansas, burned tons of manure. A gale kicked up. A choking duststorm swept out over the land—a stinging, stinking yellow haze. The sun went dead black in Kansas.

Two days later—on March 11th, 1918—an Army private reported to the camp hospital before breakfast. He had a fever, sore throat, headache . . . nothing serious. One minute later, another soldier showed up. By noon, the hospital had over a hundred cases; in a week, 500.

That spring, forty-eight soldiers—all in the prime of life—died at Fort Riley. The cause of death was listed as pneumonia. . . .

That summer and fall, over one and a half million Americans crossed the Atlantic for war. But some of those doughboys came from Kansas. And they'd brought something with them: a tiny, silent companion.

Almost immediately, the Kansas sickness resurfaced in Europe. American soldiers got sick. English soldiers. French. German. As it spread, the microbe mutated—day by day becoming more and more deadly.

By the time the silent traveller came back to America, it had become a relentless killer. . . .

When the strange new disease was finally identified, it turned out to be a very old and familiar one: influenza: the flu. But it was unlike any flu that any one had ever seen.

[According to] Dr. Alfred Crosby, author [of], "America's Forgotten Pandemic," "One of the factors that made this so particularly frightening was that everybody had a preconception of what the flu was: it's a miserable cold and, after a few days, you're up and around. This was a flu that put people into bed as if they'd been hit with a 2 [by] 4, that turned into pneumonia, that turned people blue and black and killed them. It was a flu out of some sort of a horror story. They never had dreamed that influenza could ever do anything like this to people before."

Soldiers carried the disease swiftly from one military base to the next. They did it . . . just by breathing.

If an individual with influenza were standing in front of a room full of people coughing, each cough would carry millions of particles with disease-causing organisms into the air. All the people breathing that air would have an opportunity to inhale a disease-causing organism. It doesn't take very long for one case to become 10,000 cases. . . .

There were two enormously important things going on at once and they were at right angles to each other. One, of course, was the influenza epidemic, which dictated that you should sort of shut everything down and the war which demanded that everything should speed up, that certainly the factories should continue operating, you should continue to have bond drives, soldiers should be put on boats and sent off to France. . . . It's as if we could, as a society, only contain one big idea at a time and the big idea was the war.

With America's tunnel vision focused on the war, throngs turned out for enormous parades supporting Liberty Loan drives.

In Philadelphia, 200,000 [people] sardined in the streets. The crowd linked arms, sang patriotic songs—breathed on each other—infected each other. . . .

Hospitals overflowed; emergency relief centers sprang up in parks and playgrounds. But practically every available doctor and nurse had been sent to Europe. The ones who remained were asked to perform the impossible. . . .

In many places, officials rushed through laws requiring people to wear masks in public. . . .

But masks didn't help. They were thin and porous—no serious restraint to tiny microbes. It was like trying to keep out dust with chicken wire.

In Washington, D.C., Commissioner Louis Brownlow banned all public gatherings. He closed the city's schools, theaters and bars. He quarantined the sick. He did everything he had the power to do.

But the death rate in Washington kept rising. . . .

[Biochemists] thought it was caused by a bacteria, so they made up a vaccine with the bacteria they thought was influenza. . . . But you can't make a vaccine if you're looking at the wrong causative organism. They were on the wrong track; the influenza was caused by a virus.

In the month of September, some 12,000 people died of influenza in America. But those numbers would be dwarfed. For the full horror now began. October would be the cruelest month. . . .

No one was safe. In Washington, Victor Vaughan [acting Surgeon General of the Army] was working late, trying to make sense of the hellish chaos. He uncovered an unnerving fact. Usually, influenza kills only the weak—the very young and very old—but this time it had a different target. People in the very prime of life—from 21 to 29—were the most vulnerable of all. . . .

For example: soldiers. In Europe, the flu was devastating both sides. Seventy-thousand American soldiers were sick; in some units, the flu killed 80% of the men. General John Pershing made a desperate plea for reinforcements. But that would mean sending soldiers across the Atlantic on troop ships.

There's nothing more crowded than a troop ship, it's just being jammed in there like sardines and if somebody has a respiratory disease, everybody's going to get it.

President Woodrow Wilson now faced an agonizing decision. Sending the soldiers would be signing thousands of death warrants. Wilson gazed out of his office window. After a long moment, he nodded. The troop shipments would [have to] continue. . . .

In New York, 851 people died of the flu in a single day. But the greatest horror came to Philadelphia. In one week in October, the death rate there was seven hundred times higher than normal. . . .

In 31 shocking days, the flu would kill over 195,000 Americans. It was the deadliest month in the nation's history. . . .

If the epidemic continue[d] its mathematical rate of acceleration, civilization could easily disappear from the face of the earth.

But a miraculous thing began to happen. As mysteriously as it had come, the terror began to slip away. By early November, the flu had virtually disappeared from Boston; the toll in Washington fell below 50 a week; even in ravaged Philadelphia, life was slowly returning to normal.

Then, on November 11, the Armistice ended The Great War. In San Francisco, the scene was surreal. Thirty thousand people paraded through the streets—all dancing, all singing, all wearing masks. The country had a lot to celebrate—not only was the war over, but the worst of the epidemic was passing. . . .

The epidemic killed. At a very, very conservative estimate, it killed 550,000 Americans in ten months. That's more Americans than had died in combat in all the wars of [the twentieth] century, and the epidemic had killed at least 30 million in the world and infected the majority of the human species. . . .

(excerpted)

MULTIPLE-CHOICE QUESTIONS

Directions (1–6): Use your notes to answer the following questions about the passage read to you. Select the best suggested answer and write its number in the space provided on the answer sheet. The questions may help you think about ideas and information you might use in your writing. You may return to these questions anytime you wish.

1 According to the speaker, the influenza of 1918 spread by means of
  1 water-borne contaminants
  2 undercooked food
  3 insect bites
  4 air-borne particles

2 The speaker implies that the war effort affected the epidemic by
  1 increasing the chance of exposure
  2 decreasing health care funds
  3 restricting the flow of information
  4 undermining the public confidence

3 In the sentence "In Philadelphia, 200,000 [people] sardined in the streets," the word "sardined" emphasizes the crowd's
  1 destination
  2 mood
  3 density
  4 motivation

4 According to the speaker, laws requiring people to wear masks in public did not stop the epidemic because
1 the masks helped to spread the virus
2 the masks allowed the virus to pass through
3 people would not wear the masks
4 people did not know about the masks

5 According to the speaker, how did the influenza of 1918 differ from previous flu outbreaks?
1 Its victims were primarily young adults.
2 It occurred primarily during the spring.
3 It received less attention from the government.
4 Its symptoms included fever and headache.

6 The speaker implies that troop ships were hazardous because of
1 poor maintenance
2 low morale
3 limited supplies
4 crowded quarters

LOOKING AT THE QUESTIONS

Note the key terms

1 **4** *According to the speaker*, the influenza of 1918 spread by means of "air-borne particles." The speaker points out that soldiers "carried the disease . . . just by breathing"; and, the coughing of just one person could "carry millions of particles with disease-causing organisms." There is no reference in the text to water-borne contaminants, under-cooked food, or to insect bites.

2 **1** *The speaker implies* that the war effort affected the epidemic by "increasing the chance of exposure." The examples of how the war effort affected the spread of influenza include large public gatherings, such as the one in Philadelphia, and the need to send large numbers of troops in crowded ships.

3 **3** In the sentence "In Philadelphia, 200,000 [people] sardined in the streets," *the word "sardined" emphasizes* the crowd's "density." This sentence makes reference to the popular expression "packed like sardines" to create a verb "sardined," meaning large numbers jammed close together. The expression is used later in the passage to describe conditions on troop ships.

4 **2** *According to the speaker*, laws requiring people to wear masks in public did <u>not</u> stop the epidemic because "the masks allowed the virus to pass through." The masks are described as "thin and porous. . . . It was like trying to keep out dust with chicken wire."

5 **1** *According to the speaker*, how did the influenza of 1918 differ from previous flu outbreaks? "Its victims were primarily young adults." The speaker reports that "Usually, influenza kills only the weak . . . but this time . . . [people] from 21 to 29 were the most vulnerable of all. . . . "

6 **4** *The speaker implies* that troop ships were hazardous because of "crowded quarters." "There's nothing more crowded than a troop ship . . . jammed in there like sardines, and if somebody has a respiratory disease, everybody's going to get it."

Summing Up

The passages selected for listening comprehension measure a number of skills beyond those of simple recall. They require the listener to interpret, to infer, to sense tone, and to comprehend the author's purpose. The listening passages may include anecdote, persuasive argument, personal reflection, or historical texts; the arguments may be direct and explicit, or they may be indirect and metaphoric. The good listener, like the good reader, understands and appreciates a variety of expressive methods.

The written responses in this part of the Regents exam will not always require a simple report. The task of writing to inform may include a feature article for publication, a persuasive essay in the form of a thesis/support paper to endorse a position, or an informational guide. The next chapter, on Reading and Writing for Information and Understanding, offers additional examples and review. You may also wish to consult Chapter 7, Writing on Examinations, and the *Glossary of Terms for Writing* on page 164.

Chapter 2

READING AND WRITING FOR INFORMATION AND UNDERSTANDING

Much of the work you do in high school or college requires reading for information and understanding and writing to demonstrate your ability to understand, analyze, and organize information and ideas. It is during Part B of the first session of the English Regents exam that your work in subjects other than English—science, social studies, or health, for example—will be especially relevant. It is in those subjects, as well as in writing courses, that you are expected to do many of the following:

* Use both primary and secondary sources of information for research.
* Select and limit topics for informational writing.
* Analyze and integrate data, facts, and ideas to communicate information.
* Take notes and organize information from lectures, documents and texts, video presentations, and on-line sources.
* Synthesize information for different contexts and purposes.
* Use paraphrase and quotation to integrate sources into your own text.
* Understand charts, graphs, and diagrams that support informational text.

These are, of course, skills you use when you do research in any subject, and you will find them in the Regents Learning Standards for English Language Arts.

WRITING TO INFORM OR PERSUADE: A GENERAL REVIEW

In writing for the first session of the English Regents exam you are directed to:

* Tell your audience what they need to know.
* Use specific, accurate, and relevant information.
* Use a tone and level of language appropriate for the task and audience.
* Organize your ideas in a logical and coherent manner.
* Follow the conventions of standard written English.

These guidelines are also reminders of what your teachers mean when they direct you to compose a "well-written essay" on a given topic.

PERSONAL NARRATIVE

Here is an example of a piece based on personal experience, written in response to a task in which the purpose and audience are clearly defined. It is a good example of what is meant by tone and level of language appropriate for the audience. Also, it is organized in a logical and coherent manner.

Task: A representative of a junior high school in your district has invited you to speak at the junior high [or middle school] graduation ceremonies on the topic "Getting Off to a Good Start in High School." Write a brief speech that you would give to the students, stating your recommendations for a successful start in high school. Use specific reasons, examples, or details to support your recommendations.

Not so long ago, I too was sitting where you are now, thinking and worrying about what my life in high school would be like. Would I stick out? Would I make friends? How should I approach people? Would my classes be too difficult? Would I be able to cope with the stress? These questions kept badgering me throughout the summer before the ninth grade. I was especially nervous about starting school because I had just moved to a new neighborhood and did not know a single person.

By the end of the summer, the thought that especially frustrated me was that I would have no one to eat lunch with on the first day of school. This does not seem like such a big deal but it bothered me a lot. I knew that at the high school people went out to eat with a group of friends. I had no one to go out with. I told myself that I still had a week before school started and did not need to worry.

The first day of school finally arrived. As I neared the school, I felt helpless and lonely. I wanted to plead with Mom to turn the car around and go back home. But I reluctantly got out of the car and slowly approached the front entrance of the school.

Luckily, I found my first class and quickly took a seat in the front. I felt as if all eyes were on me. The new kid. The freak. While everyone was talking and laughing about their summer, I sat in my seat trying to look as though I was busy fiddling with my notebook. I couldn't wait to get out of the classroom. I wanted to run home and hide, for this was one of the most difficult experiences of my life.

Things started to look better around fifth period. I got up the courage and started talking to people. I even went out to lunch with a few girls and had a comfortable time. I was not totally relaxed but knew that I would adapt and soon make more friends.

I have just finished my junior year in high school. I have many friends and am very happy in my school. I will be a senior this coming September and expect to experience new ideas and challenges. I am now starting to think about what I want to do with my life and what colleges I might want to attend. Soon I will be leaving high school and will feel again the nervousness and anxiety which all of you are going through in preparing for high school. I guess what we are experiencing is not trepidation but life, and what to expect in the future. You may be scared now, but be confident that you will overcome those fears and the experiences will only make you stronger.

Analysis

Although this speech is more a personal narrative than a list of recommendations, the writer/speaker clearly understands both the purpose of the task and her audience: "Not so long ago, I too was sitting where you are now . . . ." The diction is informal, the tone is conversational, and the first-person narrative is highly appropriate for the occasion.

The theme is established in the opening sentence, but the speaker's main point is not stated until the very end: "You may be scared now, but . . . you will overcome those fears . . . and [be] stronger." She leads her audience to this conclusion by narrating her own feelings and experiences, starting with a series of "fears" she knows her listeners have. The narrative covers a period of many weeks, but it is made coherent by specific references to time: "throughout the summer . . . by the end of summer . . . on the first day of school . . . my first class . . . around fifth period . . . lunch." She also uses a reference to time to come back to the present and bring the speech to a close: "I have just finished my junior year . . . ."

The ideas are well expressed, and the paragraph in which the writer describes what it was like to sit in her first class—"The new kid. The freak"—pretending to be busy with her notebook is especially vivid and convincing. We also trust the speaker when she tells us that she had "a comfortable time" at lunch but that she "was not totally relaxed" either. If she had claimed that after lunch all her fears had disappeared, we would not believe her. This is a good example of what is meant by honesty in writing: It rings true in our ears.

This response would be even better if the writer had included more specific examples of how she overcame her fears.

PERSUASIVE WRITING

Here are two examples of what is called persuasive writing, pieces that develop and support an opinion on a particular topic. Note what makes each a successful argument.

Task: The students in your science class have been invited to submit essays on topics of current interest or controversy for possible publication on the Op-Ed page of the school newspaper.

Using Animals for Scientific Research

The question of whether or not to use animals as subjects for scientific research is a difficult one. Those in opposition claim that using animals in research is inhumane, while those holding a diametrically opposing view maintain that it is a necessary evil whose long-term benefits far outweigh the sacrifice of a handful of animals. I am an ardent supporter of the latter view. I feel that the use of animals is justified by the benefits that are reaped by all of mankind, and that halting the use of animals as subjects would greatly impede advancements in the field of medicine.

One example of the tremendous benefits which animal research can bring about is the discovery of insulin by Dr. William Banting and his assistant, Charles Best. Before this amazing discovery, diabetes mellitus was a devastating and inevitably fatal disease. The extent of treatment that doctors could offer afflicted patients was a starvation diet which prolonged life for only a short time and caused the obviously detrimental and painful effects of virtual starvation.

When Dr. Banting came up with a unique idea that linked the cause of the disease to a hormonal secretion of the pancreas, a potential way to control this deadly disease became apparent. But the idea had to be tested and proven successful before it could be offered to human patients. Dr. Banting proceeded with his experiments, using 15 dogs as his subjects. Although several of the dogs did die as a result of the experiment, the benefits that society gained because of the tests are infinitely greater. If those opposed to utilizing animals in testing had their way, the concept would have died prematurely because there would have been no way to test the idea. Fortunately for the field of science and for the millions of diabetics that have lived in the past few decades, Dr. Banting was able to find this treatment.

As a diabetic, I am greatly indebted to the work of Dr. Banting and the studies he conducted using animals as subjects. Today, I am not only alive, but healthy and active. I cannot help but be a supporter of animal testing because I owe my life to it. I understand how one may object to senseless cruelty to animals and the wasting of their lives worthlessly. Using animals strictly for scientific purposes is not "senseless cruelty," however, and it is clearly justified.

Analysis

This is a good example of a short essay of opinion because the student has chosen a subject that he could develop with expertise and compelling personal experience; it also demonstrates his skill in organizing and presenting an argument.

One of the most effective ways to approach a controversial topic is to "acknowledge the opposition," that is, to recognize, even respect, the opposing view. This writer agrees that the question "is a difficult one," but goes on to say he is "an ardent supporter" of animal testing. Note that he very skillfully saves his most personal reason for the end, developing first a factual but dramatic example of the benefits of testing for millions of people. Introducing his personal reason earlier would have made the argument less persuasive because he would have appeared less objective. The conclusion is emotionally effective: "I cannot help but be a supporter of animal testing because I owe my life to it." More important, the writer demonstrates skillful argument when he says, "I understand how one may object . . ." and closes with a distinction between scientific experiment and "senseless cruelty." This essay would be a good contribution to an Op-Ed page.

Task: The editor of your local newspaper has proposed that businesses that hire high school graduates pay them salaries in proportion to their grades for the last two years of high school; that is, the higher a graduate's grades for those last two years, the higher the salary. Write a letter to the editor in which you state your opinion of the proposal. Use specific reasons, examples, or details.

I vehemently oppose the proposal that graduates be paid salaries in proportion to their grades for the last two years of high school.

First, grades should not affect the equal opportunity of all workers to receive the same paycheck for the same work. It must be taken into account that many factors influence a student's grades in high school. For example, a student may have a harder course load than another student with higher grades. It is unfair to compare grades from courses that differ in difficulty. Perhaps a student does not do well on tests, but is an excellent student in class. Participation and the ability to speak one's mind are very beneficial in a career, yet these qualities are not reflected by grades. Furthermore, if a student has an inborn proficiency in a subject (and gets good grades), it is unfair to assume that that student works hard to achieve his scores. An average student works harder and may still not get the same scores. Hard work and dedication are important factors in choosing an employee, but these factors cannot always be relayed by report card.

There are other factors besides grades that play a role in whether a student is right for a job. The applicant may have experience in the field of interest, but the proposed system would not take this into account. Perhaps a student has been a volunteer or has been active in clubs and organizations outside of school. By looking at his track record with reference to involvement in organizations, the student's ability to follow through would be noted. This is an important factor to take into account when hiring a worker.

Also, grades do not indicate strength of personal character, an important determinant in the selection of an employee. One must not make the generalization that a student with good grades is also a good person, and that a student with poor grades is not a good person. Only a personal interview can give the employer some sense of personal character of the worker. Positive interactions with other workers are vital to the success of a business.

Finally, by locking-in different salaries and pay rates based on high school grades, the employer is creating unnecessary competition and tension in the workplace. A worker with a lower salary may not work as hard, as a result. The worker with the lower salary might be treated differently, or unfairly by the employer by not being encouraged to work up to potential.

Thank you for your attention to this matter. Perhaps now an employee will be viewed as a person, and not as a report card. Everyone deserves a fair chance.

Analysis

This essay is effective because it expresses a clear and thoughtful opinion, it is well organized, and it is excellent in its development. It is weakened because it is not always focused on the specific topic. The letter begins well, with a clear statement of position, and the first section makes several important points about the limited significance of grades. Note, however, that the argument shifts from a discussion of how workers should be paid to how they should be hired in the first place. The second section makes several good points, but it too refers to *hiring* workers. The writer comes back to the topic of differentiated pay only in the third full paragraph.

If the writer had followed her statement of opinion with a *because* statement and a summary of her main points, she could have established the focus she needs. She clearly took time to gather good examples and reasons, but she did not always show how they related to the topic. The task directed the student to write a letter to an editor and to write *the body of the letter only,* but such letters are really essays of argument and must have focus and coherence to be effective. Composing "letters" of this kind is a very good way to practice writing persuasive essays. Keep in mind also that the essay "task" on the SAT will require students to develop a point of view on an issue.

SESSION ONE, PART B: READING AND WRITING FOR INFORMATION AND UNDERSTANDING

Sample Texts, Tasks, Questions, and Essays

In this part of the examination, you will first read an informational article and accompanying chart or other graphic presentation, then answer ten multiple-choice questions on basic comprehension of main ideas, on key vocabulary, and on interpretation. The essay requires an informative or a persuasive piece of writing that is supported by the information in both documents.

Below are two examples of actual tasks for this part of the examination. In the first, the task is to prepare a report on the subject of child labor laws, based on a summary text and a chart. In the second, the task is to write a position paper in which you agree **or** disagree with a ratings system for television programs. Model student essays follow each.

39

SAMPLE TASK I

Directions: Study the chart and read the text on the following pages, answer the multiple-choice questions, and write a response based on the situation described below. You may use the margins to take notes as you read and scrap paper to plan your response.

> **The Situation:** Your social studies class has been studying the history of child labor. You have chosen to write a report summarizing some provisions of current New York State law regarding the employment of children and discussing the conditions that may have led to those provisions.

> **Your Task:** Using relevant information from **both** documents, write a report summarizing some provisions of current New York State law regarding the employment of children and discussing the conditions that may have led to those provisions.

Guidelines:
Be sure to

- Tell your audience what they need to know about some provisions of current New York State law regarding the employment of children
- Discuss the conditions that may have led to those provisions
- Use specific, accurate, and relevant information from the chart **and** the text to support your discussion
- Use a tone and level of language appropriate for a report for your social studies class
- Organize your ideas in a logical and coherent manner
- Indicate any words taken directly from the text by using quotation marks or referring to the author
- Follow the conventions of standard written English

Chart

PERMITTED WORKING HOURS FOR MINORS UNDER 18 YEARS OF AGE

The following chart is a summary of the permitted working hours provisions of the New York State Labor Law (1993) relating to minors under 18 years of age.

AGE OF MINOR (girls and boys)	INDUSTRY OR OCCUPATION	MAXIMUM DAILY HOURS	MAX. WKLY. HRS.	MAX. DAYS PER WK.	PERMITTED HOURS
MINORS ATTENDING SCHOOL When School is in Session 14 and 15	All occupations except farm work, newspaper carrier, and street trades	3 hours on school days[1] 8 hours on other days	18	6	7 a.m. to 7 p.m.
16 and 17	All occupations except farm work, newspaper carrier, and street trades	4 hours on days preceding school days (i.e., Mon, Tues, Wed, Thurs)[2] 8 hours on Fri, Sat, Sun, and holidays	28	6	6 a.m. to 10 p.m.[3]
When School is Not in Session (Vacation) 14 and 15	All occupations except farm work, newspaper carrier, and street trades	8 hours	40	6	7 a.m. to 9 p.m. June 21 to Labor Day
16 and 17	All occupations except farm work, newspaper carrier, and street trades	8 hours	48[4]	6[4]	6 a.m. to midnight[4]
MINORS NOT ATTENDING SCHOOL 16 and 17	All occupations except farm work, newspaper carrier, and street trades	8 hours	48[4]	6[4]	6 a.m. to midnight[4]
FARM WORK 12 and 13	Hand harvest of berries, fruits, and vegetables	4 hours	—	—	7 a.m. to 7 p.m. June 21 to Labor Day/ 9 a.m. to 4 p.m. day after Labor Day to June 20
14 and older	Any farm work	—	—	—	—
NEWSPAPER CARRIERS 11 to 18	Delivers or sells and delivers newspapers, shopping papers, or periodicals to homes or business places	4 hours on school days 5 hours on other days	—	—	5 a.m. to 7 p.m. or 30 minutes prior to sunset, whichever is later
STREET TRADES 14 to 18	Self-employed work in places selling newspapers or work as a shoeshiner	4 hours on school days 5 hours on other days	—	—	6 a.m. to 7 p.m.

[1] Students 14 and 15 enrolled in an approved work-study program may work 3 hours on a school day; 23 hours in any one week when school is in session.

[2] Students 16 and 17 enrolled in an approved Cooperative Education Program may work up to 6 hours on a day preceding a school day other than a Sunday or holiday when school is in session, as long as the hours are in conjunction with the program.

[3] 6 a.m. to 10 p.m. or until midnight with written parental and educational authorities' consent on a day preceding a school day and until midnight on a day preceding a non-school day with written parental consent.

[4] This provision does not apply to minors employed in resort hotels or restaurants in resort areas.

Child Labor

Child labor is work performed by children that either endangers their health or safety, interferes with or prevents their education, or keeps them from play and other activity important to their development. Child labor of this character has long been considered a social evil to be abolished.

Early History of Child Labor

(5)   Industrial child labor first appeared with the development of the domestic system. In this type of production an entrepreneur bought raw material to be "put out" to the homes of workmen to be spun, woven, sewn, or handled in some other manner. This permitted a division of labor and a degree of specialization among various families. Pay was by the piece, and children were used extensively at

(10)   whatever tasks they could perform. This system was important in England, on the Continent, and in North America from the 16th to the 18th century and lingers until the present in some industries and in some countries.

The domestic system was largely replaced by the factory system associated with the Industrial Revolution, which gained impetus in the 18th century.

(15)   Machinery, driven by waterpower and later by steam, took over many functions formerly performed by hand labor and was centralized in factories situated at the source of the power. Children could and did tend the machines in ever increasing numbers from as early an age as five. Child labor also proliferated in coal mining. Half-naked children as young as six labored incredibly long hours in the

(20)   damp and dark. Many of them carried coal in packs on their backs up long ladders to the surface.

Mistreatment of Children. In the 1830's, the English Parliament set up a commission to look into the problems of working children. The testimony the commission took is revealing. One worker in a textile mill testified that he first

(25)   went to work at the age of 8 and that he customarily had worked from 6 a.m. to 8 p.m., with an hour off at noon. When business was brisk, however, he worked a 16-hour span, from 5 a.m. to 9 p.m. When asked how he could be punctual and how he awoke, the boy said:

(30)   "I seldom did awake spontaneously; I was most generally awoke or lifted out of bed, sometimes asleep, by my parents."

A boy whose services had been sold by his parents to a mill owner (for 15 shillings for 6 years) testified that the child laborers in that mill were locked up night and day. He said that twice he ran away, was pursued and caught by his overseer, and was thrashed with a whip.

(35)   A girl who worked in the mines testified:

"I never went to day school; I go to Sunday school, but I cannot read or write; I go to the mine at 5 o'clock in the morning and come out at

(40)

5 in the evening; I get my breakfast of porridge and milk first; I take my
dinner with me, a cake, and eat it as I go; I do not stop or rest any time
for that purpose; I get nothing else until I get home, and then have
potatoes and meat, not every day meat. I work in the clothes I have now
got on, trousers and ragged jacket; the bald place upon my head is
made by carrying the coal buckets. I carry the buckets a mile and more
under ground and back; I carry 11 a day; I wear a belt and chain at the

(45)

workings to get the buckets out; the miners that I work for sometimes
beat me with their hands if I am not quick enough. They strike me
upon my back. I would rather work in a mill than in a coalpit."

Pauper Children. During the great social dislocations of the early Industrial
Revolution, there were many children who had no parents or whose parents

(50)

could not support them. Under the English Poor Law then in effect, local government officials were supposed to arrange for these children to become apprentices so that they would learn a trade and be cared for. In thousands of cases these
so-called "pauper children" were simply turned over in large numbers to a distant
mill owner by the local officials. After having been thus "apprenticed," they had

(55)

virtually no one to care or intercede for them and were little better than slaves.

Other working children were indentured—their parents sold their labor to
the mill owner for a period of years. Others lived with their families and worked
for wages as adults did, for long hours and under hard conditions.

Effects of Economic Doctrines. The situation was made possible by the

(60)

economic doctrines widely believed at the time. Employers felt that the government should not meddle in business. They believed that economic affairs should
be allowed to run according to their own "natural laws," much as the physical
world was regulated by such laws as the law of gravity. One of the "natural laws"
of economics that businessmen thought they perceived was the "iron law of

(65)

wages"—it held that wages could not possibly rise above a subsistence level. So
low wages and long hours seemed inevitable.

Furthermore, idle hands were looked upon as the devil's tools, while work was
thought to be morally uplifting. Employers felt that they were helping the poor
to become more virtuous by providing them with useful work. Such ideas were

(70)

widely accepted.

Regulation of Child Labor

The movement to limit child labor sprang from several sources. The crowded
and unsanitary conditions existing when children lived in factory dormitories gave
rise to epidemics that spread to the nearby population. Concerned medical men
warned that the rigors of childhood employment resulted in a permanently weak-

(75)

ened and damaged labor force. Some people were concerned because child
laborers had no time for religious instruction. (Sunday schools, when they were
first started, taught reading and writing as well as religious subjects. They were

intended for working children who received no other schooling.) There was concern about this lack of education and also about the immoral atmosphere of fac-
(80) tory dormitories.

United States. Children worked in the American colonies, most of all on the family farm but also in various kinds of household industries, as apprentices, at sea, as indentured servants, and as slaves. In 1789 textile manufacturing on the English pattern was transplanted to the northern and middle states. As in
(85) England, children were the bulk of the labor force at first, but the United States did not have a great supply of pauper children as did England at the time, so that before long, women—many of them young—became the mainstay of the labor force in textiles.

State Legislation. Some states passed protective legislation, if it can be called
(90) that. In 1836 a Massachusetts law required that working children receive some schooling. In 1842, Connecticut and Massachusetts limited the work of children in textile factories to 10 hours a day. Pennsylvania in 1848 outlawed the hiring of children under 12 in the mills. The struggle for free compulsory public education that characterized the years before the Civil War was indirectly a campaign
(95) against excessive child labor.

By 1900 about half of the states placed some sort of restrictions on child labor, but only about 10 made a serious effort to enforce such laws as there were. The South was finally industrializing as textile manufacturing moved from New England to be close to its raw materials (and to take advantage of cheap labor).
(100) In the process, the South appeared destined to repeat all the horrors of the early Industrial Revolution. The number of child laborers in the South tripled between 1890 and 1900.

Elsewhere in the country, the glass industry employed young boys for 12-hour shifts in front of fiery furnaces. The domestic system lingered on in the garment
(105) industry where whole families labored for subcontractors in tenement sweat-shops. In the coalfields, boys manned the "breakers." Here they sat hunched over chutes as coal poured beneath them, picked out the stone and slate, and breathed coal dust for 10 hours at a stretch. The tobacco industry employed thousands of children under 10 to make cigars and cigarettes. In silk spinning, artificial flower
(110) making, oyster shucking, berry picking, canning, and shrimp packing, the story was the same.

National Legislation. The limited value of state laws soon became apparent. Labor and the progressives had little influence in a number of states, especially in the South, so that state laws there were out of the question. As a result busi-
(115) nesses in such states had a competitive advantage, and this stiffened resistance to strengthening or even enforcing laws in more progressive states. A national law appeared to be the only answer, and a campaign for one began. Public support was mobilized by several of the "muckrakers," the journalists who exposed intol-

erable conditions. The cause was helped by an angry bit of verse penned by one
(120) of the reformers, Sarah N. Cleghorn:

> The golf links lie so near the mill
> That almost every day
> The laboring children can look out
> And see the men at play.

(125)   In 1912, Congress was persuaded to establish a Children's Bureau.

The battle appeared won in 1916 when, during the high tide of the progressive
crusade, President Wilson wrestled through Congress the Keating-Owen Act,
which barred from interstate commerce articles produced by child labor. The victory was brief, however, for a conservative Supreme Court in 1918 declared the
(130) law unconstitutional because it infringed on states' rights and denied children the
"freedom" to contract to work.

The only road still open was the tortuous one of a constitutional amendment.
Congress proposed one in 1924 and sent it to the states for ratification. But the
national mood in the 1920's was far different from what it had been 10 years before.
(135) Among those who opposed ratification of the proposed amendment were the
American Farm Bureau Federation, the National Association of Manufacturers,
and the southern textile industry. They were joined by most of the Roman
Catholic hierarchy of the country, who argued that the amendment threatened
parental discipline and invaded the privacy of the home. Faced with this weighty
(140) array of enemies, the amendment was defeated in most states.

During the New Deal years, the political pendulum had swung again, and new
national efforts were made. In 1938 the far-reaching Fair Labor Standards Act
once again struck at child labor. This act, also known as the Wages and Hours Act,
with its amendments, is now the basic child labor act for the United States. It
(145) bans employers engaged in interstate commerce from employing workers under
16 or under 18 in hazardous occupations. Under certain circumstances, children
14 to 16 may be employed after school hours. The states may further control child
labor so long as their legislation does not conflict with federal law.

Current Developments

In the United States child labor remains a problem in only one sector of the
(150) economy, agriculture. Federal law requires only that children under 16 may not
be employed in agriculture during school hours. Therefore, small children may
be worked long hours in farming during other times, especially because state laws
covering child labor in agriculture are generally lax or nonexistent. Hardest hit
are the children of migrant farm laborers. There were 400,000 migrant farm
(155) laborers in the United States in the late 1960's.

—Hugh G. Cleland

MULTIPLE-CHOICE QUESTIONS

Directions (1–10): Answer the following questions by selecting the number of the correct choice. The questions may help you think about ideas and information you might want to use in your writing. You may return to these questions anytime you wish.

1   According to the chart, which occupation would have the fewest restrictions regarding working hours for 14-year-olds?
   1   farm worker
   2   newspaper carrier
   3   shoeshiner
   4   dishwasher

2   According to the chart, the conditions under which minors can work depend upon the type of job, the age of the minor, and the
   1   rate of pay
   2   approval of parents
   3   time of year
   4   availability of insurance

3   Lisa is a 15-year-old with a job in a store. According to the chart, what is the latest she can legally work during vacation?
   1   7 p.m.
   2   9 p.m.
   3   10 p.m.
   4   midnight

4   The first paragraph of the text defines "child labor" in terms of its effects on
   1   employers
   2   officials
   3   taxpayers
   4   workers

5   According to the text, the Industrial Revolution increased the demand for child labor because children
   1   were able to work on machines
   2   could work faster than adults
   3   were skilled in specialized hand work
   4   preferred factory work to farm work

6 The section subtitled "Mistreatment of Children" (lines 22 through 47) is developed mainly through the use of
   1 definitions
   2 comparisons
   3 anecdotes
   4 reasons

7 One argument used by employers to justify child labor (lines 59 through 70) was the idea that work helped to improve a worker's
   1 business sense
   2 moral character
   3 physical health
   4 social status

8 The function of the paragraph beginning with the words "The movement to limit child labor" (line 71) is to
   1 disprove some theories of economics
   2 explain the areas of concern
   3 promote religious instruction
   4 question the motives of reformers

9 The text implies that Sarah N. Cleghorn wrote her verse (lines 121 through 124) in order to
   1 alert the public to a problem
   2 criticize the publisher of the newspaper
   3 inform the readers about a sport
   4 amuse the children in the mill

10 As a result of the 1938 Wages and Hours Act, children are *not* allowed to
   1 earn minimum wage
   2 work after school
   3 hold dangerous jobs
   4 pay income taxes

LOOKING AT THE QUESTIONS

1 **1** "farm worker." The chart shows that there are no restrictions for minors 14 or older in this category. All other categories have some restrictions.

2 **3** "time of year." Many of the restrictions outlined in the chart reflect whether or not the minor is in school. The chart makes no reference to rate of pay or availability of insurance. There is only limited reference to parental consent in the footnotes.

3 **2** "9 p.m." The chart (in the second category of the left-hand column) shows that permitted hours for students 14–15 when school is not in session are 7 a.m. to 9 p.m.

4 **4** "workers." The information in the paragraph is about the conditions under which workmen, including their children and whole families, worked under what was called the "domestic system."

5 **1** "[children] were able to work on machines." The second paragraph points out that "children could and did tend the machines . . . from as early an age as five." There is no reference to whether children worked faster, were more skilled, or preferred factory work.

6 **3** "anecdotes." An anecdote is a brief story or recounting of an experience. This passage is developed chiefly through first-hand testimony of child workers in the 1830's.

7 **2** "moral character." The answer is in the last paragraph of the section: ". . . idle hands were looked upon as the devil's tools, while work was thought to be morally uplifting." There is no reference to improving a worker's business sense, physical health, or social status.

8 **2** "explain the areas of concern." The paragraph uses the term "concern" or "concerned" several times. The issues include unsanitary working conditions, lack of education, and an inappropriate moral atmosphere for children.

9 **1** "alert the public to a problem." Cleghorn's "angry bit of verse" is reported to have helped the cause of the "muckrakers," and she is referred to as "one of the reformers."

10 **3** "hold dangerous jobs." Line 146 points out that the Wages and Hours Act of 1938 "bans employers . . . from employing workers . . . under 18 in hazardous occupations."

Part B, Sample Student Response Essay

In 1993, New York State passed a labor law that established the permitted working hours for minors under 18 years of age. Looking back on the history of child labor both in America and around the world reveals a clear picture as to why such regulations are a necessary part of modern-day society.

The use of children as industrial labor began with what was called the "domestic system." Owners bought raw materials to be "put out" to workmen and their families. Because these workers were paid by the piece, "children were used extensively at whatever tasks they could perform." Greater exploitation of children began with the advent of the Industrial Revolution. As early as age five, children were used to tend machines, which replaced tedious hand labor. Factory work presented many dangers to children. These dangers were increased because of the lengthy work days children were forced to endure, often 14 hours a day. Essentially these children were treated as slaves, and many children of poor families were indentured — sold by their parents to a mill owner for a period of years. Such practices were justified as good economic policy and "employers felt that they were helping the poor to become more virtuous by providing them with useful work."

Since the 1800's, attempts have been made to regulate child labor in the United States, but few have prevailed. Initial regulation of child labor began in the 1830's, when a Massachusetts law required that working children receive some form of education. Other states followed with so-called protective legislation, but few made serious efforts to enforce such laws. In 1918, the Keating-Owen Act, which "barred from interstate commerce articles produced by child labor," was declared unconstitutional by the Supreme Court because it "infringed on states' rights and denied children the freedom to contract to work."

It wasn't until after the Great Depression that anything successful and serious was done to prevent the exploitation of children in the workforce. In 1938 the Fair Labor Standards Act was established as part of Roosevelt's New Deal. It limited the use of child labor in hazardous occupations. Additional room was left for states to "further control child labor so long as their legislation does not conflict with federal law."

The New York State law sets the permitted working hour provisions for minors. Limits are set based on age, type of occupation, and time of year (whether school is in session or not). Children are not permitted to work until the age fourteen, with the exception of light farmwork and delivering newspapers. Age isn't the only restrictive factor. Children are limited in the number of hours they are permitted to work a week, especially when school is in session. The lateness of the work day is also regulated, depending on the age of the child and whether school is in session. These limits are to ensure that minors receive an education and are not exploited by employers.

Although concerns with child labor in the agriculture sector remain, the U.S. government and state governments like New York's have come a long way in regulating child labor, making the work place safer for children.

49

Analysis

This is an excellent response because it conveys a thorough understanding of the documents in its discussion of historical background, attempts at reform, and provisions of the New York State law. The connection between the task and the documents is made clear in the opening paragraph and in the conclusion. The essay is well developed with relevant details and quotations from the text and with a general discussion of the information in the chart.

The writer maintains the focus on child labor conditions and laws, and the chronological structure gives a clear organization. The writer also moves skillfully from one paragraph to another. Overall, the use of language is mature and sophisticated, and the essay contains essentially no errors in conventions. This essay fits the criteria for a high score on all qualities. (See Appendix F for the complete rubric for this part of the examination.)

In this example, from the August 2000 English Regents examination, the student must choose to agree or disagree with a proposal and use both the documents to develop a persuasive argument.

Directions: Read the text and study the graphic on the following pages, answer the multiple-choice questions, and write a response based on the situation described below. You may use the margins to take notes as you read and scrap paper to plan your response.

The Situation: Students in your communications class are studying the television ratings system developed by the television industry. For a class debate, your teacher has asked you to write a position paper indicating whether you agree *or* disagree that the ratings system will help parents and guardians monitor their children's television viewing.

Your Task: Using relevant information from *both* documents, write a position paper for your communications class in which you agree *or* disagree that the television ratings system will help parents and guardians monitor their children's television viewing.

Guidelines:
Be sure to

- Tell your audience what they need to know about the controversy surrounding the television ratings system

- Indicate whether you agree *or* disagree that the ratings system will help parents and guardians monitor their children's television viewing
- Use specific, accurate, and relevant information from the text *and* the graphic to support your position
- Use a tone and level of language appropriate for a position paper for communications class
- Organize your ideas in a logical and coherent manner
- Indicate any words taken directly from the text by using quotation marks or referring to the author
- Follow the conventions of standard written English

Television Ratings System

Parents of young children may soon see a familiar sight on television: a bearded, rotund fellow wearing a bright blue coat, surrounded by animals and accompanied by a lanky helper with the improbable name of Mr. Green Jeans.

That's right: Captain Kangaroo is back! Four decades of kids grew up with the
(5) original Captain. Now, with a new cast, the show is being revived.

"It's a big, wonderful show that you and I grew up watching and that you don't see on TV that much anymore," says Saban Entertainment's Robert Loos, one of the producers of "The All New Captain Kangaroo." "It's entertaining as well as educational, it's kind and gentle, and it keeps you laughing while you learn."

(10) The Captain Kangaroo formula had an enviable record of holding audiences and advertisers during its commercial TV run. But the show has an added appeal: producers are designing the series to help commercial TV stations meet the new Federal Communications Commission (FCC) requirement to provide at least three hours a week of "core educational programming" for children.

(15) "This is the first time that there is a clear quantitative guideline on children's programming," says Kathryn Montgomery, president of the Center for Media Education, which led the lobbying drive for the rule. "It's clear that the industry knows it has to respond."

The FCC adopted the rule last summer after broadcasters acceded to pressure
(20) from a coalition of advocacy groups and a nudge from the White House. Broadcasters, however, say they were already meeting kids' needs for educational shows.

"We have done a good job with children's programming," says Dennis Wharton, vice president of media relations for the National Association of Broadcasters
(25) (NAB). Wharton says the industry "voluntarily agreed" to the adoption of the FCC rule, which put a concrete number on a more generally worded requirement included in the Children's Television Act of 1990.

"We've been producing at least three hours a week [of children's programs] ever since we started," says Margaret Loesch, who founded the popular Fox Children's
(30) Network (now Fox Kids) in 1990. "We felt [the rule] was appropriate," Loesch says, "because it was an important issue and because we're parents."

In fact, the TV offerings for kids have never been greater or more varied. The seemingly endless cartoon and action shows are supplemented by an assortment of educational offerings and a few teen-oriented dramas.

(35)   Even longtime critics of children's television are begrudgingly complimentary. "It is getting better, and it will get better," Montgomery says.

Children's television is not a charitable enterprise, however, but a business, and a lucrative one. Advertisers spent nearly $1 billion on children's programming in 1996. Animated programs accounted for about $688 million, or 76 percent of the total.
(40) Educational and instructional programs pulled in just $1.4 million.

"There's money to be made in kids' entertainment," says Cyma Zarghami, senior vice president of programming and general manager of Nickelodeon, a children's cable network.

But young people watch more than children's programs in the 15–20 hours a week
(45) they spend watching TV. With the expanding number of broadcast and cable channels—and the expanding number of TV sets in the home—kids can now watch violent adult dramas and sex-tinged situation comedies almost any time of day. As a result, many parents now view TV as a decidedly unwholesome influence in their children's lives.

(50)   That widespread concern fueled the drive over the past 18 months to persuade the television industry to adopt a ratings system to help parents decide what their children should watch. Initially, an age-based system was devised that mimicked the ratings used for movies. But the system was criticized as inadequate by a coalition that included groups specializing in children's television issues as well as the National
(55) PTA, National Education Association (NEA), and American Medical Association (AMA). They argued that parents needed more specific information about the content of programs—specifically violence, sex, and language.

Those arguments had strong support in official Washington. President Bill Clinton helped persuade the TV industry to agree to a rating system, and Vice
(60) President Al Gore had long paid close attention to children's television issues. On Capitol Hill, lawmakers of both parties were criticizing the amount of sex and violence on television and urging the industry to help parents limit children's intake of inappropriate fare.

Faced with the combination of public and political pressure—and an unenthusi-
(65) astic public response to the limited ratings system—most of the TV industry agreed last month to more detailed advisories. The new system will rate programs both by age and by content, as indicated below. The new ratings system begins with the age-

based ratings symbols first instituted by the industry and adds a letter when appropriate to denote potentially objectionable content: "V" for violence, "S" for sexual
(70) situations, "L" for coarse language, "D" for sexually suggestive dialogue, and "FV" for fantasy violence in children's programs.

Ratings for Children's Programs

 Programs designed for all children, not expected to frighten younger children.

(75) Programs designed for children ages 7 and older. May contain fantasy or comedic violence or may frighten younger children. Programs with more intense or combative fantasy violence will be designated **TV-Y7-FV**.

Ratings for All Audiences

 Programs for general audiences that most parents would find suitable for
(80) all ages. Little or no violence, sexual situations, or strong language.

 Programs that require parental guidance, containing material that parents might find unsuitable for young children. Programs may also carry V, S, D and/or L designations (for moderate violence, some sexual situations, infrequent coarse language, and some suggestive dialogue), as
(85) appropriate.

Programs with material that many parents would find unsuitable for children under age 14. Parents are urged to monitor these programs, which will also carry V, S, D and/or L designations (for intense violence, intense sexual situations, strong, coarse language, and intensely suggestive dialogue), as appropriate.
(90)

Programs designed to be viewed only by adults ("mature audiences") and that may be unsuitable for children under age 17, which will carry V, S and/or L designations (for graphic violence, explicit sexual activity and crude, indecent language), as appropriate.

(95)   "This is designed to be a consumer device," says Arnold Fege, director of governmental relations for the National PTA, "to give parents more information about programs, similar to the information they get from a nutrition label on the back of food."

Having been dragged into the change, broadcasters now are taking credit for it. "We're trying to give parents a little extra tool to monitor what their kids are watch-
(100) ing," says the NAB's Wharton.

Some people in the TV industry, however, worry that the rating system will be inherently subjective and necessarily incomplete—with no indication of the context for sexual material or violent scenes. Many writers and producers also worry that watchdog groups could use ratings to galvanize boycotts of programs or advertisers *(105)* or that skittish network executives could lean on them to tone down programs to the detriment of "the creative process."

Those concerns contributed to a decision by one of the broadcast networks, NBC, not to participate in the new rating system. "There is no way that there will be any consistency in application or any consistency in its use," says Rosalyn Weinman, *(110)* NBC's executive vice president for broadcast standards and content. "The system is at best confusing and at worst totally incoherent."

From the opposite perspective, some critics of TV programming say even the revised rating system still provides too little information. "Our concern is that without identifying the extent and degree of sex, language, and violence, parents will *(115)* have little more information than they do now," says Mark Honig, executive director of the conservative-leaning Parents Television Council.

Other critics say the rating system has no direct effect on TV sex and violence. "Garbage labeled is still garbage," says Sen. Joseph I. Lieberman, D-Conn.

The new system is designed for use in conjunction with the new "V-chip"("V" for *(120)* violence), a computer-encrypted microchip that can screen out objectionable programs. The Telecommunications Act of 1996 requires new TV sets to have V-chips once the rating system has been reviewed by the FCC.

Even supporters of the new rating system, however, are uncertain how families will use the new TV screening tools or what effects they will have.

(125) "It may be that nothing happens in terms of programming," Montgomery says, "but it's my hope that parents will have a tool they can use to make effective decisions in their own homes."

—Kenneth Jost, 1997

America's Love Affair With TV

- **Average amount of daily TV-watching:** 2.1 hours
- **Parents who think kids watch too much TV:** 21 percent

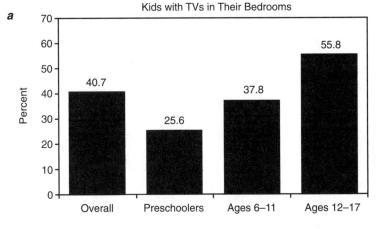

Kids with TVs in Their Bedrooms

a

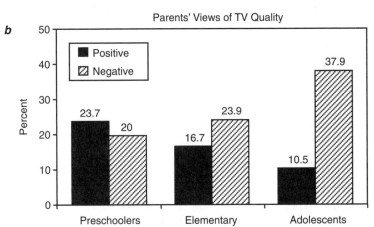

Parents' Views of TV Quality

b

Source: *Television in the Home: The 1997 Survey of Parents & Children,* Annenberg Public Policy Center, University of Pennsylvania, June 6, 1996

MULTIPLE-CHOICE QUESTIONS

Directions (1–10): Answer the following questions by selecting the number of the correct choice. The questions may help you think about ideas and information you might want to use in your writing. You may return to these questions anytime you wish.

1 The author refers to the "Captain Kangaroo" show as an example of television programming that is
   1 outdated
   2 economical
   3 educational
   4 unpopular

2 Both the new FCC programming regulation and the ratings system aim to
   1 restrict children's access to television advertising
   2 limit the time children spend watching television
   3 make children's television programming more entertaining
   4 provide control over the quality of children's television programming

3 The first system for rating children's programs was criticized because it did not provide information about
   1 alternative programming
   2 objectionable content
   3 age appropriateness
   4 participating networks

4 According to the author, some people fear that use of the ratings system will lead to
   1 censorship
   2 greed
   3 corruption
   4 propaganda

5 In line 104, the word "galvanize" most nearly means
   1 celebrate
   2 stimulate
   3 oppose
   4 interrupt

6   According to the author, NBC declined to participate in the new ratings system because the network objected to the
   1 equipment needed to use the ratings
   2 time required to use the ratings
   3 groups responsible for assigning ratings
   4 method of assigning ratings

7   The "V-chip" required by the Telecommunications Act of 1996 (lines 119 through 122) allows parents to
   1 prevent viewing of unsuitable programs
   2 observe the ratings symbol directly on the screen
   3 record the time children spend watching television
   4 remove violent scenes from televised programs

8   The main purpose of the text is to
   1 criticize the use of sex and violence on television
   2 persuade people to support the television ratings system
   3 inform people about issues surrounding the television ratings system
   4 describe children's views about the quality of television

9   According to graph *a*, entitled "Kids with TVs in Their Bedrooms," what percentage of American children have televisions in their bedrooms?
   1 25.6%
   2 37.8%
   3 40.7%
   4 55.8%

10   Which statement is best supported by the data in graph *b*, entitled "Parents' Views of TV Quality"?
   1 Television is a more positive experience for adolescents than for preschoolers.
   2 Parents' opinions of television quality decline as the ages of their children increase.
   3 Elementary students have more negative views of television quality than do adolescent students.
   4 Parents of adolescents have more positive views of television programming than do parents of preschoolers.

LOOKING AT THE ANSWERS

1   **3** "educational." In the third paragraph, the author quotes one of the producers as saying, "It's entertaining as well as educational. . . ." The author goes on to say the Captain Kangaroo formula is designed to help commercial TV stations meet FCC requirements to provide a minimum number of hours a week of educational programming.

2   **4** "provide control over the quality of children's television programming." This statement captures the overall theme of this piece. None of the other statements represents a point made in the article.

3   **2** "objectionable content." The paragraph about the first age-based ratings system, which begins at line 50, points out that "parents needed more specific information about the content of programs — specifically violence, sex, and language."

4   **1** "censorship." At lines 105–106, the author's reference to the possibility of "skittish" executives influencing writers and producers to "tone down" programs at the expense of the "creative process" is an expression of fear of censorship from within the industry.

5   **2** "stimulate." The sense of the passage is that groups could use ratings to <u>encourage</u> or <u>strengthen</u> efforts to boycott programs or advertisers.

6   **4** "method of assigning ratings." The objections attributed to NBC (lines 107–111) are that there would be no "consistency in application . . . or use. . . ." NBC argued that the system is confusing if not incoherent. There is no reference to equipment or time involved, nor is there a reference to particular groups.

7   **1** "prevent viewing of unsuitable programs." The passage points out that the V-chip makes it possible to "screen out objectionable programs," that is, prevent them from being seen altogether.

8   **3** "inform people about issues surrounding the television ratings system." Examples of criticism are offered for information but are not the purpose of the article, nor is there an evident effort to persuade the readers, and there are no references to children's views on the quality of television programming. This is a good example of writing meant to inform: The author offers background information on the issue and explains the current controversy, offering details of the rating system itself, and he includes the positions of both those who are in favor of a rating system and those who oppose one.

9   **3** "40.7%." This is the percentage "overall," that is, of all kids with TVs in their bedrooms. The other parts of the graph represent different age groups.

10   **2**   "Parents' opinions of television quality decline as the ages of their children increase." The graph shows that the percentage of parents with negative views of TV quality is highest for adolescents. The figure is nearly twice that of parents of preschoolers and is substantially higher than for parents of elementary-age children.

Part B, Sample Student Essay Responses

Essay 1

We are all familiar with those little symbols that appear on our television screens, showing whether the program is suitable for all ages. How did those symbols get there and how effective are they?

The symbols are a result of pressure by the public to protect children from the usual television fare of violence, sex, and offensive language. The Federal Communications Commission requires stations to air at least three hours a week of "core educational programming" for children, but with kids watching 15–20 hours of TV per week (according to Kenneth Jost), the FCC rule doesn't begin to cover most of what kids are actually watching.

Parents have not been happy with what TV offers children. According to a 1997 survey of parents and children conducted by the Annenberg Public Policy Center, only 21% of parents think their kids watch too much TV, but rarely do those parents consider the shows they're watching to be of good quality. Only 23.7% of parents of preschoolers think that TV shows have a positive quality; that figure shrinks to 10.5% among parents of adolescents. Nevertheless, over half of the adolescents surveyed reported having their own television sets in their bedrooms. It seems that although parents don't mind if their kids watch TV for a couple of hours every day, they do wish they would watch better programs.

That's where the ratings system comes in. The system labels each show with a symbol that indicates age-appropriateness and also reveals whether the show contains anything parents find bothersome. For example, a rating of Y7-FV indicates a program suitable for children who are 7 or older and which contains some fantasy violence. Parents can then use the rating to help them determine whether or not to let junior watch. With the new "V-chip," parents can block shows with objectionable content altogether.

The system is not universally applauded. Some TV producers feel that programs or advertisers could be boycotted, resulting in shows that may be squeaky clean, but lacking artistic merit and creativity. The Parents' Television Council, on the other hand, thinks the ratings aren't explicit enough. NBC, concerned about inconsistency in its application, has decided not to use the system at all.

Is the system effective? I think that it does provide parents with a way to monitor their children's viewing. It's true that the system doesn't tell the parents everything. Does that (for violence), for example, mean that the viewer is exposed to the gruesome but natural sight of a lion ripping apart a gazelle, which many parents would find acceptable, or does it refer to murder by chain saw, which most parents would choose to avoid? But it probably gives the parents enough information to make a decision. Without the system, parents would have to watch every show with their children, ready to cut the power immediately if something objectionable comes on. Clearly, the ratings system is a better way.

There is no guarantee, of course, that programs that survive the screening are of high quality or interest. They may be free not only of sex, violence, and bad words, but also of any meaningful content. At some point, parents have to sit down, watch the program, and determine if it's good for the kids. But the ratings system, along with the V-chip, is a good way for parents to protect their kids from the absolute worst that TV has to offer.

Essay 2

In response to political pressure, the majority of the television industry agreed recently to adopt a more specific system of program ratings, as opposed to the age-based movie system that had previously been in use.

Arguments for a better method of rating were supported by both President Bill Clinton and Vice-President Al Gore. These men have witnessed the outrage on Capitol Hill, in which both parties came to a similar expression of disapproval over the content of television. There has been an outcry against children's access to sexually explicit and violent material. This outcry, apparently, had been echoed by consumers, which prompted the creation of a more detailed system that indicates a particular type of content, such as coarse language or fantasy violence in children's programming.

This system, however, is not without its critics. NBC, one of television's major broadcast networks, refuses to take part in the newly devised rating system, arguing that "the system is at best confusing and at worst, totally incoherent." According to Roslyn

Weinman, NBC's executive vice-president for broadcast standards and content, the use and application of this system will be minimal.

On the other hand, many critics of television programming claim that even the new system provides too little information on the degree of severity of the sex, language, and violence. Some say that parents will have little more information than they do now. Others, still, say that the rating system has no effect on the content itself.

The new rating system is intended for use in conjunction with the new "V-chip." This microchip has the ability to block out questionable content. The Telecommunications Act of 1996 stipulates that all new television sets be installed with this "V-chip," to be used at the consumer's discretion. This is no surprise, taking into account that the number of parents who are dissatisfied with their children's programming continues to increase.

Personally, I disagree that the new ratings system will help parents to monitor their children's programming. Many children have sole control of their own private televisions. According to the information provided in the graph, an overall percentage of 40.7% of minors have TVs in their bedrooms. Another startling statistic is that 55.8% of teenagers have their own TVs as well.

Furthermore, I also disapprove of the new ratings system because I believe that it will promote censorship. Many members of the television industry have been fearful that the network executives could pressure writers to tone down content to the "detriment of the creative process." If we censor ourselves to the point of artistic inhibition, we will have no means of truly free expression. I do not believe that children should be exposed to obscene or inappropriate materials intentionally, but let us remember that there is a major difference between vulgar, indecent content and artistic expression that benefits the viewer despite being edgy or shocking.

But I digress. The most important reason that the new ratings system will not be effective is that parents should take these matters into their own hands. Rather than relying on the FCC to protect their children's minds, they should take into consideration what may be done on their own parts.

Analysis

Essay 1 reveals an in-depth analysis of the documents and shows skill in developing a detailed argument in support of the ratings system. The writer clearly understands the complexity of the issue by acknowledging the system's weaknesses and the views of some of its critics. The writer makes especially skillful use of the chart by pointing out that parents seem willing to allow children to watch but become more critical of the quality of television programming as their children get older. Development of ideas is especially good in this essay, and the organization is logical. Transitions are also effective in keeping the reader's attention focused on the issues. Language is precise and appropriate, and the writer shows command of the conventions.

Essay 2 makes good use of the material in the article and the graph to argue against the proposed new ratings system. While the writer reveals an in-depth analysis of the documents, the argument is less focused than in Essay 1, primarily because the writer does not state a clear position at the beginning; it is only in the sixth paragraph that the writer declares, "Personally, I disagree. . . ." In comparison with the development of ideas in the first part of the essay, the arguments in support of the writer's view are less developed, especially in the concluding paragraph. The use of transitions, appropriate language, and sentence structure is effective, and the writer has command of the conventions.

Both essays meet the criteria for a high score. The first, overall, is better written and more effective as an argument; the second is effective in showing how the documents may be used to support an opposing view.

See Chapter 7 for a more detailed discussion of writing on examinations.

Chapter 3

READING PROSE

One of the characters in Moliere's satire *Le Bourgeois Gentilhomme (The Bourgeois Gentleman)* makes an astonishing discovery: "For over forty years I have been speaking prose without knowing it!" Prose writing is composed in the rhythms and patterns of spoken discourse. When we read novels and short stories, essays and reports, journals and letters, we are usually reading prose. In our daily lives and as students, we read prose that varies widely in purpose, in method of development, and in tone. Prose serves the purposes of personal expression, persuasion, literary effect, and information.

WHAT WRITERS DO:
A LIST OF USEFUL TERMS

A group of high school juniors recently was asked to list all the verbs they could think of to denote what writers *do*. Here is the list they came up with:

address	affirm	alert	amuse	analyze
appraise	argue	assert	assess	capture
caution	censure	cite	clarify	classify
comment	conclude	condemn	conjecture	convey
create	create images	criticize	declare	defend
define	delineate	depict	describe	discern
discover	dramatize	edit	emphasize	enhance
enrich	establish	evaluate	examine	explain
explore	expose	expound	forewarn	formulate
illustrate	imply	infer	influence	inform
inspire	interpret	invent	judge	note
observe	offer	persuade	play	ponder
portray	present	probe	produce	propose
provoke	question	reassure	recreate	refine
reflect	refute	remind	reveal	revise

scrutinize	see	select	shock	show
suggest	summarize	support	symbolize	teach
theorize	uncover	view	work(!)	

As you consider these terms, you will note that they are not separated by categories; many of them denote both purpose and tone, and many suggest a method of development as well. While this list may not include everything writers "do," it is a useful reminder of the great variety in written expression. (Because command of this vocabulary will also help you to express your understanding and appreciation of what you read, you will find examples showing how many of these words are applied to discussions of nonfiction and, in Chapter 5, to writing about literature.)

To read well you must be listening actively to the narrator's voice, thinking with the author. If you are reading a piece for information or direction, ask questions; expect them to be answered. If you are reading a work of argument or persuasion, question it; actively agree or disagree; follow how the argument is developed. If you are reading a piece of personal expression, try to imagine, even share, the experience. If you are reading a piece of vivid description, recreate the images and feelings for yourself. Reading well offers us the entire range of human history and experience expressed in language.

Works of fiction are usually narrative in form. They tell us stories of what *happened* in the lives of the characters and, more important, *why it happened.* Nonfiction takes many forms, and its subjects touch on nearly everything in the human and natural worlds.

READING FICTION

When we speak of fiction, we are generally referring to narrative works—works in which events are recounted, are *told,* and have been imagined and structured by the author. (Although not narrative in form, drama shares many of the essential characteristics of fiction.) The subjects of fiction, however, are no less real than those of history or of what we call the actual or real world. In *Aspects of the Novel,* E. M. Forster shows how "fiction is truer than history." He reminds us that only in narrative fiction and drama can we truly know what is in a character's heart or mind; that is, only in a novel, short story, or play can we fully understand the motives, desires, and reasons for characters' actions. The historian draws conclusions from records of the past; the psychologist interprets interviews and tests; a jury weighs evidence and testimony; and our experience indicates that these are highly reliable ways to understand people and their lives. But only the author of a fictional work can offer an absolutely reliable account of what a character feels, believes, and desires, of why things happen as they do.

Plot and Story

The primary pleasure for most readers of narrative fiction is the story. The reason why we become involved in a novel or short story is that we want to know how it turns out; we want to know what is going to happen to those characters. An author creates a **plot*** when he or she gives order and structure to the action: in a plot, the incidents, or episodes, of the story have meaningful relationships to one another. A story becomes a plot when we understand not only *what happened* but also *why.* In good fiction we are *convinced* of the causal relationship among incidents, and we are convinced by the relationship of characters' motives and feelings to the action.

For most readers of fiction, the first response is to keep track of the plot. We do this spontaneously. If you are preparing a novel or story for class discussion, one of the first things your instructor will expect you to know is, "What happens in . . . ?" This is not a trivial question, because you cannot fully understand the significance of character, theme, or structure if you do not first understand the action as it is presented. Understanding plot, of course, requires memory, and remembering the major incidents of a plot is usually a natural and relatively easy response. The more extensively you read, however, the more skilled you become in remembering and relating the key incidents in a complex plot and in recalling details when their full significance becomes evident—sometimes well after the incidents themselves occur. Keeping notes on the development of a complex plot is very useful, especially for students whose reading of a novel is broken up over days or weeks.

For a class, or as part of your preparation for the Regents exam questions on literature, practice summarizing the plots of works you know or are reading. Be able to tell the story of a novel or play to someone who does not know it in a narrative of your own words, including all the major incidents and their consequences. Be able to tell the story in the same way you would retell a familiar children's story or narrate a significant experience of your own.

Plot and Conflict

At the end of any meaningful story, something has *happened;* something is significantly different in the world and lives of the characters from what it was at the beginning. **Conflict** in the most general sense refers to the forces that move the action in a plot. Conflict in plot may be generated from a search or pursuit, from a discovery, from a deception or misunderstanding, from opportunities to make significant choices, or from unexpected consequences of an action. Although the term *conflict* connotes an active struggle

---

*Terms in bold are featured in A Glossary of Literary Terms and Techniques at the end of the chapter.

between opposing or hostile forces, conflict in fiction may refer to any progression, change, or discovery. The resolution of conflict in a plot may be subtle and confined to the inner life of a character or it may be dramatic and involve irreversible change, violent destruction, or death.

This term may identify an actual struggle between characters, anything from dominance or revenge to simple recognition or understanding. A plot may also focus on conflict between characters and the forces of nature or society. These are essentially **external conflicts**. A work may also center on **internal conflicts**, characters' struggle to know or change themselves and their lives. Most works of fiction and drama contain more than one aspect of conflict.

In Shakespeare's *Romeo and Juliet*, the most dramatic conflicts are external, vivid, and literal: the street brawls between followers of the rival Capulets and Montagues, the fatal fight with Tybalt that leads to Romeo's banishment, and the tragic deaths of the young lovers. In *Macbeth,* however, the primary interest is in the internal conflict between Macbeth's ambitious desires and his understanding of the moral consequences of the actions he takes to achieve those desires. The action in Edith Wharton's most famous story, "Roman Fever," is ironically serene and pleasant: two middle-aged women, longtime friends now both widowed, sit on a terrace overlooking the splendors of Rome and reflect on their common experiences and lifelong friendship. At the end of the conversation—and the story—their actual feelings of rivalry have surfaced, and one of the two learns something that reveals how little she truly knew her husband or understood her marriage or the life of her friend. The conflict between the two women emerges almost imperceptibly, and its meaning is fully understood only in the completely unexpected revelation of the last line.

Plot and Chronology

Narrative is not necessarily presented in chronological order, but it does have a chronology. In other words, incidents may be presented out of the order in which they actually occurred, but by the end of the work the reader understands their order and relationship and appreciates why the story was structured as it was. Plots that are narrated in flashback or from different points of view are common examples.

The Great Gatsby, by F. Scott Fitzgerald, and *Ethan Frome,* by Edith Wharton, are novels in which the narrators first introduce themselves and their interest in the story, then tell the story in a narrative flashback whose full significance to the narrator (and reader) is revealed only at the end. Tennessee Williams's play *The Glass Menagerie* has a similar structure, in which the character of Tom serves both as a narrator in the present and as a principal character in the series of memory scenes that make up the drama. The memory scenes in Arthur Miller's play *Death of a Salesman,* however, are not flashbacks in the same way. Willy Loman relives incidents from the past while the other characters and the action of the play continue in the present. As the play progresses, the shifts in time occur only within Willy's mind.

Shakespeare's tragedies are dramas in which normal chronology is preserved, as it is in such familiar novels as William Golding's *Lord of the Flies* and Mark Twain's *Huckleberry Finn.*

Plot and Time

Related to understanding of chronology is appreciation of how an author creates understanding of *elapsed time*. In the several hours required to read a novel, the two to three hours for a full-length play, and the half-hour to an hour for a one-act play or short story, how much time in the lives of the characters has been accounted for? In one-act plays and many short stories, the time covered by the action is equal to the time to read them. In Wharton's "Roman Fever," for example, the action of the story is contained in a few hours of one afternoon—little more time than it takes to read the story. That conversation, however, completely transforms the women's, and the reader's, understanding of their lives over twenty-five years. The time required for the action in Shirley Jackson's widely read story "The Lottery" is also roughly equal to the time required to read it, yet the plot accounts indirectly for events that have taken place for longer than anyone in the story can even remember. Miller's play *Death of a Salesman* takes place over a period of only twenty-four hours, but the plot and Willy's memories tell us the story of an entire lifetime. Awareness of how an author uses and accounts for time adds considerably to the reader's appreciation of a work.

Narrative Point of View

The **narrator** of a work is the character or author's **persona** that tells a story. **Point of view** is the standpoint, perspective, and degree of understanding from which the narrator speaks. For many students and scholars, how a story is told is one of the most interesting questions. What is the narrative point of view? Is the narration **omniscient**, essentially the point of view of the author? If not, who is the narrator? What is the narrator's relationship to the story? What is the narrator's understanding of the story? How much does the narrator really know? Appreciating how, or by whom, a story is told is often essential to understanding its meaning.

One of the most easily discerned narrative points of view is the first person (*I*), in which either the central character or another directly involved in the action tells the story. J. D. Salinger's novel *Catcher in the Rye* is a vivid and popular example of such narration. Fitzgerald's *The Great Gatsby* is also told in the first person. In each of these works, the fundamental meaning of the novel becomes apparent only when the reader understands the character of the narrator. In each of these works, what the narrator experiences and what he learns about himself and the world are the novel's most important themes.

In first-person narration, the incidents of the plot are limited to those that the narrator himself experiences. First-person narrators can, however, report what they learn from others. In Wharton's *Ethan Frome,* the engineer who narrates tells us that he has "pieced together the story" from the little he has been able to learn in the town of Starkfield, from his limited conversations with Frome himself, and from his brief visit to the Frome house. Wharton's method, of course, dramatizes Frome's inability to express or fulfill the desires of his heart and reveals the reluctance of the people of Starkfield to fully understand the lives of those around them.

Authors may also use first-person narration to achieve an ironic or satiric effect. In Ring Lardner's well-known story "Haircut," a barber in a small midwestern town narrates a story about a local fellow who kept the town entertained with his practical jokes on people. As the story progresses, the reader understands how cruel and destructive the fellow's pranks were, but the barber does not. The narrative method in this story reveals, indirectly, a story of painful ignorance and insensitivity in the "decent" citizens of a small town. Mark Twain's masterpiece, *Huckleberry Finn*, is told by Huck himself. Through the morally naive observations of Huck, Twain satirizes the evils of slavery, fraud, hypocrisy, and virtually every other kind of corrupt human behavior. Edgar Allan Poe's story "The Tell-Tale Heart" is the confession of a cunning madman.

In third-person narration (*he, she, it, they*) a story is reported. The narrative voice may be *omniscient* and, therefore, able to report everything from everywhere in the story; this voice can also report on the innermost thoughts and feelings of the characters themselves. In many novels of the eighteenth and nineteenth centuries, the omniscient narrator even speaks directly to the reader, as if taking him or her into the storyteller's confidence. In Nathaniel Hawthorne's *The Scarlet Letter,* the narrator pauses from time to time to share personal feelings with the reader, as does Nick Carraway, the narrator of *The Great Gatsby.* The method is not common, however, in contemporary fiction.

A widely used narrative method is the **limited omniscient** point of view. The narrative is in the third person but is focused on and even may represent the point of view of a central character. The actions and feelings of other characters are presented from the perspective of that character. Hawthorne's short story "Young Goodman Brown" is an excellent example.

Some third-person narration is dramatically **objective** and detached; it simply reports the incidents of the plot as they unfold. This narrative method, too, can be used for intensely **ironic** effect. Jackson's "The Lottery" is one of the best examples. The real horror of the story is achieved through the utterly detached, nonjudgmental unfolding of the plot.

In some plays, too, there is a character who serves a narrative role: the Chorus in Shakespeare's *Henry V*, the character of Tom in Williams's *The Glass Menagerie,* and the Stage Manager in Thornton Wilder's *Our Town* are familiar examples.

In each of the works discussed here, the narrative method is not simply a literary device; it is an intrinsic part of the meaning of the work.

Setting

The setting of a work includes the time and places in which the action is played out; setting may also include a significant historical context. In drama, setting may be presented directly in the set, costumes, and lighting. In narrative fiction, it is usually presented directly through description. In some works, the physical setting is central to the plot and developed in great detail; in other works, only those details necessary to anchor the plot in a time or place will be developed. Regardless of detail, responsive readers recreate images of setting as they read.

In addition to the physical and natural details of the fictional world, setting also includes mood and **atmosphere**. In some works, social or political realities constitute part of the setting. *The Scarlet Letter* is not only set in Puritan Boston, it is also *about* that society; and *The Great Gatsby* presents a vivid picture of life in New York during Prohibition and the roaring twenties.

For some works, the author may create specific details of setting to highlight a theme. In Golding's novel *Lord of the Flies*, the island on which the story takes place has everything essential for basic survival: food and water are available, and the climate is temperate. In order to explore the moral questions of the boys' regression into savagery, Golding carefully establishes a setting in which survival itself is not a primary issue. In *Ethan Frome,* details of the harsh winter and of the isolation of a town "bypassed by the railroad" intensify the story of a man's desperately cold and isolated life.

Character

We understand characters in fiction and drama, as we do the people in our own lives, by what they say and do and by what others say about them. Because characters are imagined and created by an author, we can even understand them more reliably and fully than we can many of the people around us. Many students find their greatest satisfaction in reading works about characters to whom they can relate, characters whose struggles are recognizable and whose feelings are familiar.

Understanding character in fiction means understanding a person's values and **motivation**, beliefs and principles, moral qualities, strengths and weaknesses, and degree of self-knowledge and understanding. To fully appreciate a work, the reader must understand what characters are searching for and devoting their lives to.

Literature also seeks to account for the forces outside individuals that influence the directions and outcomes of their lives. These "forces" range from those of nature and history to the demands of family, community, and society. The response of characters to inner and outer forces is what literature depicts and makes comprehensible.

When you review the tasks for the literature part of the Regents exam, you will find that discussion of character is usually the focus of the best responses. (See Chapter 5 for a detailed review.) The reason is that any meaningful or convincing plot stems from human thought, motive, and action. Depending on the narrative point of view (see page 67), a character's thoughts and feelings may be presented directly through omniscient narrative or first-person commentary. In "Young Goodman Brown," the narrator tells us directly what the title character is thinking and feeling; in "Roman Fever," the reader discovers the most important revelations of character simultaneously with the two central characters. Character in drama is revealed directly in dialogue and action, but it may be expanded through soliloquies and asides. In Shakespeare's *Othello,* for example, the full extent of Iago's evil is revealed through the variety of methods Iago uses to manipulate different characters and through his **soliloquies.**

In some works, the author's primary purpose is to reveal character gradually through plot; in others, the author establishes understanding of character from the beginning in order to account for what happens. In the opening pages of *The Great Gatsby,* the narrator, Nick, who is also a character in the novel, introduces himself and declares his judgment of the moral quality of the people and events he is about to narrate. With Nick's own character and motives clearly established, the reader then shares his *gradual* discovery of the truth about Gatsby and his life.

Theme

The subjects of literature may come from any aspect of human experience: love, friendship, growing up, ambition, family relationships, conflicts with society, survival, war, evil, death, and so on. **Theme** in a work of literature is the understanding, insight, observation, and presentation of such subjects. Theme is what a work *says about* a subject. Themes are the central ideas of literary works.

One way to think about theme is to consider it roughly analogous to the topic or thesis of an expository essay. If the author of a novel, story, or play had chosen to examine the subjects of the work in an essay, what might be the topic assertions of such an essay? The student is cautioned, however, not to overinterpret the analogy. Themes in literature are rarely "morals," such as those found at the end of a fable, but neither are they are "hidden meanings." Although scholars and critics often express thematic ideas in phrases, students are often required to state themes in full sentences. In the next paragraph are some examples of statements about theme.

Macbeth is a play about the temptation to embrace evil forces and about the power of ambition to corrupt; Macbeth himself makes one of the most important statements of theme in the play when he says, "I do all that becomes a man/who does more is none." *Ethan Frome* and Lardner's "Haircut" both illustrate that people in small towns do not truly understand the innermost needs and desires of other people they *think* they know. William Golding's novel *Lord of the Flies* illustrates the bleak view that human beings' savage nature will prevail without external forces of authority, that human beings are not civilized in their fundamental natures. In contrast, in *Adventures of Huckleberry Finn,* Twain presents civilization as the source of corruption and finds truly moral behavior only in the runaway slave, Jim, and the ignorant boy, Huck.

In Chapter 5 you will find an extensive list of literature topics, many of which are expressed in terms of theme.

READING NONFICTION

Fiction and nonfiction share many common elements; they also make similar demands and offer comparable rewards to the thoughtful reader. In broad contrast to fiction, where characters and plot are imaginative creations of the author, nonfiction is about actual persons, experiences, and phenomena. Nonfiction also speculates on abstract and philosophical questions of history and politics, ethics and religion, culture and society, as well as the natural world. In biography and autobiography, the writer focuses on what is meaningful and interesting in the life of an individual. The purpose of this section is to review some of the distinctive features of formal and informal essays and to illustrate some of the methods authors use to develop arguments in persuasive writing. The glossary at the end of the chapter also features extended definitions and examples of many important terms.

Questions for the Critical Reader

Here are the questions you are urged to keep in mind as you prepare for the listening and reading tasks on the Regents exam:

What is the purpose of this piece? Its tone or mood? Its overall effect?

What does the author say? believe? recall? value? assert?

What does the author mean? imply? suggest? agree with? disagree with?

How are language and imagery used?

What conclusions or inferences is the reader led to?

What experience is meant to be shared and understood?

Purpose

In speaking of fiction, the central ideas of a work are identified as its themes. In essays, purpose refers both to the central ideas and to their intended effect on the reader. For example, many authors of essays develop a thesis with a view to influencing opinion or urging action. We encounter such writing daily on the editorial and Op-Ed pages of a newspaper. Many of the verbs on the list of "what writers do" (page 63) identify such purposes: *affirm, alert, argue, assert, caution, censure, condemn, criticize, declare, defend, evaluate, expose, forewarn, imply, inspire, judge, persuade, propose, provoke, reveal, scrutinize, support.*

Much nonfiction, of course, has as its purpose to explain and inform. The verbs used to identify informative writing include *analyze, assess, clarify, define, describe, explore, formulate, illustrate, interpret, recreate, summarize.*

Other purposes may be likened to conversations between the author and the reader; these "conversations" may be about anything from the most personal experiences to reflections on the nature of life and the universe. Some useful verbs here might be *address, amuse, capture, comment, conjecture, depict, discover, enhance, enrich, examine, explore, invent, observe, offer, ponder, probe, propose, question, recreate, reflect, shock.*

Methods of Development and Patterns of Organization

The ability to use a variety of methods to organize and express ideas is one of the most important skills a student writer learns. The thoughtful reader should also be able to appreciate how a writer develops material. Here is a review of some of the most common patterns of organization.

FROM ABSTRACT TO CONCRETE/FROM GENERAL TO SPECIFIC

Going from the general to the specific is the most common and natural pattern for explanation, illustration, and reasoning. A passage by Sandy Asher is an especially good example:

As a child, I sensed there was something I desperately needed from books. As a writer for young readers, I've tried to figure out what that something was. It turned out to be a combination of three things: companionship, a sense of control, and magic.

In her essay, Asher goes on to develop a paragraph about each of the three things that make up the "something" she is explaining. (See page 2.)

Here is how Ernie Pyle begins his explanation of what "The awful waste and destruction of war" really means:

I walked for a mile and a half along the water's edge of our many-miled invasion beach. I walked slowly, for the detail on the beach was infinite.

The wreckage was vast and startling. The awful waste and destruction of war, even aside from the loss of human life, has always been one of its outstanding features to those who are in it. Anything and everything is expendable. And we did expend on our beachhead in Normandy during those first few hours.

For a mile out from the beach there were scores of tanks and trucks and boats that were not visible, for they were at the bottom of the water—swamped by overloading, or hit by shells, or sunk by mines.

His description of a Normandy beach following the D-Day invasion in 1944 is developed in a series of vivid images and poignant details that make the waste and destruction of war comprehensible to those who have not experienced it.

FROM CONCRETE TO ABSTRACT/FROM SPECIFIC TO GENERAL

Reversing the more common pattern, going from the specific to the general can also be a very effective way to develop understanding of a general concept. This is the pattern William Kittredge uses in the **anecdote** about his boyhood encounter with a sage grouse. The passage recounts a specific experience, which leads to the closing general observation:

> **For that childhood moment I believed the world to be absolutely inhabited by an otherness which was utterly demonic and natural, not of my own making. But soon as that bird was enclosed in a story which defined it as a common-place prairie chicken, I was no longer frightened. It is a skill we learn early, the art of inventing stories to explain away the fearful sacred strangeness of the world. Storytelling and make-believe, like war and agriculture, are among the arts of self-defense, and all of them are ways of enclosing otherness and claiming ownership.**

FROM QUESTION TO ANSWER

Another method of developing **argument** and explanation is to pose a question, which the paragraph or essay then answers. Here is an example from the conclusion of Thoreau's *Walden:*

> **Why should we be in such desperate haste to succeed, in such desperate enterprises? If a man does not keep pace with his companions, perhaps it is because he hears a different drummer. Let him step to the music which he hears, however measured or far away.**

And here is a passage from "The Almost Perfect State," an essay by Don Marquis:

> **You have seen the tall towers of Manhattan, wonderful under the stars. How did it come about that such growths come from such soil—that a breed lawless and prosaic has written such a mighty hieroglyphic against the sky? How is it that this hideous, half-brute city is also beautiful and a fit habitation for demi-gods? How come? . . . It comes about because the wise and subtle deities permit nothing worthy to be lost. It was with no thought of beauty that the builders labored . . . the baffled dreams and broken visions and the ruined hopes and the secret desires of**

each one labored with him . . . the rejected beauty, the strangled appreciation, the inchoate art, the submerged spirit—these groped and found each other and gathered themselves together and worked themselves into the tiles and mortar of the edifice and made a town that is a worthy fellow of the sunrise and the sea winds.

The passage by Sandy Asher (see page 2) is also an example of this method; the final paragraph reveals that the essay is an answer to the question, "Why do I write for children?"

Magic, companionship, a sense of control. The wonder of ourselves, of each other, and of life—this is the true subject matter of all novels. The best children's literature speaks not only to children but to the human condition. Writing for children simply means writing for human beings in the beginning, when you can still take part in creation, before habit, cynicism and despair have set in, and while there is still hope and energy, a willingness to learn, and a healthy sense of humor. These qualities I find irresistible in the young people I write about and for, qualities I want to hang onto and to cultivate in myself. So I write for children, not just for their sakes—but for my own.

CHRONOLOGICAL ORDER/NARRATION

Although narration is the primary mode of development for fiction, it is also widely used in **exposition** and argument. The historian uses narration and chronology in recounting significant events; the scientific writer may use narration to explain a process. Narration is also an essential part of biography and the personal essay. Annie Dillard, in a passage that appeared on a past Regents exam, uses narration to explain what she means by the "unwrapped gifts and free surprises" of Nature.

I walked up to a tree, an Osage orange, and a hundred birds flew away. They simply materialized out of the tree. I saw a tree, then a whisk of color, then a tree again. I walked closer and another hundred blackbirds took flight. Not a branch, not a twig budged:

the birds were apparently weightless as well as invisible. Or, it was as if the leaves of the Osage orange had been freed from a spell in the form of red-winged blackbirds; they flew from the tree, caught my eye in the sky, and vanished. When I looked again at the tree, the leaves had reassembled as if nothing had happened. Finally I walked directly to the trunk of the tree and a final hundred, the real diehards, appeared, spread, and vanished. How could so many hide in the tree without my seeing them? The Osage orange, unruffled, looked just as it had looked from the house, when three hundred red-winged blackbirds cried from its crown. I looked upstream where they flew, and they were gone. Searching, I couldn't spot one. I wandered upstream to force them to play their hand, but they'd crossed the creek and scattered. One show to customer. These appearances catch at my throat; they are the free gifts, the bright coppers at the roots of trees.

CAUSE AND EFFECT

Formal development of cause and effect arguments is essential to the historian, the scientist, and the lawyer. It also serves as a basic method for much of the expository writing students do. This paragraph from a speech by Madeleine Kunin offers a good example of explanation through cause and effect:

In my own case, most essential to my political evolution was a strong desire to have an effect on events around me, whether that was a flashing red light at the railroad crossing in my neighborhood, to protect my children on their way to school, or whether it was a new environmental law for the state of Vermont. The fact that I succeeded in obtaining the flashing red light, as a private citizen, enabled me to change the environmental laws as governor. Each step builds a new self-image, enabling us to move from the passive to the active voice.

In these paragraphs, historian Bruce Catton in "Lee and Grant: A Study in Constrasts," brings to a close his extended discussion of the contrasts between Ulysses S. Grant and Robert E. Lee and introduces the discussion of how the two men were alike:

So Grant and Lee were in complete contrast, representing two diametrically opposed elements in American life. Grant was the modern man emerging; beyond him, ready to come on the stage, was the great age of steel and machinery, of crowded cities and a restless burgeoning vitality. Lee might have ridden down from the old age of chivalry, lance in hand, silken banner fluttering over his head. Each man was the perfect champion of his cause, drawing both his strengths and his weaknesses from the people he led.

Yet it was not all contrast, after all. Different as they were—in background, in personality, in underlying aspiration—these two great soldiers had much in common. Under everything else, they were marvelous fighters. Furthermore, their fighting qualities were really very much alike.

Here, from *Life on the Mississippi* (1883), is Mark Twain's comparison of how the North and South treated the Civil War as a topic of conversation, years after it ended:

In the North one hears the war mentioned, in social conversations, once a month; sometimes as often as once a week; but as a distinct subject for talk, it has long ago been relieved of duty. There are sufficient reasons for this. Given a dinner company of six gentlemen to-day, it can easily happen that four of them—and possibly five—were not in the field at all. So the chances are four to two, or five to one, that the war will at no time during the evening become the topic of conversation; and the chances are still greater that if it becomes the topic it will remain so but a little while. If you add six ladies to the company, you have added six people who saw so little of the

dread realities of the war that they ran out of talk
concerning them years ago, and now would soon
weary of the topic if you brought it up.

The case is very different in the South. There, every
man you meet was in the war; and every lady you
meet saw the war. The war is the great chief topic of
conversation. The interest in it is vivid and constant;
the interest in other topics is fleeting. Mention of the
war will wake up a dull company and set their
tongues going, when nearly any other topic would
fail. In the South, the war is what A.D. is elsewhere:
they date from it . . . . It shows how intimately every
individual was visited, in his own person, by the
tremendous episode. It gives the inexperienced
stranger a better idea of what a vast and comprehensive calamity invasion is than he can ever get by reading books at the fireside.

DEVELOPMENT THROUGH EXTENDED METAPHOR

An extended metaphor or **analogy** is a very effective way to develop an
argument or illustrate a concept. It uses the known and familiar to explain
the unfamiliar. Here is the introduction to an essay written by a student on
the topic "All the World's a Stage." (See Chapter 7 for the complete essay
and analysis.)

All the world is indeed a stage. And we are the performers. Everything we do in life is a production, and
we must constantly perform our best because, in life,
there are no rehearsals. Each of us performs on a separate stage, some for a larger audience than others.
But each performance, regardless of the size of the
audience, is of equal importance, and each performer
must meet the standard of life's most important
critic—himself.

Here is a passage from Stephen Crane's novel *The Red Badge of Courage:*

The ground was cluttered with vines and bushes,
and the trees grew close and spread out like bouquets.
The creepers, catching against his legs, cried out

harshly as their sprays were torn from the barks of trees. The swishing saplings tried to make known his presence to the world. He could not conciliate the forest. As he made his way, it was always calling out protestations. When he separated embraces of trees and vines the disturbed foliage waved their arms and turned their face leaves toward him.

DEFINITION OR CLASSIFICATION

In this paragraph from a speech by Madeleine Kunin, she develops a key term by classifying its component parts:

Political courage stems from a number of sources: anger, pain, love, hate. There is no lack of political motivation within women. We feel it all. Anger at a world which rushes toward saber-rattling displays of power. Pain at a world which ignores the suffering of its homeless, its elderly, its children. Hatred toward the injustice which occurs daily as the strong overpower the weak. And love for the dream of peace on earth.

The essay by Sandy Asher employs the same method, developing each part of the definition in a full paragraph.

EXAMPLES IN ORDER OF IMPORTANCE

The most persuasive arguments are those in which the reasoning has a cumulative effect. The skilled writer does not present the supporting details of a thesis in random order; rather, the skilled writer presents details in an order that stresses importance and significance. Here is the closing argument from a piece by Robert Finch:

To consume whales solely for their nourishment of human values is only a step from consuming them for meat. It is not only presumptuous and patronizing, but it is misleading and does both whales and men a grave disservice. Whales have an inalienable right to exist, not because they resemble man or because they

are useful to him, but simply because they do exist, because they have a proven fitness to the exactitudes of being on a global scale matched by few other species. If they deserve our admiration and respect, it is because, as Henry Beston put it, "They are other nations, caught with ourselves in the net of life and time, fellow prisoners of the splendor and travail of life."

These models offer examples of only some of the ways in which writers develop ideas. As you read more widely, you will appreciate the extent to which every writer, especially the writer of essays, creates a form best suited to the subject and purpose. When you find a piece of writing you especially admire or find convincing, note how the author developed the ideas.

Tone

When we speak of **tone** in writing we are referring to the attitude of the writer toward the subject and/or toward the reader. It is closely related to what we mean when we refer to someone's "tone of voice." Tone may range from *harsh* and *insistent* to *gentle* and *reflective*. There is as much variety of tone in writing as there is in human feeling. Some pieces—essays of opinion, for example—usually have a very distinct tone; other works, especially in fiction or personal expression, may have a more subtle and indirect tone.

Here is a list of adjectives to help you identify the tone or mood of a prose passage. Many have been gathered by students in their reading of Op-Ed page essays; most have appeared in the comprehension questions of the Regents English exam in recent years. Each reflects a distinctive feeling; be sure to look up in a dictionary any that you are not sure about.

admiring	advisory	affectionate	alarmed
amused	anguished	appalled	apprehensive
argumentative	arrogant	assured	(with) awe
bewildered	bitter	boastful	candid
cautionary	cautious	challenging	concerned
credible	critical	curious	cynical
defensive	disappointed	dismayed	eerie
frank	grateful	haughty	humorous
indifferent	indignant	informed	inquiring
instructive	intense	ironic	knowledgeable

melancholy	mocking	mysterious	nonchalant
nostalgic	objective	offended	optimistic
outraged	peaceful	probing	provocative
questioning	reasoned	reflective	sad
sarcastic	satirical	sentimental	skeptical
surprised	thoughtful	troubled	understanding
whimsical	wondering		

The Op-Ed pages of most newspapers offer daily examples of essays on current topics, representing widely varied methods of argument, style, and tone. Many national magazines such as *Newsweek, Time,* and *Sports Illustrated* also offer good examples of feature writing and reporting on current issues. *Harper's Magazine, The Atlantic Monthly,* and *The New Yorker* include excellent selections of essays and other examples of literary nonfiction. The list of Recommended Reading on page 255 also offers titles of books of nonfiction available in paperback.

A GLOSSARY OF LITERARY TERMS AND TECHNIQUES

abstract In contrast to the *concrete,* abstract language expresses general ideas and concepts apart from specific examples or instances. Very formal writing is characterized by abstract expression. An *abstract* (n.) is a brief summary of the key ideas in a scientific, legal, or scholarly piece of writing.

analogy An expression of the similarities between things that are not wholly alike or related. (See, for example, the student essay on page 78.) See *metaphor* in A Glossary of Poetic Terms and Techniques, Chapter 4.

anecdote A very brief, usually vivid, story or episode. Often humorous, anecdotes offer examples of typical behavior or illustrate the personality of a character. Writers of biography and autobiography make extensive use of anecdote to reveal the lives of their subjects.

antithesis In formal argument, a statement that opposes or contrasts with a *thesis* statement. Informally, we use the term to refer to any expression or point of view completely opposed to another. In literature, even an experience or feeling may be expressed as the *antithesis* of another. See also *thesis.*

argument In persuasive writing or speaking, the development of reasons to support the writer's position; also the method of reasoning used to persuade. Informally, we may use the term to describe the development of a topic in any piece of exposition. Historically, it has also denoted a summary of a literary work's plot or main ideas.

atmosphere Closely related to *tone* or mood, it refers to a pervasive feeling in a work. Atmosphere often stems from setting and from distinctive characters or actions. For example, the atmosphere in many of Poe's stories is mysterious, troubling, even sinister, and Hawthorne's "Young Goodman Brown" reflects the threatening and ambiguous world of its Puritan setting.

autobiography A formally composed account of a person's life, written by that person. While we must trust, or be skeptical of, the reliability of the account, we often appreciate the firsthand narration of experience. Autobiography is also a rich source of information and insight into an historical period or into literary or artistic worlds. Autobiography, like the novel, has *narrative* and chronology. (See also *journal.*) We describe literary works that are closely based on the author's life as "autobiographical." Eugene O'Neill's *Long Day's Journey into Night* and Tennessee Williams's *The Glass Menagerie* are plays that reflect many details of their authors' lives.

biography A narrative, historical account of the life, character, and significance of its subject. Contemporary biography is usually researched in detail and may not always paint an admiring portrait of its subject. A critical biography of a literary figure includes discussion of the writer's works to show the writer's artistic development and career. Biographies of figures significant in history or public affairs also offer commentary on periods and events of historical importance.

character Characters are the imagined persons, created figures, who inhabit the worlds of fiction and drama. E. M. Forster distinguished between *flat* and *round* characters: Flat are those, like stereotypes, who represent a single and exaggerated human characteristic; round are those whose aspects are complex and convincing, and who change or develop in the course of a work. In good fiction, plot must develop out of character. The desires, values, and motives of characters account for the action and conflict in a plot.

characterization The method by which an author establishes character; the means by which personality, manner, and appearance are created. It is achieved directly through description and dialogue and indirectly through observations and reactions of other characters.

concrete Refers to the particular, the specific, in expression and imagery. That which is concrete can be perceived by the senses. Concrete also refers to that which is tangible, real, or actual, in contrast to the *abstract,* which is intangible and conceptual.

conflict In the most general sense, it identifies the forces that give rise to a plot. This term may identify an actual struggle between characters, anything from revenge to simple recognition or understanding. A plot may focus on conflict between characters and the forces of nature or society. These are essentially **external conflicts**. A work may also center on **internal conflicts**, characters' struggles to know or change themselves and their lives. Most works of fiction and drama contain more than one aspect of conflict. (See the discussion on page 65.)

denouement A French term meaning "untying a knot," it refers to the way the complications or conflict of a plot are finally resolved. It also refers to what is called the "falling action" in a drama, that part of the play that follows the dramatic climax and reveals the consequences of the main action for minor characters; it also accounts briefly for what happens in the world of the play after the principal drama is resolved. In Arthur Miller's *Death of a Salesman*, the "Requiem" may be considered a denouement; it accounts for the response to Willy's death by his wife, sons, and only friend. In Shakespeare's *Macbeth,* the climax is in the scene following the death of Lady Macbeth in which Macbeth understands that he has destroyed all capacity for feeling and has rendered his life meaningless; the denouement includes the battle in which Macbeth comprehends the treachery of the witches and is killed by MacDuff, thus restoring the throne to the rightful heir, Malcolm.

determinism The philosophical view that human existence is determined by forces over which humans have little or no control. The concept that fate predestines the course of a character's life or a tragic figure's downfall is a form of determinism.

episode A series of actions or incidents that make up a self-contained part of a larger narrative. Some novels are structured so that each chapter is a significant episode. Fitzgerald's *The Great Gatsby* and Mark Twain's *Huckleberry Finn* are good examples of this structure. A *scene* in a play is often analogous to an episode in a narrative. Many television series are presented in weekly episodes.

essay A general term (from French *essai,* meaning an attempt, a trying out of something) to denote an extended composition, usually expository, devoted to a single topic. Essays may be composed to persuade, to reflect on philosophical questions, to analyze a subject, to express an opinion, or to entertain. As a literary form, the essay dates from the sixteenth century and remains a popular and widely practiced form. See *formal/informal* essay.

exposition Writing whose purpose is to inform, illustrate, and explain. In literature, exposition refers to those passages or speeches in which setting, offstage or prior action, or a character's background is revealed. In *The Great Gatsby,* Nick Carraway pauses in the narrative to give the reader additional information about Gatsby's background. The prologue to Shakespeare's *Romeo and Juliet* is an example of exposition.

flashback A presentation of incidents or episodes that occurred prior to the beginning of the narrative itself. When an author or filmmaker uses flashback, the "present" or forward motion of the plot is suspended. Flashback may be introduced through the device of a character's memory or through the narrative voice itself. William Faulkner's "Barn Burning" and *Light in August* include vivid passages of memory and narrative flashback. Jack Burden's recounting of the Cass Mastern story in Robert Penn Warren's *All the King's Men* is also a form of flashback.

foreshadowing A technique in which an author establishes details or mood that will become more significant as the plot of a work progresses. Thoughtful readers usually sense such details and accumulate them in their memories. In one of the opening scenes of *Ethan Frome*, Ethan and Mattie talk about the dangers of sledding down Starkfield's steepest hill; and, in the second paragraph of "The Lottery," the boys are stuffing their pockets with stones or making piles of them on the edge of the square.

form The organization, shape, and structure of a work. Concretely, form may refer to *genre* (see below), for example, the sonnet form, the tragic form. More abstractly, form also refers to the way we sense inherent structure and shape.

formal/informal essay The formal essay emphasizes organization, logic, and explanation of ideas, whereas the informal essay emphasizes the voice and perspective of the writer. In the latter, also called a *personal essay*, the reader is aware of the author's *persona* and is asked to share the author's interest in the subject.

genre A type or form of literature. Examples include *novel, short story, epic poem, essay, sonnet, tragedy.*

image Although the term suggests something that is visualized, an image is an evocation through language of *any* experience perceived directly through the senses. See also A Glossary of Poetic Terms and Techniques, Chapter 4.

irony In general, a tone or figure of speech in which there is a discrepancy (a striking difference or contradiction) between what is expressed and what is meant or expected. Irony achieves its powerful effect indirectly: in satire, for example, which often uses *understatement* or *hyperbole* to express serious criticism of human behavior and social institutions. We also speak of *dramatic irony* when the narrator or reader understands more than the characters do.

journal A diary or notebook of personal observations. Many writers use journals to compose personal reflection and to collect ideas for their works; the journals of many writers have been published. Students are often urged to keep journals as a way to reflect on their reading, compose personal pieces, and practice writing free of concern for evaluation.

melodrama A plot in which incidents are sensational and designed to provoke immediate emotional responses. In such a plot, the "good" characters are pure and innocent and victims of the "bad" ones, who are thoroughly evil. The term refers to a particular kind of drama popular in the late nineteenth century and, later, in silent films and early Westerns. A work

84

becomes melodramatic when it relies on improbable incidents and unconvincing characters for strong emotional effect.

memoir A form of autobiographical writing that reflects on the significant events the writer has observed and on the interesting and important personalities the writer has known.

monologue In a play, an extended expression or speech by a single speaker that is uninterrupted by response from other characters. A monologue is addressed to a particular person or persons, who may or may not actually hear it. Ring Lardner's short story "Haircut" is an example of monologue as a method of narration. In it, a barber tells the story to a customer (the reader) who is present but does not respond. See also *dramatic monologue* in A Glossary of Poetic Terms and Techniques, Chapter 4.

motivation The desires, values, needs, or impulses that move characters to act as they do. In good fiction the reader understands, appreciates, and is convinced that a character's motivation accounts for the significant incidents and the outcome of a plot.

narrative point of view The standpoint, perspective, and degree of understanding from which a work of narrative fiction is told. See *omniscient point of view, objective point of view.*

narrator The character or author's *persona* that tells a story. It is through the perspective and understanding of the narrator that the reader experiences the work. In some works, the narrator may inhabit the world of the story or be a character in it. In other works, the narrator is a detached but knowledgeable observer.

naturalism Closely related to *determinism,* naturalism depicts characters who are driven not by personal will or moral principles but by natural forces that they do not fully understand or control. In contrast to other views of human experience, the naturalistic view makes no moral judgments on the lives of the characters. Their lives, often bleak or defeating, simply *are* as they are, determined by social, environmental, instinctive, and hereditary forces. Naturalism was in part a reaction by writers against the nineteenth century Romantic view of man as master of his own fate. It is important to note, however, that none of the Naturalistic writers in America (Crane, Dreiser, London, Anderson, and Norris chief among them) presented a genuinely deterministic vision. Several of these authors began their careers in journalism and were drawn to the Naturalistic view of life as a result of their own experience and observation of life in the United States. See also *realism.*

objective point of view In fiction or nonfiction, this voice presents a story or information, respectively, without expressed judgment or qualification. A fundamental principle of journalism is that news *reports* should be objective. Ernest Hemingway's short story "The Killers" is an example of fiction rendered in a completely detached, objective point of view.

omniscient point of view Spoken in third person (*she, he, it, they*), this is the broadest narrative perspective. The omniscient narrator speaks from outside the story and sees and knows everything about the characters and incidents. Omniscient narration is not limited by time or place. In **limited omniscient** point of view, the author may choose to reveal the story through full understanding of only one character and limit the action to those incidents in which this character is present.

persona A term from the Greek meaning "mask," it refers in literature to a narrative voice created by an author and through which the author speaks. A narrative persona usually has a perceptible, even distinctive, personality that contributes to our understanding of the story. In Nathaniel Hawthorne's *The Scarlet Letter,* the omniscient narrator has a distinctive persona whose attitudes toward Puritan society and the characters' lives are revealed throughout the novel.

plot The incidents and experiences of characters selected and arranged by the author to create a meaningful narrative. A good plot is convincing in terms of what happens and why.

poetic justice The concept that life's rewards and punishments should be perfectly appropriate and distributed in just proportions. In Ring Lardner's short story "Haircut," Jim Kendall's ironic fate is an example of poetic justice: He is a victim of one of his own crude and insensitive practical jokes.

point of view In nonfiction, this denotes the attitudes or opinions of the writer. In narrative fiction, it refers to how and by whom a story is told: the perspective of the narrator and the narrator's relationship to the story. Point of view may be *omniscient,* where the narrator knows everything about the characters and their lives; or it may be *limited* to the understanding of a particular character or speaker. Point of view may also be described as *objective* or *subjective. Third-person* narrative refers to characters as "he, she, it, they." *First-person* narrative is from the "I" point of view. J. D. Salinger's *Catcher in the Rye* and Twain's *Huckleberry Finn* are told in the first person. *Second-person* narrative, the "you" form, is rare but is found in sermons addressed to a congregation or in essays of opinion addressed directly to a leader or public figure: "You, Mr. Mayor (Madame President), should do the following . . ." Thomas Friedman and William Safire occasionally write pieces in the second-person voice for the Op-Ed page of *The New York Times.*

prologue An introductory statement of the dramatic situation of a play or story. Shakespeare's *Romeo and Juliet* begins with a brief prologue. The first two pages of Fitzgerald's *The Great Gatsby* are a prologue to the story Nick Carraway will tell.

prose Most of what we write is prose, the expression in sentences and phrases that reflect the natural rhythms of speech. Prose is organized by paragraphs and is characterized by variety in sentence length and rhythm.

protagonist A term from Ancient Greek drama, it refers to the central character, the hero or heroine, in a literary work.

realism The literary period in the United States following the Civil War is usually called the Age of Realism. Realism depicts the directly observable in everyday life. Realistic writers seek to *present* characters and situations as they would appear to a careful observer, not as they are imagined or created by the author. After 1865, American writers became increasingly interested in the sources of power and force, and in the means to survival and success, in an increasingly materialistic society. For writers of this period, realism was a literary mode to express a *naturalistic* philosophy. See also *naturalism, verisimilitude.*

rhetoric From Ancient Greece, the art of persuasion in speech or writing achieved through logical thought and skillful use of language.

rhetorical question A question posed in the course of an *argument* to provoke thought or to introduce a line of reasoning.

romance A novel or tale that includes elements of the supernatural, heroic adventure, or romantic passion. Hawthorne's *The Scarlet Letter* is a romance, not because it is a love story but because it goes beyond *verisimilitude* in dramatizing elements of demonic and mystical forces in the characters and their lives.

satire A form or style that uses elements of irony, ridicule, exaggeration, understatement, sarcasm, humor, or absurdity to criticize human behavior or a society. All satire is **ironic** (see above) in that meaning or theme is conveyed in the discrepancy between what is said and what is meant, between what is and what should be, between what appears and what truly is. While satire is often entertaining, its purpose is serious and meant to provoke thought or judgment. The verses of Alexander Pope are often extended satire, and many poems by e. e. cummings are satiric. In prose, much of the writing of Mark Twain is satire; *Huckleberry Finn* is the most striking example. Other American writers of satire include Sinclair Lewis, Dorothy Parker, Edith Wharton, Joseph Heller, and Tom Wolfe. On television, *The Colbert Report, Saturday Night Live*, and *The Simpsons* are good examples of contemporary satire.

short story This form is distinguished from most novels not simply by length but by its focus on few characters and on a central, revealing incident. In short stories, however, there is as much variety in narrative point of view, subject, and technique as there is in novels. Edgar Allan Poe characterized the short story as "a short prose narrative, requiring from a half-hour to one or two hours in its perusal."

soliloquy A form of *monologue* in which a character expresses thoughts and feelings aloud but does not address them to anyone else or intend other characters in the work to hear them. In essence, the audience for a play is secretly listening in on a character's innermost thoughts. Macbeth's reflection on "Tomorrow, and tomorrow, and tomorrow . . . " is the best-known soliloquy in the play.

speaker The narrative voice in a literary work (see *persona*). Also, the character who speaks in a *dramatic monologue.*

symbol Most generally, anything that stands for or suggests something else. Language itself is symbolic; sounds and abstract written forms may be arranged to stand for virtually any human thought or experience. In literature, symbols are not Easter eggs or mushrooms—they are not "hidden meanings." Symbols are real objects and *concrete* images that lead us to *think about* what is suggested. They organize a wide variety of ideas into single acts of understanding. They embody not single "meanings" but suggest whole areas of meaning.

theme Roughly analogous to thesis in an essay, this is an observation about human experience or an idea central to a work of literature. The *subject* of a work is in the specific setting, characters, and plot. Theme in a work of fiction is what is meaningful and significant to human experience generally; themes are the ideas and truths that transcend the specific characters and plot. Shakespeare's *Macbeth* is about an ambitious nobleman who, encouraged by his equally ambitious wife, murders the king of Scotland in order to become king himself. The themes in *Macbeth* include the power of ambition to corrupt even those who are worthy and the mortal consequences of denying what is fundamental to one's nature.

thesis The central point, a statement of position in a formal or logical argument. Also used to refer to the topic, or controlling, idea of an essay. Use of the term *thesis* implies elaboration by reasons and examples. See *antithesis.*

tone The attitude of the writer toward the subject and the reader. See also A Glossary of Poetic Terms and Techniques, Chapter 4.

transition A transition is a link between ideas or sections in a work. In prose arguments, single words such as *first, second . . . moreover,* and *therefore* or phrases such as *in addition, on the other hand,* and *in conclusion* serve as transitions. In fiction, a brief passage or chapter may serve as a transition. In *The Great Gatsby,* the narrator pauses from time to time to "fill in" the reader and to account for the passage of time between the dramatic episodes that make up the novel's main plot.

turning point In drama and fiction, the moment or episode in a plot when the action is moved toward its inevitable conclusion.

verisimilitude A quality in fiction and drama of being "true to life," of representing that which is real or actual. Verisimilitude in fiction is often achieved through specific, vivid description and dialogue; first-person narration also creates the effect of verisimilitude. In drama it may be enhanced through means of set, costumes, and lighting that are realistic in all their details.

See also, in Chapter 4, A Glossary of Poetic Terms and Techniques.

Chapter 4

READING POETRY

INTRODUCTION

How should you read a poem? Aloud. Several times. And never quickly. Here is a short poem about baseball. As you read, pay attention first to what the poem by Robert Francis says.

Pitcher

His art is eccentricity, his aim
How not to hit the mark he seems to aim at,
His passion how to avoid the obvious,
His technique how to vary the avoidance.
The others throw to be comprehended. He
Throws to be a moment misunderstood.
Yet not too much. Not errant, arrant, wild,
But every seeming aberration willed.
Not to, yet still, still to communicate
Making the batter understand too late.

Now, read the poem again, with particular attention to the varied length of the statements; read from comma to comma or period to period as you would in prose. When you reach the end of the first and fifth lines, for example, pause very slightly—but do not stop. After several readings, you will not only appreciate what Robert Francis undertands about the art of pitching but also feel the way in which the rhythm of the poem is also the rhythm of pitching.

In poetry we are meant to sense a structure and to feel the rhythm. (See **meter*** and **rhythm**.) The structure and rhythm of poetry may be formal, informal, even "free." Poetry is also characterized by its directness of effect and by its concentration—ideas and feelings are expressed in relatively few words. Karl Shapiro says, "Poems are what ideas *feel like.*" Robert Francis's poem is about what good pitching *feels like.*

---

*Terms in bold type are defined in A Glossary of Poetic Terms and Techniques at the end of the chapter.

This poem, by Emily Dickinson (1830–1886), recalls the feeling of mourning:

After great pain, a formal feeling comes—
The nerves sit ceremonious, like Tombs—
The stiff Heart questions was it He, that bore,
and Yesterday, or Centuries before?

The Feet, mechanical, go round—
Of Ground, or Air or Ought—
A Wooden way
Regardless grown,
A Quartz contentment, like a stone—

This is the Hour of Lead—
Remembered, if outlived,
As Freezing persons, recollect the Snow—
First—Chill—then Stupor—then the letting go—

In this poem, Dickinson recreates what it feels like suddenly to encounter a snake in the grass:

A narrow Fellow in the Grass
Occasionally rides—
You may have met Him—did you not
His notice sudden is—
The Grass divides as with a Comb—
A spotted shaft is seen—
And then it closes at your feet
And opens further on—

He likes a Boggy Acre
A Floor too cool for corn—
Yet when a boy, and Barefoot—
I more than once at Noon
Have passed, I thought, a Whip lash
Unbraiding in the Sun
When stooping to secure it
It wrinkled, and was gone—

Several of Nature's People
I know, and they know me—

90

I feel for them a transport
Of cordiality—

But never met this Fellow
Attended, or alone
Without a tighter breathing
And Zero at the Bone—

Where the writer of prose may seek immediate clarity of meaning above all, the poet often seeks **ambiguity**, not to create "confusion," but to offer multiplicity of meaning, in single words, in images, in the meaning of the poem itself. Look again at "Pitcher." Might this poem also be a reflection on the art of poetry itself? It is because of such richness in meaning that poems often require several readings.

The experience of poetry is conveyed in vivid **imagery**, which appeals to the mind and to the senses. It is often expressed in **figurative language**, that is, words and comparisons that are not literal but that imaginatively create original, vivid, and often unexpected images and associations. (See **metaphor** and **simile**.) Finally, in poetry there is particular significance in the way words and lines sound. The story or experience is enhanced through musical effects. A poem must be felt and heard!

STRUCTURE AND LANGUAGE IN POETRY

All the traditional poetic forms stem from an oral tradition, in which poetry was sung or recited. The **epic** and the **ballad** are the oldest forms of **narrative poetry**, but modern poets also tell stories in narrative verse. (Robert Frost's "Out, Out—" is a well-known example.) Most of the poetry we read today, however, is **lyric** poetry.

Think of the lyric poem as a song; in the Ancient Greek tradition, the lyric poem was meant to be sung to the accompaniment of a lyre, a small harplike instrument. Indeed, we speak of the words for a song as its lyrics. The ancient form is evident in the songs for Shakespeare's plays, in the tradition of the nineteenth-century art song, and in the twentieth-century ballads and songs you associate, for example, with Rogers and Hart, Cole Porter, and Jerome Kern as sung by Ella Fitzgerald, Tony Bennett, Frank Sinatra, and Barbra Streisand, among others.

Lyric poems are relatively brief and are expressed in the voice (that is, from the point of view) of a single speaker. They express a powerful emotion, usually captured in a significant experience or dramatic situation. A lyric poem, like a song, often tells a story, but it does so in nonnarrative form. The **speaker** (or "poet") may recall an experience, or render it directly, in order to understand its meaning and then reveal it to the reader. Thus, many lyric poems are *meditations, reflections,* or *recollections* of experience that lead to a *discovery*, to an emotionally powerful *recognition* of the meaning of the experiences. The effect of the poem is to convey that meaning directly, to engage readers in such a way that they share the experience, feel the emotion, with the speaker. The poems by Robert Francis and Emily Dickinson on the previous pages are examples of lyrics.

This poem by Robert Penn Warren appeared on the June 1993 New York State Regents exam.

Old Photograph of the Future

That center of attention—an infantile face
That long years ago showed, no doubt, pink and white—
Now faded, and in the photograph only a trace
Of grays, not much expression in sight.

(5)   That center of attention, swathed in a sort of white dress,
Is precious to the woman who, pretty and young,
Leans with a look of surprised blessedness
At the mysterious miracle forth-sprung.

In the background somewhat, the masculine figure
(10)   Looms, face agleam with achievement and pride.
In black coat, derby at breast, he is quick to assure
You the world's in good hands—lay your worries aside.

The picture is badly faded. Why not?
Most things show wear around seventy-five,
(15)   And that's the age this picture has got.
The man and woman no longer, of course, live.

They lie side by side in whatever love survives
Under green turf, or snow, and that child, years later,
      stands there
While old landscapes blur and he in guilt grieves
(20)   Over nameless promises unkept, in undefinable despair.

In this poem, the speaker expresses the profound feelings of guilt and despair he feels in looking at an old photograph of himself and his parents when he was an infant. The **tone** of the poem is reflective, that of an elegy. The mood at the end is one of regret and loss as the speaker recalls his dead parents, confronts his own age, "the age this picture has got," and grieves at the "nameless promises unkept." Although the narrator speaks of "that child, years later" who "stands there . . . and . . . in guilt grieves," the intensity and privacy of feeling at the end indicate that the speaker is that child. The narrative voice and the lack of specific identification of the characters serve to emphasize the passage of time and underscore the fact that looking at the photograph leads the "child," now old, to reflect on his entire life.

The structure is simple and easy to observe: five **quatrains** with alternating **rhyme**; each quatrain is self-contained—ends with a period—and tells a part of the story. The first fifteen lines of the poem describe the picture and the "characters" in it. Note that the final section of the poem begins with the last line of the fourth quatrain, the description having concluded in line 15. Line 16 both ends the narrator's rendering of the photograph and also begins the "conclusion," which is the significance of the experience of looking at the photograph.

The rhythm within lines is varied and often broken by dashes or other pauses; this rhythm allows us to share the speaker's questions and reflections. The rhythm of the fourth stanza slows as each line completes a thought. In contrast, the final stanza should be heard as a single, long gesture of recognition and regret.

The experience of looking at the picture—in which he is the "center of attention"—leads the speaker to reflect on whether he has satisfied the "promises" that the "mysterious miracle" of his birth meant to his awed and proud parents. The photograph also leads the speaker to reflect on the unfulfilled promises of his own life.

There is little in the way of figurative language in this poem. The imagery, however, reveals more than a description of a photograph, and the paradox in the title reveals one of the poem's central **themes**, the cycle of birth, life, and death. On rereading Warren's poem, with our appreciation of the poet's experience in mind, we see how the third and fourth lines are more than a description of the photograph—they also suggest the speaker's age. He sees himself (in the photo and metaphorically) as "faded . . . only a trace of grays, not much expression in sight." The repetition of the fact that he was the "center of attention" (in the photograph and in his parents' lives) makes more poignant the grief over "promises unkept" at the end.

The poet offers only a few details of the photograph, but they are the details we all recognize from our own photographs of grandparents and great-grandparents: the father "In the background somewhat" and in formal pose—"in black coat, derby at breast"—the child (girl or boy) in "a sort of white dress." It is, of course, such widely shared experience that is both the poem's form and its theme.

In this poem by Theodore Roethke, the speaker recalls a significant experience from childhood:

Child on Top of a Greenhouse

The wind billowing out of the seat of my britches,
My feet crackling splinters of glass and dried putty,
The half-grown chrysanthemums staring up like accusers,
Up through the streaked glass, flashing with sunlight,
A few white clouds all rushing eastward,
A line of elms plunging and tossing like horses,
And everyone, everyone pointing up and shouting!

Try repeating just the verbs of this poem, feeling their dramatic energy. The repetition of "-ing" forms also creates what is called **internal rhyme**, while the words "like," "sunlight," "white," "line" form the pattern of sound called **assonance**.

In this poem by Donald Hall the speaker also recalls an important childhood experience:

The Sleeping Giant
(A Hill, So Named, in Hamden, Connecticut)

The whole day long, under the walking sun
That poised an eye on me from its high floor,
Holding my toy beside the clapboard house
I looked for him, the summer I was four.

I was afraid the waking arm would break
From the loose earth and rub against his eyes
A fist of trees, and the whole country tremble
In the exultant labor of his rise;

Then he with giant steps in the small streets
Would stagger, cutting off the sky, to seize
The roofs from house and home because we had
Covered his shape with dirt and planted trees;

And then kneel down and rip with fingernails
A trench to pour the enemy Atlantic
Into our basin, and the water rush,
With the streets full and the voices frantic.

That was the summer I expected him.
Later the high and watchful sun instead
Walked low behind the house, and school began,
And winter pulled a sheet over his head.

In this poem, a child's fearful and vivid imagination is sparked by **personification** of the hill near his house. This poem is particularly effective because it recalls for us the fact that small children are literal and that they tend to give names and human character to inanimate things. This child actually sees—and fears—the sleeping giant. Note too how the images of the sun in the first and last stanzas both unify the poem and denote the passage of time. Finally, there is a gentle **irony** in the final line that suggests that the child, no longer fearful, can now "play" with the metaphor of the sleeping giant, as "winter pulled a sheet over his head."

Shakespeare's Sonnet 30 illustrates several of the formal aspects of verse:

When to the sessions of sweet silent thought

When to the sessions of sweet silent thought
I summon up remembrance of things past
I sigh the lack of many a thing I sought
And with old woes new wail my dear time's waste:

(5)   Then can I drown an eye, unused to flow,
For precious friends hid in death's dateless night,
And weep afresh love's long-since-canceled woe,
And moan th'expense of many a vanished sight;

        Then can I grieve at grievances forgone,
(10) And heavily from woe to woe tell o'er
The sad account of fore-bemoaned moan,
Which I new pay as if not paid before.
  But if the while I think on thee, dear friend,
  All losses are restored and sorrows end.

The structure of the Shakespearean **sonnet** is three **quatrains** and a closing **couplet**. The **rhyme scheme** is *abab/cdcd/efef/gg*. This pattern allows us to hear the structure of the poem, to hear the development of the ideas. The couplet, with its similar end rhyme and self-contained thought, contrasts the feelings expressed in the previous 12 lines and concludes the poem.

We find in this Shakespearean sonnet, as well, examples of **alliteration** and assonance: In the first quatrain, we hear alliteration in the many words that begin with "s." In lines 7 through 12 we hear assonance in the repetition of "oh" sounds, which are also examples of **onomatopoeia**—that is, the sounds reflect the meanings of the words. Lines 4 and 10 also illustrate what is called internal rhyme.

THEME IN POETRY

Some lyric poems may assert a belief. Others may be a comment on the nature of human experience—love, death, loss or triumph, mystery and confusion, conflict and peace, on the humorous and the ironic, on the imagined and the unexpected in all its forms. Some poems reflect on the nature of time, of existence. Many lyrics are about poetry itself. These aspects of human experience are what we refer to as the themes of poetry.

In this well-known sonnet, Number 55, Shakespeare asserts that poetry confers immortality, that it can prevail over the most powerful forces of time. Note how the central idea is developed in the three quatrains and how the couplet—in its thought and its rhyme—concludes the development of that idea.

Not marble, nor the gilded monuments

Not marble, nor the gilded monuments
Of princes, shall outlive this pow'rful rhyme;
But you shall shine more bright in these contents
Than unswept stone besmeared with sluttish time.

When wasteful war shall statues overturn,
And broils root out the work of masonry,
Nor Mars his sword nor war's quick fire shall burn
The living record of your memory.

'Gainst death and all-oblivious enmity
Shall you pace forth; your praise shall still find room

Even in the eyes of all posterity
That wear this world out to the ending doom.
 So, till the judgment that yourself arise,
 You live in this, and dwell in lovers' eyes.

The best-known lyrics, however, are probably love poems—Sonnet 116 of Shakespeare, for example:

Let me not to the marriage of true minds

Let me not to the marriage of true minds
Admit impediments. Love is not love
which alters when it alteration finds,
Or bends with the remover to remove.

O, no, it is an ever-fixed mark
That looks on tempests and is never shaken;
It is the star to every wand'ring bark,
Whose worth's unknown, although his height be taken.

Love's not Time's fool, though rosy lips and cheeks
Within his bending sickle's compass come;
Love alters not with his brief hours and weeks,
But bears it out even to the edge of doom.
 If this be error and upon me proved,
 I never writ, nor no man ever loved.

This modern lyric by Langston Hughes is also a love poem.

Juke Box Love Song

I could take the Harlem night
and wrap around you,
Take the neon lights and make a crown,
Take the Lenox Avenue buses,
Taxis, subways,
And for your love song tone their rumble down.
Take Harlem's heartbeat,
Make a drumbeat,
Put it on a record, let it whirl,

And while we listen to it play,
Dance with you till day—
Dance with you, my sweet brown Harlem girl.

TONE

Tone in poetry, as in prose and all forms of human communication, expresses the *attitude* of the speaker toward the reader or listener and toward the subject. Tone in literature is as varied as the range of human experience and feeling it reflects. When we speak of the *mood* of a piece of writing, we are also speaking of tone, of an overall feeling generated by the work.

Here are some terms to help you recognize and articulate tone or mood:

ambiguous*	amused	angry	bitter
celebratory	elegiac (from elegy*)	grateful	harsh
humorous	insistent	ironic*	melancholy
mournful	mysterious	nostalgic	optimistic
paradoxical*	questioning	reconciled	reflective
regretful	reminiscent	satiric*	sorrowful
thoughtful	understated*		

WRITING ABOUT POETRY/EXPLICATION

When you are asked to *explicate* a poem, you are being asked to look closely at it and "unfold" its meaning, line by line, idea by idea. Explication combines paraphrase with close reading of form. You are explaining both the content *and* the form: the ideas and meaning as well as the structure and poetic elements.

To begin an explication, read the poem several times to discover what it says. Who is the speaker? What is the subject? the dramatic situation? What theme or experience is central to the poem? What is the tone or mood? Try to summarize or paraphrase the poem as a whole. Then note the formal details: What is the pattern of organization? What is the movement of ideas and feeling? of images and metaphors? How do stanzas or arrangement of lines reveal that? How do rhyme, meter, and rhythm contribute to the experience, to the meaning of the poem? (The commentary that follows Robert Penn Warren's "Old Photograph of the Future" on page 92 is an example of explication.)

---

*These terms are defined in A Glossary of Poetic Terms and Techniques.

POETRY ON EXAMINATIONS

On examinations, such as the English Regents exam and the AP Literature and Composition exam, the multiple-choice questions are designed to measure your skill at close reading and *explication.* You are expected to recognize and identify the elements of poetry. (See A Glossary of Poetic Terms and Techniques.) Part A of Session Two of the English Regents exam may include a poem for close reading and discussion as well as a prose passage. In addition, you are usually required to compose an essay/explication of a poem on the AP Literature and Composition exam, and such essays are commonly assigned in high school and college literature courses. *Analysis,* which requires detailed examination of particular elements of a poem or passage, is usually reserved for course assignments. The thoughtful student will, of course, develop skill in both explication and analysis.

A HANDFUL OF POEMS FOR FURTHER READING

In this **prose poem**, Karl Shapiro offers a definition of the poet and the power of poetry.

As You Say (Not Without Sadness), Poets Don't See, They Feel

As you say, (not without sadness), poets don't see, they feel.
And that's why people who have turned to feelers seem
like poets. Why children seem poetic. Why when the
sap rises in the adolescent heart the young write poetry.
Why great catastrophes are stated in verse. Why lunatics
are named for the moon. Yet poetry isn't feeling with
the hands. A poem is not a kiss. Poems are what ideas
feel like. Ideas on Sunday, thoughts on vacation.

Poets don't see, they feel. They are conductors of the senses
of men, as teachers and preachers are the insulators.
The poets go up and feel the insulators. Now and again
they feel the wrong thing and are thrown through a wall
by a million-volt shock. All insulation makes the poet
anxious. Clothes, strait jackets, iambic five. He pulls at
the seams like a boy whose trousers are cutting him in
half. Poets think along the electric currents. The words

99

are constantly not making sense when he reads. He
flunks economics, logic, history. Then he describes what
it feels like to flunk economics, logic, history. After
that he feels better.

People say: it is sad to see a grown man feeling his way, sad
to see a man so naked, desireless of any defenses. The
people walk back into their boxes and triple-lock the
doors. When their children begin to read poetry the
parents watch them from the corner of their eye. It's
only a phase, they aver. Parents like the word "aver"
though they don't use it.

In this excerpt from an extended essay in verse, Alexander Pope reflects
on how poets express meaning through sound and rhythm.

An Essay on Criticism

True ease in writing comes from art, not chance,
As those move easiest who have learned to dance.
'Tis not enough no harshness gives offense,
The sound must seem an echo to the sense:
Soft is the strain when Zephyr gently blows,
And the smooth stream in smoother numbers flows;
But when loud surges lash the sounding shore,
The hoarse, rough verse should like the torrent roar.

The horror and loss of war are often expressed through irony. Here is
Stephen Crane's reflection on war:

Do Not Weep, Maiden, for War Is Kind

Do not weep, maiden, for war is kind.
Because your lover threw wild hands against the sky
And the affrighted steed ran on alone,
Do not weep.
War is kind.

Hoarse, booming drums of the regiment
Little souls who thirst for fight
These men were born to drill and die.

The unexplained glory flies above them,
Great is the battle-god, great, and his kingdom—
A field where a thousand corpses lie.

Do not weep, babe, for war is kind.
Because your father tumbled in the yellow trenches,
Raged at his breast, gulped and died,
Do not weep.
War is kind.

Swift blazing flag of the regiment,
Eagle with crest of red and gold,
These men were born to drill and die.
Point for them the virtue of slaughter,
Make plain to them the excellence of killing
And a field where a thousand corpses lie.

Mother whose heart hung humble as a button
On the bright splendid shroud of your son,
Do not weep.
War is kind.

In this poem, by Walt Whitman (1819–1892), the speaker moves from the observation of a spider to a reflection on the soul's search to understand all existence.

A Noiseless Patient Spider

A noiseless patient spider,
I mark'd where on a little promontory it stood isolated,
Mark'd how to explore the vacant vast surrounding,
It launch'd forth filament, filament, filament, out of itself,
Ever unreeling them, ever tirelessly speeding them.

And you O my soul where you stand,
Surrounded, detached, in measureless oceans of space,
Ceaselessly musing, venturing, throwing, seeking the spheres
    to connect them,

Till the bridge you will need be form'd, till the ductile
anchor hold,
Till the gossamer thread you fling catch somewhere,
O my soul.

In this brief poem by Alfred, Lord Tennyson (1809–1892) the language and imagery convey the experience of both the observer and of the eagle itself.

The Eagle

He clasps the crag with crooked hands;
Close to the sun in lonely lands,
Ringed with the azure world, he stands.

The wrinkled sea beneath him crawls;
He watches from his mountain walls,
And like a thunderbolt he falls.

Here, in free verse, is Whitman's vision of eagles:

The Dalliance of Eagles

Skirting the river road, (my forenoon walk, my rest,)
Skyward in air a sudden muffled sound, the dalliance
of the eagles,
The rushing amorous contact high in space together,
The clinching interlocking claws, a living, fierce,
gyrating wheel,
Four beating wings, two beaks, a swirling mass tight
grappling,
In tumbling turning clustering loops, straight downward
falling.
Till o'er the river pois'd, the twain yet one, a moment's
lull,
A motionless still balance in the air, then parting, talons
loosing,
Upward again on slow-firm pinions slanting, their
separate diverse flight,
She hers, he his, pursuing.

Observe how Gwendolyn Brooks uses rhyme with varied line lengths to create this portrait.

The Bean Eaters

They eat beans mostly, this old yellow pair.
Dinner is a casual affair.
Plain chipware on a plain and creaking wood,
Tin flatware.

Two who are Mostly Good.
Two who have lived their day,
But keep on putting on their clothes
And putting things away.

And remembering . . .
Remembering, with twinklings and twinges,
As they lean over the beans in their rented back room that
    is full of
beads and receipts and dolls and cloths, tobacco crumbs,
vases and fringes.

In the first of these two poems by Robert Browning (1812–1889) the rich and varied imagery recreates the journey of a lover to his beloved and, in the second, his return to the "world of men."

Meeting at Night

The grey sea and the long black land;
And the yellow half-moon large and low;
And the startled little waves that leap
In fiery ringlets from their sleep,
As I gain the cove with pushing prow,
And quench its speed i' the slushy sand.

Then a mile of warm sea-scented beach;
Three fields to cross till a farm appears;
A tap at the pane, the quick sharp scratch
And spurt of a lighted match,
And a voice less loud, through its joys and fears,
Than the two hearts beating each to each.

Parting at Morning

Round the cape of a sudden came the sea,
And the sun looked over the mountain's rim:
And straight was a path of gold for him,
And the need of a world of men for me.

In this sonnet, George Meredith (1828–1909) imagines the desire of this fallen angel, now Satan, to return to the heavens he once inhabited.

Lucifer in Starlight

On a starred night Prince Lucifer uprose.
Tired of his dark dominion swung the fiend
Above the rolling ball in cloud part screened,
Where sinners hugged their spectre of repose.
Poor prey to his hot fit of pride were those.
And now upon his western wing he leaned,
Now his huge bulk o'er Afric's sands careened,
Now the black planet shadowed Arctic snows.
Soaring through wider zones that pricked his scars
With memory of the old revolt from Awe,
He reached a middle height, and at the stars,
Which are the brain of heaven, he looked, and sank.
Around the ancient track marched, rank on rank,
The army of unalterable law.

In this well-known sonnet by Percy Bysshe Shelley (1792–1822) we experience the ironic fate of a once proud and arrogant king.

Ozymandias

I met a traveler from an antique land
Who said: Two vast and trunkless legs of stone
Stand in the desert. Near them, on the sand,
Half sunk a shattered visage lies, whose frown,
And wrinkled lip, and sneer of cold command,
Tell that its sculptor well those passions read
Which yet survive, stamped on these lifeless things,
The hand that mocked them and the heart that fed;

And on the pedestal these words appear:
"My name is Ozymandias, king of kings:
Look on my works, ye Mighty, and despair!"
Nothing beside remains. Round the decay
Of that colossal wreck, boundless and bare,
The lone and level sands stretch far away.

These poems represent only a few examples of the great variety of expression in verse. Your own textbooks and anthologies offer many more examples; and the list of Recommended Reading at the end of the book includes titles of collections readily available in paperback. You will also find the addresses of some excellent web sites devoted to poetry. Your library, of course, offers collections of poetry by individual authors, and many national monthly magazines, such as *The New Yorker* and *Atlantic Monthly* publish contemporary verse. You should read as widely as possible, and always aloud!

A GLOSSARY OF POETIC TERMS AND TECHNIQUES

allegory A narrative, in prose or verse, in which abstract ideas, principles, human values or states of mind, are *personified*. The purpose of the allegory is to illustrate the signficance of the ideas by dramatizing them. *Parable* and *fable* are particular kinds of allegory, in which a moral is illustrated in the form of a story.

alliteration The repetition of initial consonant sounds in words and syllables. This is one of the first patterns of sound a child creates (for instance "ma-ma," "pa-pa"). The children's stories of Dr. Seuss use alliteration and assonance. Poets use alliteration for its rich musical effect: "Fish, flesh, and fowl commend all summer long/Whatever is begotten, born, and dies" (Yeats); for humor: "Where at, with blade, with bloody, blameful blade/He bravely broached his boiling bloody breast" (Shakespeare); and to echo the sense of the lines: "The iron tongue of midnight hath told twelve" (Shakespeare).

allusion A reference to a historical event, to Biblical, mythological, or literary characters and incidents with which the reader is assumed to be familiar. Allusion may, with few words, enrich or extend the meaning of a phrase, idea, or image. Allusion may also be used for ironic effect. In his poem "Out, out . . ." Robert Frost expects the reader to recall from Macbeth's final soliloquy the line, "Out, out brief candle!" Such expressions as "a Herculean task" or "Achilles heel" are also forms of allusion.

ambiguity Denotes uncertainty of meaning. In literature, however, especially in poetry, we speak of *intentional* ambiguity, the use of language and images to suggest more than one meaning at the same time.

assonance The repetition of vowel sounds among words that begin or end with different consonants. Sonnet 30 of Shakespeare (page 95) and "Child on Top of a Greenhouse" by Theodore Roethke (page 94), for example, are rich in assonance. Some poets may vary end rhymes with assonance; for example, Emily Dickinson (page 90) does it here: "The Feet, mechanical, go round—Of Ground, or Air, or Ought—."

ballad Narrative poem, sometimes sung, that tells a dramatic story.

blank verse Unrhymed *iambic pentameter,* usually in "paragraphs" of verse instead of stanzas. Shakespeare's plays are composed primarily in blank verse. For example, from *Macbeth* (Act I, Scene 5):

> **Your face, my Thane, is as a book where men**
> **May read strange matters. To beguile the time,**
> **Look like the time; bear welcome in your eye,**
> **Your hand, your tongue; look like the innocent flower,**
> **But be the serpent under't . . .**

connotation The feelings, attitudes, images, and associations of a word or expression. Connotations are usually said to be "positive" or "negative." See also discussion on page 218 in Chapter 10, Vocabulary.

couplet Two lines of verse with similar meter and end rhyme. Couplets generally have self-contained ideas as well, so they may function as stanzas within a poem. In the English (Shakespearean) *sonnet,* the couplet concludes the poem. (See the sonnets on pages 95–97.) Also many scenes in Shakespeare's plays end with rhymed couplets: "Away, and mock the time with fairest show/False face must hide what the false heart doth know" (*Macbeth* Act I, Scene 7).

denotation That which a word actually names, identifies, or "points to." Denotation is sometimes referred to as "the dictionary definition" of a word.

dramatic monologue A poem in which a fictional character, at a critical or dramatic point in life, addresses a particular "audience," which is identifiable but silent. In the course of the monologue, we learn a great deal, often ironically, about the character, who is speaking and the circumstances that have led to the speech. Robert Browning is the best-known nineteenth-century poet to compose dramatic monologues; "My Last Duchess" is a famous example. In the twentieth century, such poets as Kenneth Fearing, E. A. Robinson, T. S. Eliot ("The Love Song of J. Alfred Prufrock"), Robert Frost, and Amy Lowell have composed well-known dramatic monologues.

elegy A meditative poem mourning the death of an individual.

epic A long narrative poem often centering on a heroic figure who represents the fate of a great nation or people. *The Iliad* and *The Odyssey* of Homer, *The Aeneid* of Vergil, and the Anglo-Saxon *Beowulf* are well-known epics. Milton's *Paradise Lost* and Dante's *Divine Comedy* are examples of epic narratives in which subjects of great human significance are dramatized. *Omeros,* by Derek Walcott, is a contemporary example of an epic poem.

figurative language The intentional and imaginative use of words and comparisons that are not literal but that create original, vivid, and often unexpected images and associations. Figurative language is also called *metaphorical language.* See *metaphor* and *simile.*

free verse A poem written in free verse develops images and ideas in patterns of lines without specific metrical arrangements or formal rhyme. Free verse is distinguished from prose, however, because it retains such poetic elements as assonance, alliteration, and figurative language. The poetry of Walt Whitman offers striking examples.

hyperbole An exaggerated expression (also called overstatement) for a particular effect, which may be humorous, satirical, or intensely emotional. Hyperbole is the expression of folk tales and legends and, of course, of lovers: Romeo says to Juliet, "there lies more peril in thine eye/Than twenty of their swords." Hyperbole is often the expression of any overwhelming feeling. After he murders King Duncan, Macbeth looks with horror at his bloody hands: "Will all great Neptune's ocean wash this blood/Clean from my hand . . . ?" In her sleepwalking scene, Lady Macbeth despairs that "All the perfumes of Arabia will not sweeten this little hand." And every one of us has felt, "I have mountains of work to do!"

iambic pentameter The basic meter of English speech: "I think I know exactly what you need/and yet at times I know that I do not." Formally, it identifies verse of ten syllables to the line, with the second, fourth, sixth, eight, and tenth syllables accented. There is, however, variation in the stresses within lines to reflect natural speech—and to avoid a "singsong" or nursery rhyme effect. Most of the dialogue in Shakespeare's plays is composed in this meter. See *blank verse.*

image Images and imagery are the heart of poetry. Although the term suggests only something that is visualized, an image is the recreation through language of *any* experience perceived directly through the senses. For example, Tennyson's "The Eagle" (page 102) is composed of striking visual images. The feelings of fear and of mourning in Emily Dickinson's poems are also images. In "Juke Box Love Song" (page 97) we hear and feel music; and in "Pitcher" (page 89) we feel the motion of pitching.

internal rhyme A pattern in which a word or words within a line rhyme with the word that ends it. Poets may also employ internal rhyme at irregular intervals over many lines. The verbs in Theodore Roethke's poem "Child on Top of a Greenhouse" (page 94) create the effect of internal rhyme.

irony In general, a tone or figure of speech in which there is a discrepancy—(a striking difference or contradiction)—between what is expressed and what is meant or expected. Irony may be used to achieve a powerful effect indirectly. In satire, for example, it may be used to ridicule or criticize. Stephen Crane's poem "Do Not Weep, Maiden, for War Is Kind" (page 100) is intensely ironic, both in the stanzas apparently seeking to comfort those whose lovers, fathers and sons have died and in the contrasting stanzas of apparent celebration of the glories of war. We also speak of *dramatic irony* in fiction in which the reader understands more than the characters do. Ring Lardner's short story "Haircut" is an excellent example.

lyric A general term used to describe poems that are relatively brief and expressed in the voice of a single *speaker* (narrative voice). Lyric poems express a powerful emotion revealed in a significant experience or observation. (See discussion on page 91.)

metaphor A form of analogy. Through metaphor, a poet discovers and expresses a similarity between dissimilar things. The poet use metaphors to imaginatively find common qualities between things we would not normally or literally compare. As a figure of speech, metaphor is said to be implicit or indirect. This contrasts to *simile* (see page 109), where the comparison is expressed directly. In his final soliloquy, Macbeth uses a series of metaphors to express the meaninglessness of his own life: "Life's but a walking shadow, a poor player . . . it is a tale told by an idiot . . . ."

meter and **rhythm** Rhythm refers to the pattern of movement in a poem. As music has rhythm, so does poetry. Meter refers to specific patterns of stressed and unstressed syllables. See *iambic pentameter.*

ode A meditation or celebration of a specific subject. Traditional odes addressed "elevated" ideas and were composed in elaborate stanza forms. Keats's "Ode to a Nightingale" and "Ode to Autum" are particularly fine examples. Modern odes may address subjects either serious or personal. One well-known contemporary ode is Pablo Neruda's "Ode to My Socks."

onomatopoeia The use of words whose sound reflects their sense. "Buzz," "hiss," and "moan" are common examples. Shakespeare's Sonnet 30 shows how the sounds and rhythm of whole lines may be onomatopoetic.

oxymoron Closely related to *paradox,* oxymoron is a figure of speech in which two contradictory or sharply contrasting terms are paired for emphasis or ironic effect. Among students' favorite examples are "jumbo shrimp" and "army intelligence." Poets have written of the "wise fool," a "joyful sadness," or an "eloquent silence."

paradox An expression, concept, or situation whose literal statement is contradictory, yet which makes a truthful and meaningful observation. Consider the widely used expression "less is more," for example. Shakespeare's play *Macbeth* opens with a series of paradoxes to establish the moral atmosphere in which "foul is fair." John Donne's famous poem "Death Be Not Proud" ends with the paradox "Death thou shalt die," and the title of Robert Penn Warren's poem "Old Photograph of the Future" is a paradox.

personification A form of metaphor or simile in which nonhuman things—objects, plants and animals, forces of nature, abstract ideas—are given human qualities; for example, "The half-grown chrysanthemums staring up like accusers" (Roethke, page 94), "the walking sun/that poised an eye on me from its high floor" (Hall, page 94), "Time . . . the thief of youth" (Milton), and "Blow winds, and crack your cheeks! Blow! Rage!" (Shakespeare).

prose poem This form appears on the page in the sentences and paragraphs of prose yet its effect is achieved through rhythm, images, and patterns of sound associated with poetry. Karl Shapiro's poem on page 99 is an example.

quatrain Stanza of four lines. The quatrain is the most commonly used stanza form in English poetry. Quatrains may be rhymed, *abab, aabb, abba,* for example, or they may be unrhymed. The sonnets of Shakespeare (pages 95–97), "Old Photograph of the Future" (page 92), and "The Sleeping Giant" (page 94) are also composed in quatrains.

rhyme In general, any repetition of identical or similar sounds among words that are close enough together to form an audible pattern. Rhyme is most evident when it occurs at the ends of lines of metrical verse. The *quatrains* of Shakespeare's Sonnet 55 (page 96) have alternating rhyme as do those of Robert Penn Warren's poem "Old Photograph of the Future" (page 92).

rhyme scheme A regular pattern of end rhyme in a poem. The rhyme scheme in Shakespeare's sonnets, for example, is *abab/cdcd/efef/gg.*

satire A form or style that uses elements of irony, ridicule, exaggeration, understatement, sarcasm, humor, or absurdity to criticize human behavior or a society. All satire is *ironic* (see page 107) in that meaning or theme is conveyed in the discrepancy between what is said and what is meant, between what is and what should be, between what appears and what truly is. While satire is often entertaining, its purpose is serious and meant to provoke thought or judgment. The verse of Alexander Pope is often extended satire, and many poems by e. e. cummings are satiric.

simile An expression that is a direct comparison of two things. It uses such words as *like, as, as if, seems, appears.* For instance: "A line of elms plunging and tossing like horses" (Theodore Roethke); "Mind in its purest play is like some bat" (Richard Wilbur); "I wandered lonely as a cloud" (William Wordsworth).

soliloquy A form of monologue found most often in drama. It differs from a dramatic monologue in that the speaker is alone, revealing thoughts and feelings to or for oneself that are intentionally unheard by other characters. In Shakespeare's plays, for example, the principal characters' reflections on how to act or questions of conscience are revealed in their soliloquies. Hamlet's "To be, or not to be . . ." is probably the most famous dramatic soliloquy in English.

sonnet A poem of fourteen lines in *iambic pentameter* that may be composed of different patterns of stanzas and rhyme schemes. The most common forms are the English, or Shakespearean, sonnet, which consists of three quatrains and a closing couplet, and the Italian sonnet, which consists of an *octave* of eight lines and a *sestet* of six lines.

speaker The narrative voice in a poem. Also, the character who speaks in a *dramatic monologue*. The poems "The Sleeping Giant" and "Old Photograph of the Future" have distinctive speakers who are also the central characters in the dramatic experience of the poem.

stanza The grouping of lines within a poem. A stanza provides the basic organization and development of ideas, much as a paragraph does in an essay. Many stanza patterns have a fixed number of lines and a regular pattern of rhyme; the poems of Robert Penn Warren (page 92) and Donald Hall (page 94) are good examples. Poets, however, often create stanzas of varying length and form within a single poem. A stanza that ends with a period, completing an idea or image, is considered "closed," while a stanza that ends with a comma or with no punctuation, is called "open," indicating that there should be very little pause in the movement from one stanza to another. Roethke's poem "Child on Top of a Greenhouse" (page 94) is an example of a poem composed in a single stanza.

symbol Most generally, anything that stands for or suggests something else. Language itself is symbolic; sounds and abstract written forms may stand for almost any human thought or experience. Symbols are real objects and *concrete* images that lead us to think about what is suggested. Symbols organize a wide variety of ideas into single acts of understanding. They embody not single "meanings" but suggest whole areas of meaning.

tone The attitude or feeling of the speaker toward the subject. Tone may also refer to the dominant mood of a poem. (See discussion of *tone* on page 98.)

understatement Expression in which something is presented as less important or significant than it really is. The first and third stanzas of Stephen Crane's "Do Not Weep, Maiden" (page 100) ironically understate the horror of death in battle and the loss for those who mourn. Understatement is often used for humorous, *satiric,* or *ironic* effect. Much of the satire in *Huckleberry Finn* stems from Huck's naive and understated observations. One particular form of understatement, actually a double negative, includes such expressions as "I was not uninterested," which really means "I was interested," or "He was not without imagination," which really means "He had some imagination."

Chapter 5

WRITING ABOUT LITERATURE: A GENERAL REVIEW

For most students, writing papers and responding to essay questions on exams are the most challenging aspects of their course work. Writing requires that you articulate and focus your understanding of what you read. Like all good writing, writing about literature not only demonstrates to others what you understand and think but also obliges you to clarify *for yourself* what you truly know. That process is sometimes hard, but it is worthwhile. Writing is essential to developing your critical reading and thinking skills.

TOPICS FOR LITERARY ESSAYS

Much of your writing about literature is done in response to assignments and exam questions. Students are also urged to maintain notes and journals. For essays, instructors may assign very specific topics, or they may offer general subjects that require you to develop your own topic and controlling idea.

In your literature courses and exams you will find that the majority of the questions focus on **character**. Because essay topics may apply to many works of nonfiction you read—personal essay, memoir, and autobiography in particular—the term *character* should be understood to refer to any persons, not exclusively to those of fiction and drama.

As you think about characters in the literature you read, keep the following questions in mind: What are a character's values and motives? beliefs and principles? moral qualities? strengths and weaknesses? illusions or delusions? For what is a character searching? striving? devoting his or her life? What significant decisions and actions does a character take? What are the consequences of those decisions and actions? To what extent does a character "succeed" or "fail"? understand or fail to understand?

Literature also seeks to account for the forces outside individuals, that is, the external forces that influence the direction and outcome of their lives. These "forces" range from those of nature and history to the demands of family, community, and society. The response of individuals to inner and outer forces is what literature considers and dramatizes. (See Chapters 3 and 4 for discussions of reading literature and for glossaries of important terms and techniques.)

TOPIC AND FOCUS

As any essay must, your paper must have a clear purpose, a controlling idea; moreover, the development of the purpose must be convincing to the reader. *Focus* means in writing, as it does in a photograph, that the subject is clear! We can see it, even recognize it. And, if the photographer/writer has "framed" the material properly, we see the relationship of the background details to the principal subject. When you take a picture of your best friend at camp, or of the place you most want to remember from a vacation trip, you keep the lens of your camera directed at what is most important—not at the tree next to your friend, not at the bus that took you to Niagara Falls.

SELECTION OF SIGNIFICANT DETAILS

One of the most widely observed characteristics of short stories is that they are very selective in detail. The author of a short story includes only those elements of setting, character, and plot that reveal the significance of the central incident. In "The Lottery," for example, we do not know when the story takes place, we do not even know the name of the town or where it is located, and we know little about the lives of individual characters. Those details are not *significant*—they do not matter —to the story Shirley Jackson tells; comparable details *are* significant in "Haircut," and, therefore, Ring Lardner includes them.

To achieve focus in your essays about works of literature, you must exercise the same rigorous process of selection. However interesting you may find a particular incident or aspect of a character, do not include those details if they do not directly explain or clarify your topic.

DEVELOPING THE TOPIC

Many of the common methods of developing arguments are discussed in Chapter 3, Reading Prose. Here are some of those methods as they might be used to develop essays on works of literature:

Comparison/Contrast

Although *compare* means to identify similarities, and *contrast* means to identify differences, the term *comparison* is often used for a discussion that examines both similarities and differences among the items being compared. This is one of the most useful approaches, and one of the most commonly used, because the process of comparing helps sharpen thought. To compose a meaningful comparison, the writer must understand the objects of comparison in detail.

Any literary aspect found in two or more works may serve as a basis for comparison. For example, one could compare the effective use of first-person narration in *The Great Gatsby* and *Ethan Frome,* or in *The Catcher in the Rye* and *Huckleberry Finn.* Although the circumstances of their lives are vastly different, the fact that both Ethan Frome and Jay Gatsby fail to achieve what they most desire—a life with the women they love—offers a rich possibility for comparison and contrast. "Haircut" and "The Lottery" share common elements of setting and irony. *Othello* and *Romeo and Juliet* have a common theme—the tragic destruction of great love.

Comparison may, of course, focus on much narrower topics and be confined to a single work. The best way to develop notes for a comparison is first to list the aspects common to the items under comparison, then to list for each all the specific details that differentiate them. Finally, as you do in preparation for any essay, you select those that are most significant.

The essay on Part A of Session Two of the new Regents exam is a form of comparison/contrast because it requires discussion of two works of different genres.

Analysis

Analysis requires detailed examination of a particular aspect of a literary work. The purpose of an analytic paper is to show the significance of that aspect to the meaning of the work as a whole. Examples of analytic topics include the use of time in Miller's *Death of a Salesman,* the imagery of light and dark in *Othello,* and the extended metaphor in Emily Dickinson's poem "I Taste a Liquor Never Brewed."

Classification

Classification organizes objects, people, and other living things into categories; it is a process of identifying and relating. In discussions of literature, classification may be an important part of an essay, or it may constitute a topic in its own right. An essay in which the writer shows how a particular work exemplifies a **genre** is considered classification: *The Scarlet Letter* as a **romance;** Shakespeare's *Macbeth* as Elizabethan **tragedy;** Dreiser's *Sister Carrie* as **naturalism.**

Cause and Effect

Many of the topics for writing and discussion of literature may be developed by showing how circumstances or actions have direct and observable consequences. Demonstrating actual cause and effect, however, requires careful thinking and attention to detail. Cause and effect are more easily demonstrated in logic and chemistry than in human experience.

Literary topics that focus on **plot** often lend themselves to cause and effect development because essentially any plot is built on cause and effect: specific circumstances, actions, or decisions lead to others and have consequences in the lives of the characters. Plot summary alone does *not* establish cause and effect; it simply relates "what happened." Cause-and-effect argument requires the writer to show how and why incidents are related.

Exemplification

Whenever you cite specific details to support a thesis, and when you choose the works you will use to answer the literature question in Part B of Session Two, you are using exemplification. *To exemplify* means to illustrate the meaning of a general concept through use of specific examples. This method is fundamental to the development of nearly any essay or literary topic.

LOOKING AT KEY TERMS IN LITERATURE QUESTIONS

identify   To name and also to characterize and to place in context; sometimes you may be required to state the significance of what you are identifying. Often identification includes linking characters to the theme or experience that serves as the topic.

describe   To give the essential characteristics of a person, object, or experience. If you are asked to describe, your choice of details or characteristics must reveal your understanding of a larger question. Why are these details relevant to the topic? Description alone will not be the focus of a literature topic.

explain/show/discuss   These terms indicate the most important parts of a question, which will be developed in the body of an essay. Once you have identified and described your subject, you must interpret and demonstrate the significance of your examples and details; you must offer evidence, using specific references, to support your argument.

USING FLUENT AND PRECISE LANGUAGE

Effective writing is characterized by interesting and vivid language, and "use of precise and engaging language" is among the criteria for evaluation of Regents essays. From the list of what writers *do,* here are some terms to help you articulate your observations about creation of plot:

> *convey, create, delineate, depict, describe, dramatize, foreshadow, illustrate, invent, portray, present, recreate, reveal, select, shock, show, symbolize*

The following terms offer precision and variety in discussing details of a plot:

> *affair, circumstance, climax, development, episode, event, experience, incident, instance, juncture, moment, occasion, occurrence, opportunity, scene, situation*

Terms useful in referring to *character* include:

> *disposition, identity, individuality, makeup, mettle, nature, persona, personality, self, spirit, temperament*

Finally, here is a list of adjectives collected by students to describe some of the many relationships and attitudes among characters in literature (and in our own lives!):

> *admiring, affectionate, bitter, cautious, compassionate, curious, deceitful, disapproving, disdainful, dishonest, distant, envious, false, fearful, generous, hostile, indifferent, loving, optimistic, reluctant, resentful, reserved, respectful, scornful, sincere, skeptical, stern, suspicious, sympathetic, treacherous, watchful*

(See also Using Synonymies to Enhance Your Writing in Chapter 7.)

CHOOSING YOUR OWN TOPIC: REPRESENTATIVE LITERARY SUBJECTS AND THEMES

In many high school and college literature courses, students must select their own topics for writing. The subjects of literature are as varied as human experience itself, and below are some of the many themes authors dramatize. You will encounter these as topics in class discussion and as topics for essays and examination questions. These topics may, of course, serve for discussion of more than one work in an essay.

Topics That Focus on Character

- In many works of literature, an important theme is an **individual's achievement of self-knowledge as a result of undergoing an ordeal.** This self-knowledge may be a recognition of the individual's own strengths, weaknesses, values, prejudices, aspirations, or fears. Identify the individual and the self-knowledge he or she achieves. Using specific references from the work, explain how the ordeal led the individual to the self-knowledge.
- **Nature** can have different effects on different people. It can defeat someone with its power; it can inspire someone with its beauty. Identify the character; using specific references, show how he or she was either defeated or inspired by nature.
- It has been said that to live with **fear** and not be overcome by it is the final **test of maturity.** Explain what fear a character lives with; show how the character "passes" or "fails" the test of maturity on the basis of his or her response to that fear.
- A commonly held belief is that **suffering strengthens an individual's character.** The suffering can be physical, mental, or emotional. Identify the individual; describe the nature of the suffering; explain how the suffering did or did not strengthen the individual's character.
- Sometimes a person **struggles to achieve a goal** only to discover that, once the goal is achieved, the results are not what was expected.
- In many works of literature there are characters who are **troubled by injustice** in society, such as poverty, discrimination, or lawlessness, and **who try to correct** the injustice. Identify the character and the injustice, explain what actions the character takes; discuss whether or not the efforts are successful.
- In many works, characters who love one another or share a special friendship often face **obstacles to their relationship.** Sometimes characters overcome the obstacle; sometimes they are defeated by it. Identify the characters and the obstacle; explain how the characters overcome or are defeated by the obstacle; discuss the effect this outcome (the success or failure, not the obstacle) has on the relationship.
- In many works of literature, **a character sacrifices something of value** in order to achieve something of greater value.
- Sometimes a character faces a **conflict between his or her conscience** and the standards of behavior expected by others. Identify the character; explain the specific nature of the conflict; discuss how the character was affected by this conflict.
- In many works of literature, a character reaches a **major turning point** in his or her life. From that point onward, the character undergoes a significant change.
- Characters in works of literature frequently **learn about life or themselves** by taking risks.

- The phrase **"rite of passage"** describes a situation in which a young person is faced with an experience that results in his or her becoming mature. Explain the experience; discuss how the young person matures as a result of the way in which he or she deals with the experience.
- In many works of literature, characters are **challenged by unfamiliar environments.** Show how the character was or was not successful in meeting the challenge.
- Some individuals in literature **try to do what they believe is right,** even though they face opposition.
- In some works of literature, an important character **makes a mistake that advances the reader's understanding of that individual.**
- Confusion, danger, or tragedy sometimes results when **one character misunderstands the words or actions of another character.**
- In many works of literature, a character **struggles against circumstances that seem to be beyond his or her control.** Sometimes the character is victorious, sometimes not.

Topics That Focus on Literary Elements and Techniques

While topics that focus on character may be the most common in literature courses or on exams, various literary elements also provide topics for essays. The AP literature exam, for example, often features a question based on a literary element or technique. In developing the essays for the literature sections of the English Regents exam, students must show how authors use specific literary elements or techniques. (These tasks are reviewed in the next chapter.)

- Some authors are especially successful at creating **a memorable visual image** that contributes to the reader's understanding of a work. Identify the image and its importance; show how the image contributes to the meaning of the work.
- In many works of literature, the **setting** contributes to the reader's understanding of the central conflict in the plot. Describe the setting; show how it contributes to the reader's understanding of the conflict on which the plot hinges.
- Authors often create a **predominant mood** in a work of literature. Using specific references, discuss incidents that convey that mood and explain the importance of mood to the work.
- Authors sometimes use **foreshadowing** to help develop the plot of a work. Foreshadowing usually takes the form of incidents that seem to be unimportant at first, but take on added significance later. Discuss examples of foreshadowing and show how they contribute to the overall effect and meaning of the work.

- A work of literature may be defined as **a classic** because it promotes deep insight into human behavior, presents a universal theme, or uses language in an exceptional way. Show how a particular work meets the above definition of the term *classic.*
- Through their work, some **authors reveal their acceptance or rejection of values** held by society. Identify the value; state whether the author accepts or rejects it; using specific references, show how the author reveals his or her attitude toward that value.
- In literature, **symbols** are used to reinforce the central idea or to represent characters. Using specific references, explain how the symbol in a particular work enriches the reader's understanding of either the central idea or a character.
- The **narrative point of view** is significant to the effect and meaning of a literary work. Illustrate the truth of this statement by specific references to a work of literature.

AUDIENCE AND LITERATURE ESSAYS

Most teachers mention audience in the assignments they give; if it is not clear for whom you are writing, it is a good idea to ask before you complete an assignment. For most outside examinations, including the Regents, assume that you are writing the essay for a reader who is familiar with the works of literature but who has not considered the topic; background discussion and *detailed* explanation of plot are not needed.

A NOTE ON CONCLUSIONS

No essay, however brief, should simply stop. Even if you run out of time or things to say, try not to telegraph that information to the reader. A conclusion must come back to the topic, must complete the discussion, in a way that leaves the reader feeling convinced by what you have written. On examinations, most students close with a brief, summative conclusion that highlights the relationship of the literary work or works to the topic or restates the thesis of the essay. Even if the reader of a short essay does not really *need* the conclusion to appreciate your argument, the obligation to compose a conclusion keeps you focused on the topic.

Student writers are urged to avoid the following in their conclusions: the expression "what this paper has shown . . ." or "As you can see . . ."; a reminder that Shakespeare was a great playwright or that Mark Twain was an important figure in American literature; a confession that the reader *really* liked or did not like a particular work. Above all, the conclusion is not the place to introduce a new topic or tack on an idea that properly belongs in the body of the essay.

Chapter 6

WRITING ABOUT LITERATURE ON THE REGENTS EXAM

The Regents exam requires you to compose two essays on aspects of literature. Session Two, Part A requires an essay that discusses the ways in which two given passages of different literary genres reveal a common subject and that shows how specific literary elements (theme, characterization, structure, point of view) and techniques (figurative language, irony, symbolism) convey the meanings of the selected passages. This task expects you to be able to identify the distinguishing features of different literary genres and to recognize and understand the significance of a wide range of literary elements and techniques in order to interpret the works. Chapter 3 of *Let's Review* offers a detailed review of the literary elements you are expected to know and illustrates them with references to works widely read in high school. Be sure to refer also to the Glossary of Literary Terms and Techniques at the end of that chapter.

Session Two, Part B of the Regents exam allows you to choose the works on which you will write and does not limit the genres: You may write on fiction, on nonfiction, on works of book length, or on single poems, essays, or short stories. Your essay, however, must discuss "works of literature you have read . . ."; this specification does not include films. This essay gives you the opportunity to demonstrate that you recognize and appreciate the significant themes in literature and that you understand the range and complexity of literary expression. The literature essay requires you to go beyond plot summary or character description. The essay must show why and how the works chosen illustrate your interpretation of a "critical lens" (see page 146), and it must do so through clear organization and effective language. You will have three hours on the second day of the Regents examination to complete the two tasks in Parts A and B.

SESSION TWO, PART A: READING AND WRITING FOR LITERARY RESPONSE

In this part of the exam you are given two passages to read and respond to. The passages will be of different literary genres, such as poetry and fiction; passages may also be selected from nonfiction, such as memoir, journal, or reflective essay. Your task is to appreciate how these two passages develop a common theme using different literary styles and techniques. After answering ten multiple-choice questions on the passages, you will compose "a unified essay . . . in which you use evidence from both passages to develop your controlling idea, and show how each author uses specific literary elements or techniques to convey ideas." The three examples that follow are actual Part A tasks from past Regents exams. In the first two, you will read a poem followed by an excerpt from a personal essay. In the third, both passages are in prose, one from a short story and the other from a memoir. Review of the multiple-choice questions and analysis of a student essay follow each sample task.

Sample Texts, Task, Questions, and Essay

Directions: Read the passages on the following pages (a poem and an essay). Write the number of the answer to each multiple-choice question on your answer sheet. Then write the essay in your essay booklet as described in **Your Task.** You may use the margins to take notes as you read and scrap paper to plan your response.

Your Task: After you have read the passages and answered the multiple-choice questions, write a unified essay about lessons from childhood as revealed in the passages. In your essay, use ideas from *both* passages to establish a controlling idea about lessons from childhood. Using evidence from *each* passage, develop your controlling idea and show how the author uses specific literary elements or techniques to convey that idea.

Guidelines:
Be sure to

- Use ideas from *both* passages to establish a controlling idea about lessons from childhood
- Use specific and relevant evidence from *each* passage to develop your controlling idea
- Show how each author uses specific literary elements (for example: theme, characterization, structure, point of view) or techniques (for example: symbolism, irony, figurative language) to convey the controlling idea
- Organize your ideas in a logical and coherent manner
- Use language that communicates ideas effectively
- Follow the conventions of standard written English

Passage I

The Thing You Must Remember

The thing you must remember is how, as a child,
you worked hours in the art room, the teacher's
hands over yours, molding the little clay dog.
You must remember, how nothing mattered
(5) but the imagined dog's fur, the shape of his ears
and his paws. The gray clay felt dangerous,
your small hands were pressing what you couldn't
say with your limited words. When the dog's back
stiffened, then cracked to white shards
(10) in the kiln, you learned how the beautiful
suffers from too much attention, how clumsy
a single vision can grow, and fragile
with trying too hard. The thing you must
remember is the art teacher's capable
(15) hands: large, rough and grainy,
over yours, holding on.

—Maggie Anderson
from *Windfall*, 2000
University of Pittsburgh Press

Passage II

She was only about five feet tall and probably never weighed more than 110
pounds, but Miss Bessie was a towering presence in the classroom. She was the
only woman tough enough to make me read *Beowulf* and think for a few foolish
days that I liked it. From 1938 to 1942, when I attended Bernard High School in
(5) McMinnville, Tenn., she taught me English, history, civics—and a lot more than
I realized.

I shall never forget the day she scolded me into reading *Beowulf*.

"But Miss Bessie," I complained, "I ain't much interested in it."

Her large brown eyes became daggerish slits. "Boy," she said, "how dare you
(10) say 'ain't' to me! I've taught you better than that."

"Miss Bessie," I pleaded, "I'm trying to make first-string end on the football
team, and if I go around saying 'it isn't' and 'they aren't,' the guys are gonna laugh
me off the squad."

"Boy," she responded, "you'll play football because you have guts. But do you
(15) know what *really* takes guts? Refusing to lower your standards to those of the
crowd. It takes guts to say you've got to live and be somebody fifty years after all
the football games are over."

I started saying "it isn't" and "they aren't," and I still made first-string end—and class valedictorian—without losing my buddies' respect.

(20) During her remarkable 44-year career, Mrs. Bessie Taylor Gwynn taught hundreds of economically deprived black youngsters—including my mother, my brother, my sisters and me. I remember her now with gratitude and affection—especially in this era when Americans are so wrought-up about a "rising tide of mediocrity" in public education and the problems of finding competent, caring

(25) teachers. Miss Bessie was an example of an informed, dedicated teacher, a blessing to children and an asset to the nation.

Born in 1895, in poverty, she grew up in Athens, Ala., where there was no public school for blacks. She attended Trinity School, a private institution for blacks run by the American Missionary Association, and in 1911 graduated from

(30) the Normal School (a "super" high school) at Fisk University in Nashville. Mrs. Gwynn, the essence of pride and privacy, never talked about her years in Athens; only in the months before her death did she reveal that she had never attended Fisk University itself because she could not afford the four-year course.

At Normal School she learned a lot about Shakespeare, but most of all about

(35) the profound importance of education—especially, for a people trying to move up from slavery. "What you put in your head, boy," she once said, "can never be pulled out by the Ku Klux Klan, the Congress or anybody."

Miss Bessie's bearing of dignity told anyone who met her that she was "educated" in the best sense of the word. There was never a discipline problem

(40) in her classes. We didn't dare mess with a woman who knew about the Battle of Hastings, the Magna Charta and the Bill of Rights—and who could also play the piano.

This frail-looking woman could make sense of Shakespeare, Milton, Voltaire, and bring to life Booker T. Washington and W. E. B. DuBois. Believing that it was

(45) important to know who the officials were that spent taxpayers' money and made public policy, she made us memorize the names of everyone on the Supreme Court and in the President's Cabinet. It could be embarrassing to be unprepared when Miss Bessie said, "Get up and tell the class who Frances Perkins is and what you think about her."

(50) Miss Bessie knew that my family, like so many others during the Depression, couldn't afford to subscribe to a newspaper. She knew we didn't even own a radio. Still, she prodded me to "look out for your future and find some way to keep up with what's going on in the world." So I became a delivery boy for the Chattanooga *Times*. I rarely made a dollar a week, but I got to read a newspaper

(55) every day.

Miss Bessie noticed things that had nothing to do with schoolwork, but were vital to a youngster's development. Once a few classmates made fun of my frayed, hand-me-down overcoat, calling me "Strings." As I was leaving school, Miss Bessie patted me on the back of that old overcoat and said, "Carl, never fret about

(60) what you *don't* have. Just make the most of what you *do* have—a brain."

Among the things that I did not have was electricity in the little frame house that my father had built for $400 with his World War I bonus. But because of her inspiration, I spent many hours squinting beside a kerosene lamp reading Shakespeare and Thoreau, Samuel Pepys and William Cullen Bryant.

(65)   No one in my family had ever graduated from high school, so there was no tradition of commitment to learning for me to lean on. Like millions of youngsters in today's ghettos and barrios, I needed the push and stimulation of a teacher who truly cared. Miss Bessie gave plenty of both, as she immersed me in a wonderful world of similes, metaphors and even onomatopoeia. She led me to believe that I

(70) could write sonnets as well as Shakespeare, or iambic-pentameter verse to put Alexander Pope to shame.

In those days the McMinnville school system was rigidly "Jim Crow," and poor black children had to struggle to put anything in their heads. Our high school was only slightly larger than the once-typical little red schoolhouse, and its library was

(75) outrageously inadequate—so small, I like to say, that if two students were in it and one wanted to turn a page, the other one had to step outside.

Negroes, as we were called then, were not allowed in the town library, except to mop floors or dust tables. But through one of those secret Old South arrangements between whites of conscience and blacks of stature, Miss Bessie

(80) kept getting books smuggled out of the white library. That is how she introduced me to the Brontës, Byron, Coleridge, Keats and Tennyson. "If you don't read, you can't write, and if you can't write, you might as well stop dreaming," Miss Bessie once told me.

So I read whatever Miss Bessie told me to, and tried to remember the things

(85) she insisted that I store away. Forty-five years later, I can still recite her "truths to live by," such as Henry Wadsworth Longfellow's lines from "The Ladder of St. Augustine":

The heights by great men reached and kept
Were not attained by sudden flight,

(90)   But they, while their companions slept,
Were toiling upward in the night.

Years later, her inspiration, prodding, anger, cajoling and almost osmotic infusion of learning finally led to that lovely day when Miss Bessie dropped me a note saying, "I'm so proud to read your column in the Nashville *Tennessean*."

(95)   Miss Bessie was a spry 80 when I went back to McMinnville and visited her in a senior citizens' apartment building. Pointing out proudly that her building was racially integrated, she reached for two glasses and a pint of bourbon. I was momentarily shocked, because it would have been scandalous in the 1930s and '40s for word to get out that a teacher drank, and nobody had ever raised a rumor

(100) that Miss Bessie did.

I felt a new sense of equality as she lifted her glass to mine. Then she revealed a softness and compassion that I had never known as a student.

"I've never forgotten that examination day," she said, "when Buster Martin held up seven fingers, obviously asking you for help with question number seven,

(105) 'Name a common carrier.' I can still picture you looking at your exam paper and humming a few bars of 'Chattanooga Choo Choo.' I was so tickled, I couldn't punish either of you."

Miss Bessie was telling me, with bourbon-laced grace, that I never fooled her for a moment.

(110) When Miss Bessie died in 1980, at age 85, hundreds of her former students mourned. They knew the measure of a great teacher: love and motivation. Her wisdom and influence had rippled out across generations.

Some of her students who might normally have been doomed to poverty went on to become doctors, dentists and college professors. Many, guided by Miss *(115)* Bessie's example, became public-school teachers.

"The memory of Miss Bessie and how she conducted her classroom did more for me than anything I learned in college," recalls Gladys Wood of Knoxville, Tenn., a highly respected English teacher who spent 43 years in the state's school system. "So many times, when I faced a difficult classroom problem, I asked myself, *How would Miss Bessie deal with this?* And I'd remember that she would *(120)* handle it with laughter and love."

No child can get all the necessary support at home, and millions of poor children get *no* support at all. That is what makes a wise, educated, warm-hearted teacher like Miss Bessie so vital to the minds, hearts and souls of this country's *(125)* children.

— Carl T. Rowan
"Unforgettable Miss Bessie"
from *Reader's Digest*, March 1985

MULTIPLE-CHOICE QUESTIONS

Directions (1–10): Answer the following questions by selecting the number of the correct choice. The questions may help you think about the ideas and information you might want to use in your essay. You may return to these questions anytime you wish.

Passage I (the poem)—Questions 1–5 refer to Passage I.

1 In line 4, the words "how nothing mattered" help to emphasize the child's
   1 fear
   2 memory
   3 indifference
   4 concentration

2 The description in lines 6 through 8 conveys the child's feeling of
   1 anxiety
   2 control
   3 importance
   4 resentment

3 According to the poem, what is most likely the "thing you must remember"?
   1 the broken dog
   2 the hard work
   3 the teacher's support
   4 the clay's texture

4 The tone of the poem is best described as
   1 bitter
   2 reflective
   3 ironic
   4 lively

5 What aspect of the poet's craft suggests that the child and the speaker are the same person?
   1 the narrative point of view
   2 the simple words
   3 the blank verse
   4 the irregular line lengths

Passage II (the essay) — Questions 6–10 refer to Passage II.

6 Miss Bessie's remarks about learning correct grammar (lines 9 through 17) stress the importance of
   1 participating in sports
   2 avoiding peer pressure
   3 reading classical literature
   4 enforcing team spirit

7 In lines 44 through 55, the author's references to memorization and reading the newspaper serve to emphasize Miss Bessie's desire that her students be
   1 financially independent
   2 socially adept
   3 emotionally stable
   4 politically aware

8 The author's references to the world of poetry (lines 66 through 71) have the effect of stressing Miss Bessie's power to
   1 instill confidence
   2 encourage dependence
   3 predict events
   4 discourage imitation

9 Miss Bessie most likely recommended that her students remember Longfellow's verse to illustrate the value of
1 spiritual discipline
2 regular rest
3 hard work
4 heroic behavior

10 The author most likely includes the quotation from Gladys Wood (lines 116 through 120) to emphasize the extent of
1 the author's grief
2 Miss Bessie's influence
3 the student's disobedience
4 Gladys Wood's success

LOOKING AT THE ANSWERS

1 **4** "concentration." The image in this part of the poem is of the small child, working for hours, trying to shape the figure of a dog out of clay.

2 **2** "anxiety." The key image here is that the "gray clay felt dangerous . . . ." The child is not confident that she can shape the clay as she wishes, and her words are limited. The poem does not suggest a sense of importance or resentment in the child.

3 **3** "the teacher's support." The poem opens with the image of the "teacher's hands over yours"; the repetition of this image and the phrase "holding on" at the end emphasize the supporting presence of the teacher as what "you must remember."

4 **2** "reflective." *Reflective* here means looking back with thought and understanding. That captures best the tone of the poem. The feeling of the poem is not "lively," and there is nothing to suggest bitterness or irony.

5 **1** "the narrative point of view." The effect here is of the speaker addressing herself. The details are expressed with a vividness that comes from the speaker's own remembered experience; the poem captures what the speaker felt, not simply what she may have observed in another child.

6 **2** "avoiding peer pressure." The key line in this passage is when Miss Bessie says that what "really takes guts" is "refusing to lower your standards to those of the crowd."

7 **4** "politically aware." Note that the examples of what Miss Bessie thought it important to know were the "officials . . . that spent taxpayers' money and made public policy." She expected her students to

memorize the names of the members of the Supreme Court and the President's Cabinet. There is nothing to suggest that she thought it would make her students financially independent, socially aware, or more emotionally stable.

8 **1** "instill confidence." Because Carl Rowan's family had no "tradition of commitment to learning," he needed the "push and stimulation of a teacher who truly cared." She also convinced him that he could write sonnets as well as Shakespeare!

9 **3** "hard work." The image in the Longfellow verse is of great men who reach their heights by ". . . <u>toiling</u> upward in the night." Toil denotes constant effort and hard work.

10 **2** "Miss Bessie's influence." Gladys Wood's comments reveal the extent to which she would think about how Miss Bessie would have responded to a difficult classroom situation. Wood also says that Miss Bessie's memory taught her more "than anything I learned in college."

Here is an essay one student wrote in response to this task. Note how many of the key ideas are suggested by the questions and answers above.

Sample Student Response Essay

Both the poem and the prose passage detail lessons learned in an academic setting, but neither is primarily about academic content. Both pieces reveal that the most valuable lessons from childhood are those that are still valued in maturity.

Written in poetic form but employing the language of everyday speech, "The Thing You Must Remember" recalls the experience of a young child in art class trying to shape a dog out of clay. The speaker reveals how, even for a child, the creation of art transcends language—"pressing what you couldn't say with your limited words." When the dog shatters in the heat of the kiln, the speaker "must remember" that the "beautiful suffers from too much attention" and that a single vision may grow clumsy "and fragile with trying too hard." What the poet most remembers is found in the opening and in the final image of the poem, the art teacher's "hands over yours." The most important lesson from the child's effort to make a clay dog was in feeling the guidance and reassurance of her teacher.

Passage II, in the form of personal narrative, recalls a teacher who had a profound influence on the experiences of a black youth in the pre-integration South. Though much of the passage details the academic expectations of the demanding "Miss

127

Bessie," the passage reveals the more important life lessons she taught. Beginning with the initial vignette when Miss Bessie upbraids the reluctant scholar for using "ain't" and calling him "Boy," to the quote from Longfellow that represented her "truths to live by," we see how this "frail-looking woman" inspired and truly educated her students. Not only did Carl Rowan go on to become a nationally known journalist, but some of her other students who "might have been doomed to poverty" went on to professional careers of their own.

Miss Bessie taught Rowan to resist peer pressure and to be proud of his intelligence, especially when he feared it might keep him from being accepted as a football player. She also taught the importance of reading the newspaper and being an informed citizen by not only knowing who was on the Supreme Court and in the President's Cabinet, but also by cultivating opinions about those figures. Rowan's memoir reveals, however, that the most important things Miss Bessie taught came from her "inspiration, prodding . . . and infusion of learning" in a child whose family had no tradition of a commitment to learning.

In both the poem and the personal narrative, the writers are remembering teachers who gave them lessons that transcend skill, lessons, and tests. These teachers taught about confidence and gave inspiration.

Analysis

This response demonstrates insightful appreciation of the texts. The introduction establishes the controlling idea that "the most valuable lessons of childhood are those that are still valued in maturity." Relevant quotes from both passages support the development of ideas and give variety to the sentences. Although the discussion of literary elements is not extensive, discussion of the poem, in particular, shows the writer's understanding of how imagery and point of view contribute to the common theme: "What the poet most remembers is found in the opening and in the final image of the poem. . . ."

The essay is also well organized, with the discussion leading in each section to the most important point or "lesson." The conclusion is effective because it reinforces the controlling idea and heightens our appreciation of what is common to the two passages: ". . . the writers are remembering teachers who gave them lessons that transcend skill, lessons, and tests." The language of the essay is appropriate and often very sophisticated: "Beginning with the initial vignette when Miss Bessie upbraids the reluctant scholar. . . ." This essay meets all the criteria for a high score.

Directions: Read the passages on the following pages (a poem and an essay). Select the number of the correct choice to each of the questions following the passages. Then write the essay on separate sheets of paper as described in **Your Task**. You may use the margins to take notes as you read and scrap paper to plan your response.

Your Task: After you have read the passages and answered the multiple-choice questions, write a unified essay about the influence of outside forces on personal growth. In your essay, use ideas from *both* passages to establish a controlling idea about the influence of outside forces on personal growth. Using evidence from *each* passage, develop your controlling idea and show how the author uses specific literary elements or techniques to convey that idea. (Regents examination, August 2000)

Guidelines:
Be sure to

- Use ideas from *both* passages to establish a controlling idea about the influence of outside forces on personal growth
- Use specific and relevant evidence from *each* passage to develop your controlling idea
- Show how each author uses specific literary elements (for example: theme, characterization, structure, point of view) or techniques (for example: symbolism, irony, figurative language) to convey the controlling idea
- Organize your ideas in a logical and coherent manner
- Use language that communicates ideas effectively
- Follow the conventions of standard written English

Passage I

The bonsai tree
in the attractive pot
could have grown eighty feet tall
on the side of a mountain
(5) till split by lightning.
But a gardener
carefully pruned it.
It is nine inches high.
Every day as he
(10) whittles back the branches
the gardener croons,
It is your nature

> to be small and cozy,
> domestic and weak;
> *(15)* how lucky, little tree,
> to have a pot to grow in.
> With living creatures
> one must begin very early
> to dwarf their growth:
> *(20)* the bound feet,
> the crippled brain,
> the hair in curlers,
> the hands you
> love to touch.

—Marge Piercy

Passage II

My daughter is an athlete. Nowadays, this statement won't strike many parents as unusual, but it does me. Until her freshman year in high school, Ann was only marginally interested in sports of any kind. When she played, she didn't swing hard, often dropped the ball, and had an annoying habit of tittering on field
(5) or court.

Indifference combined with another factor that did not bode well for a sports career. Ann was growing up to be beautiful. By the eighth grade, nature and orthodontics had produced a 5-foot 8-inch, 125-pound, brown-eyed beauty with a wonderful smile. People told her, too. And, as many young women know, it is
(10) considered a satisfactory accomplishment to be pretty and stay pretty. Then you can simply sit still and enjoy the unconditional positive regard. Ann loved the attention too, and didn't consider it demeaning when she was awarded "Best Hair," female category, in the eighth-grade yearbook.

So it came as a surprise when she became a jock. The first indication that ath-
(15) letic indifference had ended came when she joined the high school cross-country team. She signed up in early September and ran third for the team within three days. Not only that. After one of those 3.1-mile races up hill and down dale on a rainy November afternoon, Ann came home muddy and bedraggled. Her hair was plastered to her head, and the mascara she had applied so carefully that morning
(20) ran in dark circles under her eyes. This is it, I thought. Wait until Lady Astor sees herself. But the kid with the best eighth-grade hair went on to finish the season and subsequently letter in cross-country, soccer, basketball, and softball.

I love sports, she tells anyone who will listen. So do I, though my midlife quest for a doctorate leaves me little time for either playing or watching. My love of
(25) sports is bound up with the goals in my life and my hopes for my three daughters. I have begun to hear the message of sports. It is very different from many messages that women receive about living, and I think it is good.

My husband, for example, talked to Ann differently when he realized that she
was a serious competitor and not just someone who wanted to get in shape so
(30) she'd look good in a prom dress. Be aggressive, he'd advise. Go for the ball. Be
intense.

Be intense. She came in for some of the most scathing criticism from her dad,
when, during basketball season, her intensity waned. You're pretending to play
hard, he said. You like it on the bench? Do you like to watch while your team-
(35) mates play?

I would think, how is this kid reacting to such advice? For years, she'd been
told at home, at school, by countless advertisements, "Be quiet, Be good, Be still."
When teachers reported that Ann was too talkative, not obedient enough, too
flighty. When I dressed her up in frilly dresses and admonished her not to get
(40) dirty. When ideals of femininity are still, quiet, cool females in ads whose vacant-
ness passes for sophistication. How can any adolescent girl know what she's up
against? Have you ever really noticed intensity? It is neither quiet nor good. And
it's definitely not pretty.

In the end, her intensity revived. At half time, she'd look for her father, and
(45) he would come out of the bleachers to discuss tough defense, finding the open
player, squaring up on her jump shot. I'd watch them at the edge of the court, a
tall man and a tall girl, talking about how to play.

Of course, I'm particularly sensitive at this point in my life to messages about
trying hard, being active, getting better through individual and team effort. Ann,
(50) you could barely handle a basketball two years ago. Now you're bringing the ball
up against the press. Two defenders are after you. You must dribble, stop, pass.
We're depending on you. We need you to help us. I wonder if my own paroxysms
of uncertainty would be eased had more people urged me—be active, go for it!

Not that dangers don't lurk for the females of her generation. I occasionally
(55) run this horror show in my own mental movie theater: an unctuous but handsome
lawyerlike drone of a young man spies my Ann. Hmmm, he says, unconsciously
to himself, good gene pool, and wouldn't she go well with my BMW and the
condo? Then I see Ann with a great new hairdo kissing the drone goodbye-honey
and setting off to the nearest mall with splendid-looking children to spend money.
(60) But the other night she came home from softball tryouts at 6 in the evening.
The dark circles under her eyes were from exhaustion, not makeup. I tried too
hard today, she says. I feel sick.

After she has revived, she explains. She wants to play a particular position.
There is competition for it. I can't let anybody else get my spot, she says. I've got
(65) to prove that I can do it. Later we find out that she has not gotten the much-
wanted third-base position, but she will start with the varsity team. My husband
talks about the machinations of coaches and tells her to keep trying. You're doing
fine, he says. She gets that I-am-going-to-keep-trying look on her face. The
horror-show vision of Ann fades.
(70) Of course, Ann doesn't realize the changes she has wrought, the power of her
self-definition. I'm an athlete, Ma, she tells me when I suggest participation in the
school play or the yearbook. But she has really caused us all to rethink our views

131

of existence: her younger sisters who consider sports a natural activity for females, her father whose advocacy of women has increased, and me. Because when I
(75) doubt my own abilities, I say to myself, Get intense, Margaret. Do you like to sit on the bench?

And my intensity revives.

I am not suggesting that participation in sports is the answer for all young women. It is not easy—the losing, jealousy, raw competition, and intense personal
(80) criticism of performance.

And I don't wish to imply that the sports scene is a morality play either. Girls' sports can be funny. You can't forget that out on that field are a bunch of people who know the meaning of the word cute. During one game, I noticed that Ann had a blue ribbon tied on her ponytail, and it dawned on me that every girl on the
(85) team had an identical bow. Somehow I can't picture the Celtics gathered in the locker room of the Boston Garden agreeing to wear the same color sweatbands.

No, what has struck me, amazed me and made me hold my breath in wonder and in hope is both the ideal of sport and the reality of a young girl not afraid to do her best.
(90) I watch her bringing the ball up the court. We yell encouragement from the stands, though I know she doesn't hear us. Her face is red with exertion, and her body is concentrated on the task. She dribbles, draws the defense to her, passes, runs. A teammate passes the ball back to her. They've beaten the press. She heads toward the hoop. Her father watches her, her sisters watch her, I watch her. And
(95) I think, drive, Ann, drive.

—Margaret A. Whitney

MULTIPLE-CHOICE QUESTIONS

Directions (1–10): Answer the following questions by selecting the number of the correct choice. The questions may help you think about the ideas and information you might want to use in your essay. You may return to these questions anytime you wish.

Passage I (the poem)—Questions 1–5 refer to Passage I.

1   Lines 1 through 5 focus on what aspect of the bonsai tree?
  1   its vulnerability
  2   its history
  3   its beauty
  4   its potential

2   In lines 12 through 24, the poet likens the bonsai tree to
  1   women
  2   love
  3   power
  4   gardeners

3   In line 19, the word *dwarf* most nearly means
    1   celebrate
    2   observe
    3   stunt
    4   evaluate

4   The narrator implies that the conditions described in lines 20 through 24 are ones that society
    1   ridicules
    2   imposes
    3   discounts
    4   criticizes

5   The short lines of the poem have the effect of echoing the poem's emphasis on
    1   restriction
    2   youth
    3   failure
    4   imperfection

Passage II (the essay)—Questions 6–10 refer to Passage II.

6   The author implies that her daughter's interest in athletics is inconsistent with her daughter's
    1   pride
    2   hobbies
    3   accomplishments
    4   appearance

7   As used in line 12, the word *demeaning* most nearly means
    1   appropriate
    2   belittling
    3   surprising
    4   outrageous

8   The phrase "Wait until Lady Astor sees herself" (lines 20 and 21) refers to the author's assumption that the physical effects of running would diminish her daughter's
    1   motivation
    2   affection
    3   popularity
    4   indifference

9 What is "the message of sports" to which the author alludes (line 26)?
1 Competition is unbecoming to women.
2 Competition between male athletes is more pronounced than competition between female athletes.
3 Participation in sports is more beneficial to women than to men.
4 Participation in sports fosters values that are as important to women as to men.

10 The author's references to her own uncertainties (lines 52 and 53 and lines 74 through 76) have the effect of emphasizing
1 her husband's intentions
2 her husband's advocacy
3 Ann's self-assurance
4 Ann's skill

LOOKING AT THE ANSWERS

1 **4** "its potential." In line 3, the poet says of the bonsai tree, it "could have grown eighty feet tall. . . ."

2 **1** "women." The poet is referring to once-traditional views of women when she says, "It is your nature to be small and cozy, domestic and weak. . . ." The references to "bound feet," "crippled brain," "hair in curlers," and "the hands you love to touch" are all of cultural forces historically meant to keep women compliant and attractive.

3 **3** "stunt." The sense of the passage echoes the key image of the tree kept in a pot and carefully pruned to keep it small. "Stunt" means to stifle or severely limit, in this case, the growth of women.

4 **2** "imposes." (See (2) above) "Bound feet" is the most vivid example of physical "stunting," but the others are also references to the power of a society's expectation that women be attractive to stifle growth of spirit and intellect. There is no suggestion in the poem that society ridicules, discounts, or criticizes these forces.

5 **1** "restriction." Beginning with the image of the potentially great bonsai tree confined in a pot to grow only a few inches, all of the images convey forms of restriction. The poet does not emphasize youth, and while failure or imperfection may be implied, the fundamental theme and imagery of the poem are of restriction.

6 **4** "appearance." In the second paragraph, Whitney recounts that Ann was "growing up to be beautiful . . ." and enjoyed the admiration it brought her in eighth grade. At line 14, she remarks, "So it came as a surprise when she became a jock."

7 **2** "belittling." The passage indicates that Ann did not feel at all "put down," diminished by the award for Best Hair. Ann enjoyed the attention she was getting and was probably not surprised by it.

8 **1** "motivation." The passage indicates that the mother was quite sure Ann would want to quit running when she saw what it did to her make-up and appearance. The last sentence of the paragraph reinforces the idea of Ann's motivation.

9 **4** "Participation in sports fosters values that are as important to women as to men." The sentence preceding links the author's love of sports with the goals and hopes she has for her daughters, and later in the passage, she refers to "messages about trying hard, being active, getting better through individual and team effort." At line 53, the author suggests that it might have been better for her as well if more people had urged her to "be active, go for it!" One of the key themes in this passage, therefore, is that the "message" of sports is equally important to women as it is to men.

10 **3** "Ann's self-assurance." The passage includes many examples of Ann's determination, confidence, and "self-definition." Whitney indicates that her own sense of self is enhanced when she thinks of her daughter's intensity. It is this, more than Ann's athletic skill, that the author values.

Sample Student Response Essay

Both passages deal with the influence of outside forces on personal growth. Although the passages differ in many ways, they share the same theme: society's expectations can be a highly restrictive, even destructive force in shaping the life of a female. The authors use various techniques and elements to convey this theme.

In Passage I, the author uses a powerful metaphor. The poem seems to be about a bonsai tree, but at the end we see several images that relate to women and society's expectations of them: women are supposed to have smooth, lovely hands and nicely styled hair. In China it was the custom to bind women's feet. They couldn't walk very well, but those tiny feet were considered very beautiful. These images of women who have to suffer to be beautiful make us realize that the poet wants us to think about that bonsai tree in another way. Think of it as a woman who has been trained to be "domestic and weak." The poet contrasts the size of the bonsai tree ("nine inches high") with what the tree might have been ("eighty feet tall"). As a metaphor, the bonsai

135

makes us think about a female's potential: what could she become if she didn't have to conform to society's expectations? Worse yet, all this restriction is done kindly, with the best intentions. The gardener works "carefully" and he "croons" as he makes the tree "cozy." The poet uses soft and gentle words to emphasize the gardener's kindness. The gardener calls the little tree "lucky." This is ironic. I don't think the poet considers it lucky, because we then see words that are not gentle, but painful: "bound feet," "crippled brain." Even the lines are short, like these bound feet, like that nine-inch-high tree that wants to be eighty feet tall, living in the mountains, not in a pot, no matter how "attractive." Whether it's bound feet or curled hair, society's expectations can stifle a woman if she lets them.

In Passage II, the author uses point of view to convey the idea that society's expectations can be destructive. It is Ann's mother speaking, and from this viewpoint, we can see Ann's actions, her father's actions, and the narrator's own thoughts. Ann's mother, Margaret, comes from a time when women's lives were more restricted, and she fears those restrictions for Ann too. Throughout the passage, she refers to those restrictions.

For example, she knows that "it is considered a satisfactory accomplishment to be pretty and stay pretty," and Ann knows it, too. The advice Ann has heard from school, parents, and advertisements is "Be quiet, be good." And later in life, Margaret fears that Ann may be attracted to the things society tells her to value: a "handsome lawyerlike drone" with a "BMW and the condo," happy with "a great new hairdo" and going to the mall "to spend money."

The author contrasts these "pretty" images and messages with images and messages that are better suited to her athlete daughter. Ann's "hair was plastered to her head," and her mascara was running after a hard race. Her dad doesn't tell her to sit still and be dainty. "Be aggressive, be intense" is his advice.

The author of the essay knows that society's expectations can be destructive, but she has seen that other influences in Ann's life will protect her from those destructive influences. Her father's advice, her peers' encouragement, and her own motivation will prevent her from being just a pretty face with "best hair." Margaret even points out that Ann's intensity and self-definition have revived her own.

One image suggests that Ann can accept society's demands for "prettiness" without losing her own drive, her own intensity. That is the image of her teammates, all working hard, wearing matching blue ponytail ribbons.

The author of the poem writes of the tragedy of lost potential when society imposes its will on women. The author of the essay writes of the hope for society and individuals when women break free of that oppression.

Analysis

This is an excellent response to the task because it reveals an in-depth understanding of the common theme in both passages and of the different literary techniques in them. The introduction is brief but clearly establishes the topic to be developed: "Although the passages differ in many ways, they share the same theme: society's expectations can be a highly restrictive, even destructive force in shaping the life of a female."

The discussion of the poem is especially effective in showing how metaphor, imagery, and language convey the theme. This writer's insight is further evident in the way point of view becomes the focus of the analysis of Passage II: "It is Ann's mother speaking, and from this viewpoint, we can see Ann's actions, her father's actions and the narrator's own thoughts. . . ." The essay is coherent and well organized, and the conclusion effectively summarizes the expression of the common theme in two contrasting passages. The final sentence shows how the essay takes that common theme beyond its harsh expression in the poem.

Throughout the essay, the language is precise and fluent, and the writer uses a variety of sentence structures to good effect; each paragraph shows the writer's skill in balancing lengthy, complex, or compound sentences with simple, direct assertions. This writer also demonstrates solid command of the conventions. This essay meets the criteria for a high score.

Directions: Read the passages on the following pages (a short story excerpt and an autobiographical excerpt). Write the number of the answer to each multiple-choice question on your answer sheet. Then write the essay in your essay booklet as described in **Your Task.** You may use the margins to take notes as you read and scrap paper to plan your response.

Your Task: After you have read the passages and answered the multiple-choice questions, write a unified essay about the things mothers do for their children as revealed in the passages. In your essay, use ideas from *both* passages to establish a controlling idea about the things mothers do for their children. Using evidence from *each* passage, develop your controlling idea and show how the author uses specific literary elements or techniques to convey that idea.

Guidelines:
Be sure to

- Use ideas from *both* passages to establish a controlling idea about the things mothers do for their children
- Use specific and relevant evidence from *each* passage to develop your controlling idea
- Show how each author uses specific literary elements (for example: theme, characterization, structure, point of view) or techniques (for example: symbolism, irony, figurative language) to convey the controlling idea
- Organize your ideas in a logical and coherent manner
- Use language that communicates ideas effectively
- Follow the conventions of standard written English

Passage I

     . . ."Well, Mary."Aunt Elvera heaved herself up the porch steps and drew off her gauntlet gloves. "I can see you are having a busy day."Mama's hands were fire red from strawberry juice and the heat of the stove. Mine were scratched all over from picking every ripe berry in the patch.

(5)   "One day's like another on the farm,"Mama remarked.

     "Then I will not mince words,"Aunt Elvera said, overlooking me. "I'd have rung you up if you were connected to the telephone system."

     "What about, Elvera?"She and Mama weren't sisters. They were sisters-in-law.

     "Why, the Fair, of course!"Aunt Elvera bristled in an important way. "What

(10) else? The Louisiana Purchase Exposition in St. Louis. The world will be there. It puts St. Louis at the hub of the universe."Aunt Elvera's mouth worked wordlessly.

     "Well, I do know about it,"Mama said. "I take it you'll be going?"

     Aunt Elvera waved her away. "My stars, yes. You know how Schumate can be. Tight as a new boot. But I put my foot down. Mary, this is the opportunity of a

(15) lifetime. We will not see such wonders again during our span."

     "Ah,"Mama said, and my mind wandered—took a giant leap and landed in St. Louis. We knew about the Fair. The calendar the peddler gave us at Christmas featured a different pictorial view of the Fair for every month. There were white palaces in gardens with gondolas in waterways, everything electric-lit. Castles from

(20) Europe and paper houses from Japan. For the month of May the calendar featured the great floral clock on the fairgrounds.

     "Send us a postal,"Mama said.

     "The thing is . . ."Aunt Elvera's eyes slid toward Dorothy. "We thought we'd invite Geneva to go with us."

(25)   My heart liked to lurch out of my apron. Me? They wanted to take me to the Fair?

"She'll be company for Dorothy."

Then I saw how it was. Dorothy was dim, but she could set her heels like a mule. She wanted somebody with her at the Fair so she wouldn't have to trail after
(30) her mother every minute. We were about the same age. We were in the same grade, but she was a year older, having repeated fourth grade. She could read, but her lips moved. And we were cousins, not friends.

"It will be educational for them both," Aunt Elvera said. "All the progress of civilization as we know it will be on display. They say a visit to the Fair is tantamount
(35) to a year of high school."

"Mercy," Mama said.

"We will take the Wabash Railroad directly to the gates of the Exposition," Aunt Elvera explained, "and we will be staying on the grounds themselves at the Inside Inn." She leaned nearer Mama, and her voice fell. "I'm sorry to say that there will
(40) be stimulants for sale on the fairgrounds. You know how St. Louis is in the hands of the breweries." Aunt Elvera was sergeant-at-arms of the Women's Christian Temperance Union, and to her, strong drink was a mocker. "But we will keep the girls away from that sort of thing." Her voice fell to a whisper. "And we naturally won't set foot on the Pike."

(45) We knew what the Pike was. It was the midway of the Fair, like a giant carnival with all sorts of goings-on.

"Well, many thanks, but I don't think so," Mama said.

My heart didn't exactly sink. It never dawned on me that I'd see the Fair. I was only a little cast down because I might never get another glimpse of the world.

(50) "Now, you're not to think of the money," Aunt Elvera said. "Dismiss that from your mind. Schumate and I will be glad to cover all Geneva's expenses. She can sleep in the bed with Dorothy, and we are carrying a good deal of our eats. I know these aren't flush times for farmers, Mary, but do not let your pride stand in Geneva's way."

(55) "Oh, no," Mama said mildly. "Pride cometh before a fall. But we may be running down to the Fair ourselves."

Aunt Elvera's eyes narrowed, and I didn't believe Mama, either. It was just her way of fending off my aunt. Kept me from being in the same bed with Dorothy, too. . . .

(60) I could tell you very little about the rest of that day. My mind was miles off. I know Mama wrung the neck off a fryer, and we had baking-powder biscuits to go with the warm jam. After supper my brothers hitched up Fanny to the trap and went into town. I took a bottle brush to the lamp chimneys and trimmed the wicks. After that I was back out on the porch swing while there was some daylight left. The
(65) lightning bugs were coming out, so that reminded me of how the Fair was lit up at night with electricity, brighter than day.

Then Mama came out and settled in the swing beside me, which was unusual, since she never sat out until the nights got hotter than this. We swung together awhile. Then she said in a quiet voice, "I meant it. I want you to see the Fair."

(70) Everything stopped then. I still didn't believe it, but my heart turned over.

"I spoke to your dad about it. He can't get away, and he can't spare the boys. But I want us to go to the Fair."

Oh, she was brave to say it, she who hadn't been anywhere in her life. Brave even to think it. "I've got some egg money put back," she said. We didn't keep
(75) enough chickens to sell the eggs, but anything you managed to save was called egg money.

"That's for a rainy day," I said, being practical.

"I know it," she said. "But I'd like to see that floral clock."

Mama was famous for her garden flowers. When her glads were up, every color, people drove by to see them. And there was nobody to touch her for zinnias.
(80) people drove by to see them. And there was nobody to touch her for zinnias.

Oh, Mama, I thought, is this just a game we're playing? "What'll we wear?" I asked, to test her.

"They'll be dressy down at the Fair, won't they?" She said. "You know those artificial cornflowers I've got. I thought I'd trim my hat with them. And you're
(85) getting to be a big girl. Time you had a corset."

So then I knew she meant business. . . .

—Richard Peck
"The Electric Summer"
from *Time Capsule*, 1999
Delacorte Press

Passage II

I began working in journalism when I was eight years old. It was my mother's idea. She wanted me to "make something" of myself and, after a levelheaded appraisal of my strengths, decided I had better start young if I was to have any chance of keeping up with the competition. . . .
(5) With my load of magazines I headed toward Belleville Avenue. That's where the people were. There were two filling stations at the intersection with Union Avenue, as well as an A&P, a fruit stand, a bakery, a barber shop, Zuccarelli's drugstore, and a diner shaped like a railroad car. For several hours I made myself highly visible, shifting position now and then from corner to corner, from shop
(10) window to shop window, to make sure everyone could see the heavy black lettering on the canvas bag that said THE SATURDAY EVENING POST. When the angle of the light indicated it was suppertime, I walked back to the house.

"How many did you sell, Buddy?" my mother asked.

"None."
(15) "Where did you go?"

"The corner of Belleville and Union Avenues."

"What did you do?"

"Stood on the corner waiting for somebody to buy a *Saturday Evening Post*."

"You just stood there?"
(20) "Didn't sell a single one."

"For God's sake, Russell!"

Uncle Allen intervened. "I've been thinking about it for some time," he said, "and I've about decided to take the Post regularly. Put me down as a regular customer." I handed him a magazine and he paid me a nickel. It was the first
(25) nickel I earned.

Afterwards my mother instructed me in salesmanship. I would have to ring doorbells, address adults with charming self-confidence, and break down resistance with a sales talk pointing out that no one, no matter how poor, could afford to be without the *Saturday Evening Post* in the home.
(30) I told my mother I'd changed my mind about wanting to succeed in the magazine business.

"If you think I'm going to raise a good-for-nothing," she replied, "you've got another think coming." She told me to hit the streets with the canvas bag and start ringing doorbells the instant school was out next day. When I objected that I
(35) didn't feel any aptitude for salesmanship, she asked how I'd like to lend her my leather belt so she could whack some sense into me. I bowed to superior will and entered journalism with a heavy heart.

My mother and I had fought this battle almost as long as I could remember. It probably started even before memory began, when I was a country child in
(40) northern Virginia and my mother, dissatisfied with my father's plain workman's life, determined that I would not grow up like him and his people, with calluses on their hands, overalls on their backs, and fourth-grade educations in their heads. She had fancier ideas of life's possibilities. Introducing me to the *Saturday Evening Post*, she was trying to wean me as early as possible from my father's
(45) world where men left with their lunch pails at sunup, worked with their hands until the grime ate into the pores, and died with a few sticks of mail-order furniture as their legacy. In my mother's vision of the better life there were desks and white collars, well-pressed suits, evenings of reading and lively talk, and perhaps—if a man were very, very lucky and hit the jackpot, really made
(50) something important of himself—perhaps there might be a fantastic salary of $5,000 a year to support a big house and a Buick with a rumble seat and a vacation in Atlantic City. . . .

— Russell Baker
from *Growing Up*, 1982
Congdon & Weed

MULTIPLE-CHOICE QUESTIONS

Directions (1–10): Select the best suggested answer to each question and write its number in the space provided on the answer sheet. The questions may help you think about the ideas and information you might want to use in your essay. You may return to these questions anytime you wish.

Passage I (the short story excerpt)—Questions 1–6 refer to Passage I.

1   Mama's statement, "One day's like another on the farm," (line 5) indicates that Mama felt
    1   homesick
    2   resigned
    3   jealous
    4   curious

2   The narrator concludes that she is being invited to the Fair primarily because
    1   Aunt Elvera pities her
    2   Dorothy admires her
    3   Aunt Elvera values education
    4   Dorothy wants a companion

3   In line 74 "egg money" refers to money set aside for
    1   investment
    2   supplies
    3   emergencies
    4   food

4   The narrator thinks that Mama is brave to talk about going to the Fair because Mama
    1   has never traveled before
    2   dislikes being in a crowded place
    3   fears Geneva would be embarrassed
    4   is worried about her husband and sons

5   The narrator implies that Mama's true reason for visiting the Fair is to
    1   sell the eggs and chickens
    2   find a husband for Geneva
    3   show off her new clothes
    4   give Geneva an unusual experience

6   The sentence, "So then I knew she meant business," (line 86) suggests that Mama's talk about the Fair is becoming a
    1   plan
    2   burden
    3   fantasy
    4   disaster

Passage II (the autobiographical excerpt)—Questions 7–10 refer to Passage II.

7 The list of details in lines 6 through 8 establishes the setting as
  1 an elegant residential area
  2 a busy shopping area
  3 an empty railway station
  4 a quiet office building

8 The dialogue in lines 13 through 21 reveals the mother's sense of
  1 fear
  2 greed
  3 dismay
  4 remorse

9 Uncle Allen probably decided to buy the *Post* because he
  1 preferred the *Post* to other magazines
  2 hoped to impress Russell's mother
  3 wanted a career in journalism
  4 felt sorry for Russell

10 The narrator suggests that his battle with his mother was the result of her
  1 appreciation of journalism
  2 desire to get him out of the house
  3 ideas about success
  4 admiration for her husband's work

LOOKING AT THE ANSWERS

1 **2** "resigned." To be resigned to something is to be uncomplaining, accepting. This best expresses the tone in Mama's remark.

2 **4** "Dorothy wants a companion." At line 28, the narrator says, "Then I saw how it was. . . . She wanted somebody with her at the Fair so she wouldn't have to trail after her mother every minute." Aunt Elvera certainly values education, but Geneva understands that this was probably Dorothy's idea.

3 **3** "emergencies." The narrator reminds her mother, "That's for a rainy day." This expression usually signifies setting something aside for emergencies or the unexpected.

4 **1** "[Mama] has never traveled before." In line 73, Geneva remarks on how brave her mother was, ". . . she who hadn't been anywhere in her life."

5   **4**   "give Geneva an unusual experience." The passage suggests that Geneva's mother sees this as an opportunity for her daughter to have new experiences. She probably also sensed Geneva's desire to go in her reactions to Aunt Elvera's offer. When Mama comes out to sit on the swing, she says, "I meant it. I want you to see the Fair."

6   **1**   "a plan." Geneva's mother is thinking about how to dress for the trip and has already decided how to trim her hat. She is also thinking about what Geneva will need, now that she is ". . . getting to be a big girl."

7   **2**   "a busy shopping area." The description here includes two filling stations, a grocery store and a fruit stand, a bakery, etc. There is nothing to suggest a residential area, office building, or railway station.

8   **3**   "dismay." Russell's mother is expressing her shock and exasperation at Russell's complete lack of effort to sell anything. She seems dumbfounded by his behavior.

9   **4**   "felt sorry for Russell." Russell says here that his uncle "intervened." That is, he stepped in to rescue Russell from greater anger in his mother.

10   **3**   "ideas about success." The final paragraph of the passage explains that Russell's mother was dissatisfied with her husband's plain workman's life and had "fancier ideas of life's possibilities." For her, success means white collars, suits, and a man's making "something important of himself. . . ." Baker says that from even before he could remember, his mother was battling to get him to aspire to something "better" for himself.

Sample Student Response Essay

In these two passages, a single incident offers a brief portrait of a mother who is determined that her children have a fuller or "better" life than her own. In each, the story is told from the point of view of the child as he or she remembers the experience. The setting of each suggests a time early in the 20th century and families struggling to earn a living.

Mary, the mother in the first passage, sees an opportunity to give her daughter (and herself) some knowledge and experience beyond that of life on the farm. This opportunity arises when Aunt Elvera, Mary's sister-in-law, offers to take her daughter Geneva to the Louisiana Purchase Exposition in St. Louis as a companion for her own daughter. Geneva's narration exposes Aunt Elvera as somewhat condescending when she points out that the family is not "connected to the telephone system," and suggests that Mary and her family may not even know about the Fair and how important it is. Geneva also knows that Dorothy is not as bright as she is but perceives right away that Dorothy "wanted somebody with her . . . so she wouldn't have to trail after her mother every minute." Seeing Aunt Elvera and Dorothy through Geneva's eyes helps the reader understand why Geneva's mother would reject the offer. Nonetheless, the reader can't help but share Geneva's surprise when Mary says, mildly, that ". . . we may be running down to the Fair ourselves."

The bond between mother and daughter is a unifying theme introduced in the opening images of Geneva and her mother making jam. Geneva also knows her mother is trying to fend off her aunt and does not think she really means to go to the Fair. Geneva's understanding of her mother is also revealed in Geneva's recognition of her mother's "bravery" and willingness to spend the "egg money." The image of the two of them sitting in the swing talking about what clothes would be needed makes Mary's determination to offer her daughter a special experience vivid and convincing.

In the second passage, from Russell Baker's memoir, we see a mother who is determined that her son "make something of himself," whether he wants to or not. The passage reveals his mother's battle to "wean [him]" from his father's plain workman's life. The tone of the passage is ironic from the beginning, when Baker says that he "began working in journalism when I was eight years old." His mother, of course, wants him to develop ambition and salesmanship. In a few brief lines of dialogue, we hear an account of his first day selling and his mother's exasperation with him. Although Russell Baker is writing this many years later, he allows us to see him in the way his mother did and then accounts for her determination by explaining how dissatisfied she was with her husband's life.

In both passages, narrated from the child's perspective, we have a portrait of a mother who wants a better or fuller life for her child and who selects experiences she believes will support that goal. Through dialogue and narrative of a single incident, the author offers insight into the relationship of the mother and child.

Analysis

This essay has many strengths. The introduction establishes a controlling idea in the "portrait of a mother" and indicates which literary elements will be the focus of the essay: incident and point of view. These points are elaborated to show how dialogue in particular is effective in revealing character.

Development is especially good in the discussion of the first passage. The writer shows how "Geneva's narration exposes" the character of Aunt Elvera and later reveals her appreciation of what her mother has decided to do for her. The discussion is also enhanced by the writer's reference to images that support the theme of a bond between mother and daughter. The observation that "the reader can't help but share Geneva's surprise" is also insightful and well expressed.

The discussion of the Russell Baker passage is somewhat less focused, but the writer recognizes the irony in the tone and makes an excellent observation about point of view: ". . . he allows us to see him in the way his mother did." The emphasis on narration of a single incident also links the two passages and gives the essay coherence. Sentence structure is varied and quotes are well integrated. The writer also shows good control of the conventions. This essay meets all the criteria for a high score.

Preparing for this part of the Regents exam means reviewing the important literary terms and techniques (see Chapters 3 and 4) and, more important, reviewing carefully the essays on literary topics you have written and revised throughout high school.

SESSION TWO, PART B: READING AND WRITING FOR CRITICAL ANALYSIS AND EVALUATION

This part of the Regents also assesses your ability to show how literary elements and techniques reveal theme, but it requires that you first interpret and respond to what is called a "critical lens." You will then choose from works you have read and use those works to support the critical position you have established. For most students, this will be the most challenging part of the exam. A closer look at the different parts of this task, however, will show you that much of the reading, discussion, and writing about literature you have done in high school has prepared you for it.

What Is a *Critical Lens*?

A *critical lens* does much of what the lenses in a pair of glasses or the lens in a camera does: It allows us to bring what we are looking at into focus—and, like the lens of a camera, it directs our attention to something worth looking at. We can pursue the metaphor further: Some lenses may alter or color what we are looking at; in literary terms, a critical lens expresses and shapes a point of view about how to evaluate literature.

For the Regents exam, the purpose of the critical lens is to give you the opportunity to respond to a critical point of view as a prompt for discussion of works you know and appreciate. The critical lens statements are likely to focus on what literature "is about" and how authors convey the meanings and achieve the effects of their works.

Here is a familiar example, which the developers of the Regents exam offered as a model:

Sample Tasks

Your Task: Write a position paper in which you explain what the statement below means to you, agree or disagree with the statement, and support your opinion using two works from the literature you have studied.

> **Critical Lens:** According to author Joseph Conrad, the task of a writer is "by the power of the written word, to make you hear, to make you feel—it is, before all, to make you see."

Note that there are three parts to this task: First, you must *interpret* the statement, say what it means to you; then, you must tell whether you agree or disagree with the statement; finally, you must choose two literary works for a discussion that supports your position.

To interpret what Conrad means here, you must first look at the key terms. He is talking about the *power* of the written word to make us recreate the experience of hearing, feeling, and seeing, and the power to make us understand—*to see* in the figurative sense. Remember: To interpret means to state what you think Conrad means; then you must state your response to the quote.

To agree with Conrad's statement, you might choose works of literature that are particularly vivid in imagery and show how they are effective in recreating experience for the reader. This would be a literal but perfectly valid interpretation of the quote. A more subtle discussion would emphasize Conrad's final point—the power of literature to make us understand character and theme in new and powerful ways.

147

To disagree with Conrad's statement, if you consider that the greatest power of literature is to make us feel, for example, you would choose works of literature whose effect on the reader is primarily emotional or affecting. This too would be a valid response to the task.

Here is another example of a critical lens as a prompt. Two model student essays follow, showing how one may agree or disagree with the assertion to write an effective response.

Your Task: Write a critical essay in which you discuss *two* works of literature you have read from the particular perspective of the statement that is provided for you in the **Critical Lens**. In your essay, provide a valid interpretation of the statement, agree *or* disagree with the statement as you have interpreted it, and support your opinion using specific references to appropriate literary elements from the two works. You may use scrap paper to plan your response. Write your essay on separate sheets of paper.

Critical Lens: "A story must be exceptional enough to justify its telling; it must have something more unusual to relate than the ordinary experience of every average man and woman."

—Thomas Hardy

Guidelines:
Be sure to

- Provide a valid interpretation of the critical lens that clearly establishes the criteria for analysis
- Indicate whether you agree *or* disagree with the statement as you have interpreted it
- Choose *two* works you have read that you believe best support your opinion
- Use the criteria suggested by the critical lens to analyze the works you have chosen
- Avoid plot summary. Instead, use specific references to appropriate literary elements (for example: theme, characterization, setting, point of view) to develop your analysis
- Organize your ideas in a unified and coherent manner
- Specify the titles and authors of the literature you choose
- Follow the conventions of standard written English

Sample Student Response Essay

Essay 1

Thomas Hardy's statement, "a story must be exceptional enough to justify its telling; it must have something more unusual to relate than the ordinary experience of every average man and woman" epitomizes what makes a story valuable and important to read. Everyone's lives are full of intertwining stories; however, it is stories that are not about everyday occurrences that can lead one to see things in a new light and that are worthy of telling. The novels <u>Beloved</u> by Toni Morrison and <u>Native Son</u> by Richard Wright are exceptional stories; they're worthy of reading and worthy of telling.

<u>Beloved</u> is a story of profound hardship experienced by characters who refuse to give up. The novel is a piece of history dealing with slavery, oppression, and freedom; however, this novel is not a typical view of slavery and its effects on former slaves. Woven into it are lessons on loss, family values, perseverance, and making decisions. Morrison leads us into intricate relationships, relationships as common and heartwarming as mother/daughter ties and as rare and dark as relationships between the deceased and the living. Through her extremely descriptive writing style she takes you through the main character Sethe's past as a slave and her upward climb with her daughter to freedom. The supernatural element Morrison incorporates in the story sets it apart from other books of its kind. She uses the ghost of the daughter Sethe killed, in order to keep her from slavery, to show her readers the value of life, loss, love, and family ties. This novel is anything but ordinary and is sufficiently "exceptional to justify its telling."

Richard Wright's <u>Native Son</u> also examines the effects of oppression during the Jim Crow era. Wright leads us into the main character Bigger's mind as he cracks after years of oppression and commits a gruesome murder of a white girl. However, this book is unique in the way Bigger views his crime. He feels as if he committed the murder for all Blacks and feels as if he has fulfilled a deep debt to himself. The story causes the reader to question several themes. Do the crimes society commits give someone like Bigger reason to commit these atrocities? What makes some able to deal with oppression and others crack? Is society blind to its contribution toward violence? Wright also examines themes such as family ties, religion, and idealism. <u>Native Son</u> is a moving story that is unique in its message and story. It is hardly "the experience of every average man and woman."

Beloved and *Native Son* are novels in which the stories are powerful and thought provoking. The characters' lives and struggles leave readers with questions about life to examine. While there can be enjoyable stories written about just a "slice of life" experience of every average man and woman, they do not contain the depth, importance, and intricacy that "exceptional stories" such as *Native Son* and *Beloved* possess.

Essay 2

Thomas Hardy believed that in order for a story to be great, it must be more than simply the story of the "ordinary experience of every average man and woman." However, I do not agree with this idea. I think that stories of ordinary lives can sometimes make the greatest impact. The novel The Grapes of Wrath and the play Death of a Salesman both illustrate how the story of a seemingly simple, ordinary life can be so much more.

In the novel The Grapes of Wrath, written by John Steinbeck, a migrant family is forced to leave their farm during the era of the great Depression and the Dust Bowl. They, like many others, set off on a journey west to California. Throughout the novel, Ma Joad and Tom illustrate great strength of character and perseverance. It is the story of the survival of everyday people in the face of great adversity. Even when the Joads are discriminated against and starving, they refuse to abandon one another or to give up. It is an easy story to relate to precisely because it is about simple people, but they are people who show themselves to be somehow larger than life, almost mythic in their struggle to survive and to find social justice. We can all envision ourselves in their situation: losing our jobs, working just to eat and feed our families, coping with the death of loved ones—and we might hope that we would be as dedicated to pursuing our own dream as they were to following theirs. Novels like The Grapes of Wrath give us a new outlook on life.

In Death of a Salesman, by Arthur Miller, a common man must struggle to hold on to his dream of greatness, though surrounded by proof of its falseness. Willy, a salesman, is stuck in a dead end job but is reluctant to give up his hope for a better, more prosperous life and for worldly success for his son Biff. Willy is not a great, exceptional man; rather, he is an average man with exceptional dreams and ambitions. His story teaches us that our dreams may not always come true, no matter how desperately we wish they would. It also teaches us that sometimes the fault is our own, through our failure to find the "ordinary" pleasures of life—a loving wife, devoted children, worthy work—to be the treasures they truly are. True happiness comes only through self-acceptance and honesty in dealing with others and oneself, characteristics Willy did not possess. This story is also easy to relate to because it is about "average" Willy Loman—note how his very name signals his position in the world, his un-singularity. There is nothing about him or his story that is particularly great or wonderful, and yet it is still quite powerful and tragic.

The Grapes of Wrath and Death of a Salesman are two literary works that exemplify how the story of ordinary people can be very meaningful. In my opinion, a story does not have to be about the unusual to be powerful and moving.

Analysis

These two examples show how you must interpret the critical lens and then show how you agree or disagree with what it implies. Each of the essays offers only a brief interpretation, but the choice of literary works in each case reveals the writers' understanding of Hardy's observation. The writer of Essay 1 agrees with Hardy and discusses works in which the lives and stories are dramatically different from the ordinary; the writer of Essay 2 disagrees with Hardy and discusses works about the lives of simple and unexceptional people. Neither of these interpretations fully explores the complexity of Hardy's statement, but they are adequate for the task.

The emphasis in both essays is on the stories themselves, as the critical lens would suggest. Both are strong in choice of examples, but somewhat limited in discussion of literary elements; Essay 1 is stronger in that regard. Each is organized clearly and offers language that is precise and often fluent. Both writers demonstrate command of the conventions. For many students, this is the most challenging part of the examination; and, even though the examples are not fully developed, these essays are good models of what this part of the Regents exam requires.

In this example, the critical lens requires more than a discussion of a story to be fully effective. In the essay that follows, note the excellent choice of works and how the writer uses details of the story to support discussion of literary elements and the writer's interpretation of the critical lens.

Critical Lens:

"It is not what an author says, but what he or she *whispers*, that is important."
—Logan Pearsall Smith (adapted)

Sample Student Response Essay

"It is not what an author says, but what he or she whispers, that is important." In this quote, Logan Smith comments on the importance of underlying themes in novels. The quote implies that thoughts expressed explicitly may be less important than those expressed in a more subtle fashion. The *"whispers"* of books provide insight into what the author has to say about human experience. These observations can be found in works such as <u>Lord of the Flies</u> by William Golding and <u>The Bluest Eye</u> by Toni Morrison. Both authors use symbolism and setting to convey the importance of their underlying themes.

In <u>Lord of the Flies</u>, William Golding presents the story of a group of young boys stranded on an uninhabited island after a plane crash. Since there are no adults, the boys are forced to create a society of their own. Golding focuses on conveying a warning to the reader of the importance of the rules and constraints in civilization. As the novel progresses, the reader sees the transformation of the boys' behavior from civilized to savage. Without any supervision, law, or order, the boys allowed their primitive and savage natures to emerge, resulting in destruction and chaos. Although the obvious theme of the story is about survival, the theme that Golding *"whispers"* deals with the importance of civilization. This less obvious, but more important theme serves as a warning to mankind in this novel.

Golding's use of setting is central to the themes of the novel. The boys are completely isolated, but the island has food and water, and the climate is mild. There also seem to be no great dangers from other creatures. The boys are free to create their own set of rules. Golding makes it clear at the beginning that these boys know what they should do, and they begin by electing a leader and agreeing to use a conch shell to summon everyone for meetings. But as the story progresses, the desire of some of the boys to create their own tribe and to begin hunting leads to a complete breakdown of any civilized behavior. The fear of what is unknown on the island and the desire to kill something lead to savagery.

Golding also uses symbolism throughout the story. Piggy, Simon, and the conch shell were all symbols of civilization. Piggy is not physically strong the way the other boys are, but Piggy's glasses allowed the boys to build a fire. The glasses also suggest the importance of <u>seeing</u> what the boys are doing. Piggy is wise about many things, but the boys only make fun of him, and ultimately he is killed. Simon is another character who understands the savagery in the boys, but when he comes to explain what "the beast" really is, he too is killed. When the conch is broken, the reader understands the significance of the conch as a symbol of civilization. Golding's "whispers" about the capacity of "civilized" boys to become savages convey the most important themes of the novel.

In The Bluest Eye, Toni Morrison "whispers" to us by showing through the character of Pecola how racism can destroy an individual. Although Morrison does not come out and say, "Hey, racism breaks down black people," it is evident that she is conveying this message through symbolism in Pecola's story. Pecola hates her dark eyes and longs for blue ones; she deeply envies white girls such as Shirley Temple. Pecola drinks quarts of milk a day from a Shirley Temple mug, probably hoping that one day she will look like Shirley Temple. Pecola is also the victim of abuse from her own father, and when at the end of the novel, she loses whatever sanity she had she believes that she has blue eyes. Morrison's irony is that Pecola is probably happier believing that she has blue eyes than she would be living in a society that rejects "ugly" girls like her.

Morrison also "whispers" that black people cannot survive with racism by having Claudia and her sister plant seeds, with the hope that if the marigolds grow, then so will Pecola's baby. Unfortunately, we see that the marigolds are not able to grow in the poor soil. This reflects why Pecola was not able to survive in the "soil" of a racist society. If everyone rejects who you are and what you look like, how can you possibly have the capacity to love yourself?

As Pearsall Smith suggests, we must listen carefully to the "whispers" in a story in order to appreciate what the author means.

Analysis
The writer begins with an interpretation of the critical lens that is faithful to the complexity of the statement: "The quote implies that thoughts expressed explicitly may be less important than those expressed in a more subtle fashion. The 'whispers' of books provide insight into what the author has to say about human experience." The writer has also chosen two good examples of works rich in universal themes and symbolism. This essay succeeds in avoiding plot summary to discuss the significance of certain characters, themes, and incidents.

Most of the ideas are adequately developed, especially the concept of setting in Lord of the Flies; the significance of setting in The Bluest Eye is implied in the discussion of the devastating effects of life in a racist society. This writer also reveals excellent understanding of the important symbolic elements in both works. The discussion is brief, but direct and relevant.

The organization is clear as the writer discusses first setting and symbolism in <u>Lord of the Flies</u>, then moves to discuss, less explicitly, the same elements in the Toni Morrison novel. The one-sentence conclusion effectively reiterates the central concept of the critical lens.

The language is generally fluent and appropriate for a literary essay. The touch of informality in the imagined quote from Toni Morrison, "Hey . . . ," actually complements the metaphor of "whispering" in the critical lens. The writer also has good command of sentence variety and of the conventions.

In Chapter 7 you will also find discussion of strategies for writing on examinations.

Summing Up

The Standards for English Language Arts are expressed in terms of "the knowledge, skills, and understandings that individuals can and do habitually demonstrate. . . ." The emphasis here is on the word *habitually;* that is why the tasks on the Regents exam, including Parts A and B of Session Two, engage the reading, thinking, and writing skills students develop in English courses and in many other subjects, throughout secondary school. Keep this fact in mind as you prepare for the exam.

You may wish to review the ELA Standards (Appendix C), the Performance Indicators (Appendix D), and the rubrics for scoring (Appendix F). They express widely shared goals for the education of all students.

Chapter 7

WRITING ON EXAMINATIONS

Writing has always been an important part of a student's work in school as well as an essential skill for success in college and professional life. The National Commission on Writing is only one of the most recent initiatives in American education to emphasize the importance of good writing among our students. Extended essays are a key part of the New York State English Regents examination, now required for a high school diploma; American colleges and universities also seek independent assessment of students' writing skills as part of the admissions process. In this chapter you will find some guidelines for effective writing on demand.

WRITING FROM A PROMPT

On many examinations and in high school or college courses, you will encounter the term *prompt*. This term is used to refer in general to any set of directions for a writing task. In the theater, the prompter is the one who gives an actor or singer in danger of forgetting her lines the phrase she needs to remember and continue the performance. In writing, a prompt serves to recall ideas or stimulate discussion. A prompt is also meant to inspire, even provoke. A prompt may be in the form of a task and directions, as on the Regents exam; or, it may be in the form of a quote, even a photograph—anything that offers the writer a subject and a reason to produce a piece of writing.

In Part II B of the English Regents examination, the section that assesses some of your skills in critical analysis of literature, the prompt is in the form of a quotation or "critical lens." (See Chapter 6, page 146.) On the SAT essay, the prompts will require the writer to develop his or her own point of view on an issue. The prompts will be in the form of quotations or a short passage, which leads the student to form a point of view and develop an effective discussion supporting that point of view. As on the critical lens section of the Regents exam, the student is free to agree or disagree with the point of view expressed in the prompt. On Part II B of the Regents exam, students must develop their arguments with specific reference to two literary works; on the SAT essay, students may choose whatever rhetorical strategy best suits them and may develop examples from literature or other subjects as well as personal experience and observation.

Here are two examples of persuasive writing where the prompt was in the form of a quote only; the writers had to establish controlling ideas and develop the examples on their own.

"All the World's a Stage"

William Shakespeare once wrote, "all the world's a stage and all the people players . . ." This well-known phrase has stuck in people's minds through time because theater is a prominent medium in society; whether it's an amphitheater in ancient Rome or Broadway in New York City, crowds of people are drawn to the theater every day.

The theater appeals to people for many different reasons. Some attend the theater to escape from the harsh realities of life for a little while. While sitting in a dark auditorium and watching trials and disputes played by live actors in front of you, it is very easy to forget your own problems. Other people find the theater simply entertaining. Plays and musicals involve audiences because they stimulate the senses and the mind. And some people go to the theater as a social event.

But theater is not only something to be watched. For many people, theater is their life. Every day, more and more people are becoming actors and actresses in hopes of becoming rich and famous. And for some people, that dream actually comes true. Many actors join the world of theater for their love of expressing themselves through their bodies, the tools of the trade. Nothing can compare to that adrenaline rush an actor gets just before he or she steps on stage in front of hundreds of people who all have their eyes focused on him or her, and the applause of an audience is all the gratitude some actors need to feel appreciated.

Many people don't realize that theater goes beyond the actors though, and that is where they are deceived. Sometimes the technical aspect of a production is more interesting than the acting is. A Broadway production can have a set with more complicated plans than a skyscraper building. Shows like "Phantom of the Opera" can have over twenty major trap doors and more than ninety minor ones. There are dozens of people in charge of sound, lighting, props, and costumes that no one ever sees or thinks about when sitting in the audience. There is just that wonderful feeling that these things just magically happen; no one seems to be responsible.

The theater is an art that will live on for a long time to come, as long as people take the time to support it. The magic of a show that enthralls most viewers, though, is a culmination of the hard work, time, and dedication of many people who never get credit for their actions. But Shakespeare was right because, for many people in the theater, all the world is a stage.

"All the World's a Stage"

All the world is indeed a stage. And we are the performers. Everything we do in life is a production, and we must constantly perform our best because, in life, there are no rehearsals. Each of us performs on a separate stage, some for a larger audience than others. But each performance, regardless of the size of the audience, is of equal importance, and each performer must meet the standard of life's most important critic—himself.

As a high school student, I often find that there exists much pressure to perform: pressure to perform academically, pressure to perform in sports, pressure to perform in social situations, and countless others. Furthermore, there are many individuals for whom I constantly must perform. At this juncture in life, parents, teachers, friends, and others comprise what I often perceive as an overwhelmingly large audience, which is sometimes overly critical.

As I grow older, I am learning to accept new responsibilities, and I find that my role in life is changing. Often in life, we cannot constantly adhere to a routine performance; sometimes we must improvise. The improvisation, or adjustment to new responsibility, is often difficult though of critical importance to a successful production. In life, I have come to expect the unexpected and have done my best to deal with new situations. As performers, we must not allow tragedy, depression, and self-doubt to unnerve us. Instead, we must cope, adjust, and continue to perform.

Throughout my performance I have received evaluation from many critics, some of which I have taken better than others. No matter how many critics we have, we should remind ourselves that we are our most important critics, for of life's performance we will make the ultimate evaluation. Even though all the world's a stage, each of us need be concerned with only one performance.

Analysis

The first essay stumbles at the beginning: The introduction has a central idea, but it is not well expressed and there is no coherence in the reference to ancient Rome. This essay reads like a first draft, and perhaps the writer was pressed for time. It would be improved not only in revision

---

of the opening paragraph but also in the transitions. This writer begins too many sentences with *and* or *but*, and the language is not always fluent or precise. The writer, however, does establish organization and some unity in the opening of the second paragraph: "The theater appeals to people for many different reasons."

The writer also shows skill in development by moving from the role of theater for audiences to its importance for participants. The concluding sentence also works well because it relates the major part of the essay to a fresh meaning of the quote. In this case, a good conclusion rescues an essay with a weak introduction.

The second essay is effective because of the exceptional way in which the writer developed the topic as an extended metaphor. The essay is brief, but it is absolutely focused; every detail supports the central idea, the comparison of one's life to a dramatic performance. The writer has maintained a consistent point of view and has developed the topic in a creative way.

EVALUATING COMPOSITION

Every student has seen on a paper or an essay test the comment "develop this point more." The Regents rubrics (see page 269–272) for scoring compositions are a reminder that one of the most important criteria in evaluating essays for class or for an exam is the extent to which the topic has been developed to achieve the writer's purpose. Simply to announce a subject and say that you have thoughts on that subject is not enough.

For any topic, the student must show skill in establishing a central idea and in creating an effective way to develop it. All compositions must be unified and expressed in fluent and precise language, and they must follow the conventions of standard written English. (See *Guide to Standard Written English* beginning on page 167.)

PREPARING FOR ESSAY EXAMS

Nearly all the writing you have done, both personal and for school, serves as preparation. Just as an athlete or musician practices regularly in order to have the skills to draw on in a performance, high school students are developing their skills whenever they compose written responses. Reflect on what you know your strengths and weaknesses are. To review, go over the essays and exams you have written in high school; note what is consistently strong and what needs revision; review carefully your teachers' comments. Because Part I B of the Regents exam assesses your skills in writing from research, be sure to review such papers and projects from all subjects, not just from English classes.

Good writers are also readers. Read good writing, observe what makes it effective, emulate it, and imitate for practice what you admire. In serious magazines and in the editorial pages, letters to the editor, and Op-Ed sections of newspapers you can often find good essays of argument on current topics. (See also Recommended Reading on page 255 for suggested works and authors of nonfiction.)

To succeed in any assigned task, you need to know what is expected and how you will be evaluated. Review the rubrics for the examination. These are the scoring guides that describe the criteria for scoring the essays. The rubrics for each part of the New York State English Regents exam are expressed on a scale from 1 to 6 (see Appendix F). The rubric for the SAT essay is also on a 6-point scale and is very similar to the rubrics for the Regents exam.

WRITING ON TIMED EXAMINATIONS

If you are writing an essay for an examination, you do not have time for extensive preparation, but you can learn to condense the kind of thinking and notetaking you do for course assignments into a process for planning an examination response. How to begin?

Gather Your Ideas

First, be sure you understand the task or the meaning of the topic. One way to do that is to rephrase the question into a topic assertion. This may not be original, but if a restatement of the question serves as a topic sentence for your introduction and gets you started—use it! You may not use such statements in your final essay, but the fact that you can express them for yourself means you understand what the question expects or that you have something to say about the topic

If you are creating your own topic, be sure you know what you want to say about it. This may seem obvious, but only when you sketch or outline can you be sure you have sufficient material for an essay. Use the brainstorming techniques you have learned in class or workshops. For example, if you have practiced "freewriting" in the past or have written journal entries as a way of developing ideas, take a few minutes to address the topic in that way, without regard to organization or "getting it absolutely right." Similarly, you can just note down in words or phrases everything the prompt brings to mind. It is better to note more ideas than you can use than to discover after twenty-five minutes that you have too few.

Organize

Second, take a few minutes to make a plan or outline. All essay writing requires this step. Do not leave it out, even on the new SAT, in which you have only 25 minutes for the essay. The outline may consist of only phrases or a brief list to remind you of the points you want to make. Consider possible lines of argument. That is, answer for yourself the questions "How can I prove that? What information in the text (if given) can I quote or paraphrase as evidence? How can I show or persuade someone who is interested in what I have to say? What do I know or believe that will make my discussion convincing?" Finally, decide on the order that is best: chronological? sequence of cause and effect? order of importance or intensity? (Common methods of developing ideas in essays are reviewed, with examples, in Reading Nonfiction, Chapter 3.)

Compose

The essays you write for the Regents exam and for the SAT are, of course, "tests." You are not being asked to demonstrate acquired knowledge so much as you are to demonstrate how well you can communicate in standard written English what you understand about the given subjects and texts or what you think about a particular issue. What is being assessed is your ability to articulate a controlling idea and support it with reasons and appropriate examples. On the Regents exam, you must also be able to work from given texts and write for clearly defined purposes and audiences.

Concentrate on good development—not a finished product. An essay that reveals critical thinking and coherence and effectively develops several appropriate examples or reasons with command of sentence variety and language will receive a high score even if it remains somewhat unfinished or lacks a formal conclusion. Remember, on the SAT you are writing what will be evaluated as a first draft. Regents essays are viewed as somewhat more "finished," but those too are understood to have been written in only one sitting.

Edit as You Go

The time you take in planning is also well spent because on-demand writing requires you to edit and revise as you compose your response. If you still make spelling errors in commonly used words, make a deliberate effort to look for those errors and correct them on the exams. A few neatly corrected spelling or usage errors are not only acceptable, they reveal the writer's ability to edit his or her own work. (See Chapter 8 on Grammar and Usage and Chapter 9 on Punctuation.)

USING SYNONYMIES TO ENHANCE YOUR WRITING

Included in the expectations for any well-written essay is use of language that is vivid and appropriate; the rubrics for scoring Regents essays include "use of original, fluent, and precise language." The term *synonymy* refers to words that can be grouped according to general meaning; that is, they all denote or describe a specific instance of a general concept. Reviewing and creating synonymies will help you develop the vivid and precise language characteristic of good writing. Below are some examples of synonymies for commonly used but often vague or overused expressions.

to cause

bring about	create	effect	engender
excite	generate	give rise to	incite
invent	lead to	originate	persuade
produce	promote	provoke	raise
spawn			

to change

adapt	adjust	alter	amend
become	convert	correct	depart
develop	deviate	differ	digress
diverge	diversify	edit	evolve
grow	mature	metamorphose	modify
modulate	mutate	progress	remake
revise	rework	transform	turn (into)
vary			

to look upon someone/something

analyze	appraise	censure	classify
conclude	condemn	consider	deem
discern	dismiss	distinguish	esteem
evaluate	honor	hypothesize	infer
judge	observe	perceive	ponder
reckon	regard	review	ruminate
scrutinize	stereotype	summarize	typecast
value	view	watch	

to look down upon someone/something

belittle	censure	condescend	condemn
degrade	demote	depreciate	deride
devalue	diminish	discredit	disfavor
disgrace	disparage	disregard	show disrespect
embarrass	find fault with	frown upon	have disdain for
hold inferior	humiliate	ignore	jeer
mock	rebuke	reject	ridicule
scorn	shame	shun	taunt
vilify			

bad

abhorrent	atrocious	awful	base
belittling	blemished	calumnious	catastrophic
contemptible	corrupt	counterfeit	criminal
cruel	damaged	deceptive	defective
defiled	delinquent	depraved	despicable
detrimental	devilish	dirty	disquieting
evil	false	fiendish	foul
fraudulent	grotesque	hateful	heinous
hellish	hideous	horrible	horrid
horrific	immoral	imperfect	impish
inequitable	infamous	inferior	loathsome
malevolent	malign	marred	mean
merciless	monstrous	nefarious	negative
notorious	odious	ominous	perverse
putrid	rotten	ruthless	scabrous
scandalous	scurrilous	shameless	sinful
sinister	slanderous	sour	spiteful
spoiled	squalid	tasteless	terrible
unethical	unscrupulous	vile	villainous
wicked			

effective

capable	cogent	commanding	compelling
convincing	dazzling	dramatic	effectual
efficacious	emotional	forceful	impressive

| influential | lively | moving | persuasive |
| potent | powerful | strong | telling |

caring

affectionate	benevolent	bountiful	compassionate
concerned	courteous	devoted	doting
empathetic	empathic	fond	generous
giving	goodhearted	humane	kind
loving	philanthropic	selfless	sympathetic
tender	thoughtful	warm	warmhearted

due to

as a consequence of	as a result of	because	because of
by reason of	caused by	following from	from
in light of	in view of	induced by	on account of
resulting from			

hard/difficult

arduous	bitter	challenging	complex
daunting	demanding	enigmatic	esoteric
exacting	exhausting	exigent	fatiguing
galling	grievous	grim	harsh
Herculean	impenetrable	impossible	impregnable
inflexible	insurmountable	intricate	labyrinthine
mighty	oppressive	relentless	resistant
rigorous	serious	severe	sharp
strenuous	strong	tiresome	toilsome
tough	unattainable	unbending	uncompromising
unyielding	wearisome		

sad/depressing (depressed)

abject	aching	aggrieved	bereaved
bereft	bleak	blue	cheerless
dark	dejected	desolate	despairing
disconsolate	discontent	distraught	distressing
down	forlorn	forsaken	gloomy
joyless	lugubrious	melancholy	miserable
morose	painful	saddening	somber

sorrowful	tormenting	tragic	unhappy
upset	wretched		

same

akin	alike	allied	analogous
associated	clone	cognate	collective
common	comparable	comparative	compatible
conformable	conforming	congruent	consonant
copy	correspondent	corresponding	duplicate
equal	equivalent	generic	homogeneous
identical	imitation	indiscernible	inseparable
interchangeable	joint	like	matching
mutual	parallel	photocopy	related
replica	same	shared	similar
synonymous	tantamount	twin	

A GLOSSARY OF TERMS FOR WRITING*

anecdote   A brief story or account of a single experience, often biographical, which illustrates something typical or striking about a person. Anecdotes, like parables, are effective as vivid, specific examples of a general observation or quality.

argument   The development of reasons, examples to support a thesis; narrowly, to outline a position on an issue or problem with the intent to clarify or persuade. Argument is also used in a broad sense to refer to the way a writer develops any topic. (The speech by Samuel Hazo on page 19 is a good example of argument.)

audience   For the writer this term refers to the intended reader. Awareness of an audience determines, for example, what the writer may assume a reader already knows, level of diction, and tone.

coherence   A piece of writing has coherence when the logical relationship of ideas is evident and convincing. In a coherent discussion, statements and sections follow one another in a natural, even inevitable way. A coherent discussion hangs together; an incoherent one is scattered and disorganized.

controlling idea   This refers to the writer's thesis or main idea. It asserts what the writer has to say <u>about</u> the topic or question.

---

*Many of the terms in this glossary are also discussed in Chapter 3, Reading Prose.

conventions These are the "rules" or common guidelines for punctuation, spelling, and usage.

description The expression in words of what is experienced by the senses. Good description recreates what is felt, seen, heard—sensed in any way. We also use the term describe to mean *identify, classify, characterize,* even for abstract ideas. Description permits readers to recreate the subject in their own imaginations.

development This refers to the choice and elaboration of examples, reasons, or other details that support an argument or illustrate a controlling idea. (See also the rubrics for scoring Regents essays in Appendix F.)

diction This refers to word choice. Diction may be formal or informal, complex or simple, elegant or modest, depending on the occasion and the audience. The language we use in casual conversation is different from the language we use in formal writing. The good writer uses language that is varied, precise, and vivid; the good writer has resources of language to suit a wide range of purposes.

exposition The development of a topic through examples, reasons, details, which explain, clarify, show, instruct—the primary purpose of exposition is to convey information. Much of the writing assigned to students is referred to as expository writing: Through exposition you can demonstrate what you have learned, discovered, understood, appreciated. (The passage by Sandy Asher on page 2 is a good example of exposition.)

focus This refers to the way a writer contains and directs all the information, examples, ideas, reasons in an essay on the specific topic.

narrative Because it tells a story, narrative has chronological order. Narrative method is commonly used in exposition when examples are offered in a chronological development. (The student speech to junior high school students on page 34 is an example of chronological development.)

position paper A form of persuasive writing, a position paper is meant to generate support for an issue or cause; the essay is based on specific evidence that can be cited to support the writer's argument. A position paper may also evaluate solutions or suggest courses of action. Composing a position paper is often one of the tasks in the first two sections of the English Regents exam.

prompt This refers to a set of directions for a writing task; may also be a quote or passage meant to stimulate a piece of writing. The "critical lens" in Part II B of the Regents examination is a good example of a prompt.

tone In writing, tone refers to the attitude of the writer toward the subject and/or toward the reader. Tone may range from *harsh and insistent* to *gentle and reflective.* There is as much variety of tone in writing as there is in human feeling. Some pieces, essays of opinion, for example, usually have a very distinct tone; other works, especially in fiction or personal expression, may have a more subtle and indirect tone. (See discussion of Tone on page 80 in Reading Prose and on page 98 in Reading Poetry.)

transition   Words or phrases used to link ideas and sections in a piece of writing. Common transitions include *first, second . . . in addition . . . finally; on the other hand, moreover, consequently, therefore.* Transitions make the development of an argument clear.

unity   In the narrowest sense, unity refers to focus: The ideas and examples are clearly related to the topic and to one another. In the largest sense, unity refers to a feature of our best writing: All elements—ideas, form, language, and tone—work together to achieve the effect of a complete and well-made piece.

Chapter 8

GRAMMAR AND USAGE FOR THE CAREFUL WRITER: A GUIDE TO STANDARD WRITTEN ENGLISH

The grammar of a language is its logic. We observe the conventions of standard usage in order to write and speak clearly, in order to communicate precisely what we mean. This section reviews those aspects of grammar and usage you are expected to know and to apply.

The New York State Regents Comprehensive Examination in English evaluates your mastery of standard written English by how well you write in your essays. The SAT Writing exam tests your mastery through both multiple-choice error recognition and revision questions and a brief essay.

Neither of these exams requires you to identify errors in usage by name, but a review of the essential terms and structures will help you to recognize errors and to understand how to correct them. What are the essentials?

REVIEWING THE FUNDAMENTALS

The Parts of Speech

Below are the parts of speech that you should review. These include the noun, pronoun, adjective, verb, and adverb, as well as conjunction, preposition, and interjection.

NOUN

Names or identifies persons, creatures, objects, ideas. The articles *the, a, an* usually precede and signal a noun. For example:

woman	child	book	happiness
climate	history	English	politics
education			

Pronoun

Replaces or "stands in for" nouns or other pronouns already stated; the noun or pronoun referred to (replaced) is the **antecedent**.

Subject Forms:	I, you, he/she/it, we, you, they
Object Forms:	me, you, him/her/it, us, you, them
Possessive Forms:	mine, yours, his/hers/its, ours, yours, theirs
Relatives:	that, which, who, whom, whose, whoever, whomever

Adjective

Modifies nouns, that is, it describes, limits, specifies, what a noun names. For instance:

tall woman	*young* child	*illustrated* book
temperate climate	*American* history	*public* education

Verb

Denotes any *action*: run, talk, think, intend, suggest, play, strike, have, do; or *state of being*: appear, seem, be, feel. The principal parts of a verb are as follows:

Infinitive:	to run, to talk, to think, to intend, to appear, to seem
Simple past:	ran, talked, thought, intended, appeared, seemed
Present participle:	running, talking, thinking, intending, appearing, seeming
Past participle:	(has) run, (has) talked, (has) thought, intended, appeared, seemed

Adverb

Modifies verbs; it indicates the manner, quality, or degree of an *action*.

run *swiftly*	talk *loudly*	think *clearly*
play *well*	strike *suddenly*	

Adverbs also function as *intensifiers*; that is, they indicate the degree or intensity of modifiers, both adjectives and adverbs.

rather tall woman   *very* young child

talk *too* loudly   *nearly* complete project

CONJUNCTION

A word that connects two or more words or groups of words.

Coordinating conjunctions: and, but, yet, so, for

Subordinating conjunctions: because, although, since, while, if, until, when, unless, before, after

There are a tall woman *and* a young child.

We will stay home *if* it rains.

Because he trains regularly, he plays well.

PREPOSITION

Expresses relationships of time, space, or position.

above	across	after	at
before	behind	beside	between
except	for	in	into
on	over	to	under
within	without		

INTERJECTION

An expression that begins or interrupts a sentence to express a particular feeling.

Ouch!, that hurts.   *Oh,* how interesting!   *Bravo!*

Phrases, Clauses, and Sentences

While we may express feelings and give commands with single words, our most useful expression is in words grouped in phrases, clauses, and sentences.

PHRASE

A meaningful group of words. There are many kinds of phrases in English. Here are some common examples:

A noun and its modifiers:	the large brick building
	the tall young woman

A verb and its auxiliaries:	has run
(to show different tenses):	will arrive
	should have been done

A preposition and its object:	across the room
	down the hill
	on the roof
	in the final chapter

A participle and its object or modifiers:	walking slowly
	opening the door carefully
	sensing danger
	returning after many years*

CLAUSE

A meaningful group of words that contains a verb and its subject.
Clauses are *dependent* when they form only part of a complex sentence of more than one clause:

Because he was late, . . .   If it rains tomorrow, . . .

. . . when the plane arrives   . . . that you requested

Each of these expressions contains a verb and *its* subject, but you can see that the sentence will not be complete—that is, the assertion will not be fully expressed or understood—until at least one additional clause is added.

---

* Note that prepositional phrases, which are modifiers because they function as adjectives and adverbs do, may be part of a larger participial phrase.

In these examples, one *independent* clause has been added to form a *complete sentence:*

[Because he was late], his appointment was canceled.

I will call you [when the plane arrives].

The book [that you requested] is now available.

A *sentence,* then, may be made up of a few words—a subject, and a predicate verb that establishes the action or state of being of the subject, and modifiers:

She ran.

The dog barked.

He was late.

The crowd cheered enthusiastically.

Or a sentence may be made up of more than one clause and contain several phrases as modifiers.

Because he was late, his appointment was canceled and had to be rescheduled for the following week.

The large crowd in the bleachers cheered enthusiastically as the home team took the field in the last inning.

Tests of standard usage are tests of how well you understand and can compose the many relationships of words, phrases, clauses, and sentences that make up standard written English.

Most of the problems in grammar and usage you are expected to recognize and be able to correct are considered "errors" because they result in a lack of clarity, even confusion, in the writer's expression.

Although writing that contains minor errors in standard usage may still be understood, careful writers seek expression that is precise and clear—even elegant—and that demonstrates their ability to use variety in language and structure. It is only through mastery of a wide range of expression that students may fully reveal their ideas, insights, and feelings.

AVOIDING COMMON ERRORS IN WRITING

When we refer to errors in writing, we are referring to expressions that are illogical, inconsistent, vague, or imprecise. The elements of usage reviewed here are those that high school students should be able to recognize.

Agreement of Subject and Verb

Agreement is a form of consistency and is one of the most basic elements of grammar. When you learn to conjugate verbs, for example, you are applying the concept of agreement. Singular subjects take singular verbs; plural subjects take plural verbs.

He speaks/they speak; One is/many are

Errors in agreement commonly occur in sentences where the subject follows the verb:

On the desk *are* my notebook, a few pencils, and the assignments for tomorrow.

"Desk" is not the subject of the verb; "notebook, pencils, assignments" is the subject, *they* are on the desk. In such inverted word order, the writer must hear and think ahead to choose the correct form of the verb. Similarly:

There *seems* to be only *one answer.*

There *seem* to be *several ideas* worth considering.

Here *are* the *pieces* you have been looking for.

Agreement errors may also occur when a subject followed by a phrase precedes the verb:

New York with its many historical sites and tourist attractions *is* a fascinating city to visit.

His *many talents* in sports, academics, and student leadership *make* him a popular candidate.

Subjects may be expanded by such prepositional phrases as *along with, in addition to, as well as, together with.* These phrases, however, do not form part of the *grammatical* subject; they modify the subject:

English, as well as math, science, and social studies, *is* a required subject for most high school students.

Evan, along with several of his friends, *is* planning to visit colleges in the fall.

In some sentences, the subject may be modified by one or more clauses before the predicate verb is stated. In such sentences the writer must "remember" the actual subject before composing the correct form of the verb:

The *fact* that Americans must now compete in a global economy and must recognize the necessity for higher standards in our schools *has led* to educational reform in many states.

Many common pronouns are singular and must take a singular verb:

Each one of these books *is* worth reading.

Every one of us *is* prepared to contribute.

None of these solutions *is* acceptable. (No *one* is)

Note how agreement with correlatives *either/or, neither/nor* is achieved:

Either Susan or her brother *is* home now.

(Either Susan is . . . or her brother is)

Neither rain, nor sleet, nor snow *deters* us . . . .

When the correlative contains both a singular and plural expression, the verb agrees with the one closest:

Neither Susan nor her sisters *are* at home.

Either the members of the legislature or the governor *is* authorized to submit a budget.

Do not be confused when the predicate is completed with a plural expression:

His most reliable *source* of encouragement *is* friends and family.

To avoid the correct but awkward-sounding expression above, rewrite as follows:

His *friends and family are* his most reliable source of encouragement.

Collective nouns take singular verbs because all the "members" are understood to act as a single unit:

The *jury was* unanimous in its decision to acquit.

A school *board has* extensive responsibilities.

Our *family has agreed* on plans for the vacation.

The *team practices* for two hours every day.

When there is not such unity of action, you may use a plural verb:

The *jury are* not in unanimous agreement.

The *family are* expected to arrive at different times.

It is better, however, to avoid such awkward-sounding expressions by rewriting to make the plural idea clear:

The members of the jury are not in agreement.

Players on the team are required to keep their uniforms and equipment in good order.

Family members are expected to arrive at different times.

Agreement of Pronoun and Antecedent

Because pronouns replace nouns or other pronouns, they must agree with their singular or plural antecedents.

Evelyn is very grateful to *her parents* for *their* constant support and encouragement.

Most pronoun/antecedent errors arise when we use the indefinite pronouns *anyone, anybody, everyone, everybody, someone, somebody, no one,* and so on. These pronouns are singular because they refer to *individuals:*

Everybody is responsible for *his* own work.

Someone has left *her* books on the floor.

If *anyone* calls while I am out, please tell *him* or *her* I will call back after lunch.

The common practice of replacing *him/her* with *them,* or *her/his* with *their,* solves the problem of choosing gender, but it is ungrammatical and illogical. The careful writer (and speaker) avoids these errors or rewrites:

Please tell *anyone who calls* that I will return at noon.

Someone's books have been left on the floor.

Everyone has individual responsibility for the assignments.

Form of Pronouns

Use the subject forms when pronouns are *subjects* of verbs or identify the subject after a linking verb:

> *He and I* received the information we needed.
>
> *She* is the favorite candidate of the party.
>
> *He* is the head baseball coach.
>
> The head baseball coach is *he*.
>
> (Think of the verb *is* as an = sign.)

It is easy to avoid the awkward sound of the last sentence by choosing the preceding expression, which uses the pronoun first.

Pronouns as *objects* of verbs or prepositions must be in the object form:

> Please give *him* the information.
>
> Give the information to *them*.
>
> *Whom* did you see yesterday?

Errors often occur when we have pronouns preceded by a noun; the writer no longer "hears" the preposition and is reluctant to use the object form. But,

> Please give the information to Ellen and *him*. (to Ellen . . . to him)
>
> The host was very gracious to Ellen and *me*.
> (to Ellen . . . to me; *not* to Ellen and I)
>
> Just between you and me, this is simple.

We also use the object form with infinitives:

> We understand *her to be* the favorite candidate.
>
> We understand the favorite candidate *to be her*.

Remember to use the possessive form with *gerunds* ("-ing" verb forms that function as nouns):

> I do not approve of *your staying* out so late.
> (of your "late hours")
>
> She was concerned about *his working* too hard.
> (about his excessive work)

Note the following:

Mark's mother saw *him* [*running* after the bus].

Mark's mother encouraged [*his running* on the cross-country team].

In the first example, *running* is a participle describing *him*, which is the object of the verb *saw*. In the second example, *running* is a noun; it is the object of the verb *encouraged*.

Parallelism

Parallelism is used for consistency and clarity. Parallel ideas and expressions in a series should be composed in the same form:

He wants to spend the summer *reading, sleeping, and traveling.*

He plans *to read, to sleep, and to travel.*

Use parallel phrases and clauses:

She is known *for* her talent and *for* her generosity.

We expect our presidents to be skilled *not only in* domestic affairs *but also in* foreign policy.

Our state senator was reelected *because* she is honest, *because* she works hard for the district, *and because* she has an important leadership position in the senate.

Use parallel construction when you use correlatives: *either, or; not only, but also:*

Either you will complete the work now, *or* he will complete it in the morning.

We will *either take* a train this afternoon *or take* a plane this evening.

Consistency of active and passive voice is also a form of parallelism:

The research team *formulated* its ideas and *developed* its proposal.

Ideas *were formulated* and a proposal *was developed* by the research team.

Verbs: Using the Correct Tense

Use the simple past tense for actions completed in the past:

The train *arrived* at 6:30.

He *retired* in 1993.

The Nobel prizes *were announced* in January.

Use the present perfect tense to establish facts, to assert that something *has occurred, has happened, has been done*, without reference to a specific time.

Have you done your homework yet?

The renovation of our house *has been completed.*

I *have read* Macbeth several times.

Note the correct *sequence of tenses* in the following:

The novelist *completed* the book in 1993, two years after he *had begun* it.

She *recorded* the names of everyone who *had called* the day before.

In the Middle Ages, most people *believed* that the earth *is* round.

Copernicus *demonstrated* that the earth *orbits* the sun.

If I *were* you, I *would accept* the offer.

If the congressman *were indicted,* he *would* lose the support of many constituents.

If we *had taken* more time to plan, our trip *would have been* more pleasant.

If you *had trained* harder, you *would have* made the team.

If you would have called earlier is sometimes heard but this is not an acceptable construction in standard English.

Finally, you are generally expected to write about works of literature in the *present tense.*

Macbeth *is driven* by ambition.

Jay Gatsby *believes* he can recreate the past.

Willy Loman *dies* believing his son will achieve great success.

Aspects of character, themes, plot, and setting remain constant—they *are* what they are—regardless of how the plot concludes or when we finish reading the work.

Logical Comparisons

My sister is *taller* than I [am].

She is *more* clever than he [is].

Josh is the *tallest* member of the team.

Among all of Miller's plays, *Death of a Salesman* is the *best* known.

Avoid incomplete comparisons in your writing:

Dreiser's novels are *more* popular now [than they were when they were first published].

Shakespeare's plays are *harder* to read [than modern works are].

The passages in brackets should be fully stated.
In informal speech we may use *so* as an intensifier:

I was *so* tired. He was *so* angry.

In writing, however, be sure every *so* is followed by a *that,* every *more* by a *than.*
Comparisons must be parallel and logical:

The paintings of Monet are more popular than Goya **should read**:

The paintings of Monet are more popular than *the paintings* of Goya.

You must compare paintings to paintings, not inadvertently compare paintings to a man.
And,

Anne is a better player than anyone on her team. **should read**:

Anne is a *better* player *than any other* [player] on her team.

or,

Anne is the *best player* on the team.

It is illogical to suggest Anne is better than she herself is.

Clear and Logical Modification

The careful writer must also be aware of errors in modification and in the logical relationships of ideas. Many such errors are corrected simply, with commas; others may require revision or reorganization of sentences.

Introductory subordinate (dependent) clauses must be set off by a comma:

> *After the lights had come back on,* the children were no longer frightened by the thunderstorm.
>
> *When it rains,* cats and dogs prefer not to go outside.

Without the comma, such sentences would be ambiguous.

Nonrestrictive (nonessential) phrases and clauses are set off by commas:

> My aunt, *who lives in Milwaukee,* will be flying in for a weekend visit to New York.
>
> Several stranded passengers, *feeling restless and impatient,* demanded flights on another airline.

When such phrases or clauses are restrictive* (essential to the meaning of the sentence), do not set them off with commas:

> Passengers *traveling with small children* will be permitted to board the plane first.
>
> My cousin *who lives in Milwaukee* will have to fly, but the cousins *who live in the New York area* will be able to drive to my brother's wedding.

A common error occurs when we begin a sentence with a participial phrase:

> *Feeling restless and impatient,* seats were demanded on other airlines' flights [by many travelers].
> (The seats are not restless . . .)
>
> *Barking loudly,* we were afraid the dog would wake our neighbors.
> (We are not barking, the dog is . . .)
>
> *Tired and hungry,* even cold leftovers looked good to us.
> (The leftovers are not hungry, we are . . .)

(*For additional examples, see *which/that/who* on page 186.)

The *subject* of the participle must also be stated as the subject of the clause that follows:

> *Feeling restless and impatient, many stranded travelers* sought seats on other airlines' flights.
>
> *Barking loudly, the dog* wakened our neighbors.
>
> *Tired and hungry, we* were satisfied with the cold leftovers.

You may also recompose sentences to make the modification clear:

> We were afraid our dog, *barking loudly,* would wake the neighbors.
>
> *Because we were tired and hungry,* even cold leftovers looked good to us.

EXPRESSIONS OFTEN CONFUSED, MISUSED, AND OVERUSED*

accept/except

> To **accept** is to receive, take willingly, agree to:
>
> I **accept** your offer, apology, invitation
>
> To **except** is to exclude, to separate out:
>
> I will **except** you from the requirement.
>
> **Except** is also a preposition:
>
> Everyone **except** him will be leaving on Tuesday.

affect/effect

> To **affect** (vb.) means to move, influence, or change. It also means to put on an artificial quality of personality or character; such an exaggerated or artificial person may be called **affected**.
>
> An **effect** (n.) is a consequence or result.
>
> To **effect** (vb.) means to put into action, to complete—a plan or a change, for example.

---

*See also Words Commonly Confused/Misspelled in Chapter 11, Spelling.

aggravate

To **aggravate** means to make worse. Do not use it when you really mean to irritate or annoy.

allusion/illusion

An **allusion** is a reference (see Glossary of Poetic Terms and Techniques, Chapter 4); an **illusion** is a false or deceptive idea or vision.

among/between

Use **between** for two, **among** for three or more:

between you and me

among all the members of the family

amount/number

One has an **amount** of something (the quantity as a whole) and a **number** of things (that can be counted):

an **amount** of time/a **number** of hours, days

a large **amount** of work/a **number** of tasks

See also **fewer/less** for the same distinction.

as far as . . . is/are concerned

The expression **as far as** used by itself creates an incomplete and illogical statement; it must be completed with **is/are concerned.** The expression as **far as . . . goes/go** is also widely used and correct as completed.

Faulty: **As far as** plans for school construction in the future, we expect the legislature to take action in the next session.

As far as the weather, it will be sunny and pleasant tomorrow.

Correct: **As far as** plans for school construction in the future are concerned, we expect the legislature to take action in the next session

As far as the weather goes, it will be sunny and pleasant.

bad/badly, good/well

Use **bad** and **good** (adjectives) to describe how one feels; use **badly** and **well** (adverbs) to describe how one does something.

He felt **bad** (sorry, regretful) because he caused the team to lose.

The team lost the game because he played so **badly**.

She feels **good** (in good spirits, positive) when her work is going **well.**

She is feeling **well** (no longer ill) now after a long bout with the flu.

The team lost because he did not play **well.**

being as, being that

These expressions are not standard speech. Use *because* or *since* instead.

compare to, compare with

Use **compare to** when you are expressing an analogy or similarity; use **compare with** when you are showing similarities and differences between two things.

He compared his small room **to** a closet.

The critics compared the movie **with** the book.

could of/ should of

Do not make this unfortunate confusion in the way words sound! You mean **could have/should have.**

different from (not **than**)

You should use the preposition **from** with **different** because you are making a distinction, a separation. Use **than** for comparisons, to show degrees of the same quality:

She is only slightly older **than** her sister, but her personality is very different **from** her sister's.

due to

This expression is popularly used for almost any cause and effect relationship. Avoid its overuse in your writing:

Absence **due to** illness is excused.

Delays **due to** bad weather are common in winter.

It is more precise to say:

The road was closed **because of** an accident.

The defendant was acquitted **by reason of** insanity.

There were many landslides **caused by** the heavy rains.

everybody, somebody, someone, nobody

These are *singular* forms; they may refer to many people, but they refer to *each one individually.* Singular antecedents take singular pronouns:

Everybody has *his/her* books, lunch, opinions.

Someone, a person has *his/her* opinions.

farther/further

In general, you may use **farther** or **further** for actual or figurative distance:

The nearest town is ten miles **farther** from here.

The latest agreements move us **further** toward a full peace.

Use **further** when you mean more:

We have nothing **further** to discuss.

A final agreement requires **further** negotiations.

fewer/less

One has **fewer** things and **less** something.

fewer hours/**less** time

fewer dollars/**less** money

fewer ideas/**less** content

first, second, . . .

To show transition and to enumerate examples, use these terms instead of *firstly, secondly,* . . .

hang/hanged/hung

When we use this verb in the past tense to denote an execution, we use **hanged**; for such things as clothes and pictures, we use **hung.**

The condemned man was **hanged** at dawn.

We **hung** our winter coats in the hall closet.

hopefully

This expression is popularly used to mean we hope, it is hoped, and so on. The careful writer should use it only as an adverb:

The cat looked **hopefully** at the leftover chicken.

But:

We **hope** the situation will improve.

It is hoped that research will lead to a cure.

however

Along with its cousins *therefore, moreover,* and *consequently,* **however** should be placed *within the sentence,* close to the verb it modifies; think of it as a conjunction, not as a transition at the beginning of a sentence.

if/whether

Use **if** to introduce conditional expressions; use **whether** (or not) for choices, decisions, questions:

If it rains, our game will be postponed.

If you work hard, you will succeed.

I do not know **whether** we will play or not.

infer/imply

To **infer** is to conclude, to draw an inference from evidence; to **imply** is to suggest or hint.

We can **infer** from his comments that he is pleased.

She **implied** in her speech that she is planning to run for public office.

its/it's

it's = a contraction* for it is.

its = a possessive form; do not add an apostrophe.

if . . . were/if . . . was

Use the **if . . . were** construction for *hypothetical* conditions and situations:

If you were president, what would you do?

If I were you, I would accept the offer.

---

*Contractions should be avoided in formal writing, unless you are quoting someone. Contractions are features of spoken language.

Use **if . . . was** for situations that *were possible*:

If that really **was** Linda who called yesterday, she should have left a message.

incredible/incredulous

Incredible means unbelievable, beyond belief or understanding. In formal writing, avoid using it as *hyperbole*. Use instead such terms as *astonishing* or *extraordinary*.

A person is **incredulous** when he/she utterly cannot believe what is being said.

kind of/sort of/type of

Avoid using *a* or *an* with these expressions:

That type of character is popular in children's books.

Those types of characters are . . .

This kind of fabric is best for the new sofa.

Also avoid using **kind of** or **sort of** when you mean *a little, rather, somewhat.*

lie/lay

These verbs are often confused. Note their principal parts and distinctions in meaning: to **lie (down)** means to recline, be situated, rest:

You **lie** on your bed to take a nap.

The mail **has lain** on your desk since yesterday.

Last winter the snow **lay** on the ground for weeks.

Note that to **lay** means to put or place something. (It is a transitive verb and always takes a direct object.):

You can **lay** your hat and gloves on the hall table.

Masons **lay bricks** and hens **lay eggs**.

He cannot remember where he **laid** his car keys.

like/as/as if

Use **like** as a preposition, use **as** and **as if** as conjunctions:

He looks just **like** his father.

A talent **like** hers is rare.

It looks **as if** it will rain this afternoon.

You should do the assignments **as** you were instructed to.

"Do **as** I say, not **as** I do!"

only/just

These modifiers should be placed as close as possible to the expressions they actually limit:

I have **only** two dollars for lunch.

He has time for **only** a brief conversation.

I have **just** one thing to say.

presently

This should be used to denote the immediate future; it means right *away* or in *a little while:*

I will answer your question **presently**.

He is expected to arrive **presently**.

The meeting will begin **presently**.

For current time, use **at present** or **currently**:

He is **currently** a junior at North High.

At present, she is working on her master's degree.

purposely/purposefully

Use **purposely** to mean intentionally, knowingly, deliberately, that is, to describe an action done "on purpose" and not by accident.

purposefully is best used to mean decisively, firmly, resolutely, with determination, and with a specific purpose or goal in mind.

toward/towards

Either is acceptable; **toward** is more formal.

when/where

These are terms of time and place; do not use them to introduce definitions.

which/that/who

These relative *pronouns* introduce *clauses* that describe or define. Use **that** for clauses that are *restrictive* (defining, limiting):

The books **that** you ordered will arrive tomorrow; the ones **that** Sam ordered will come next week. (those particular books . . .)

He likes the car **that** he bought last year better than any other he has owned. (that particular car)

Basketball is the game **that** he plays best.

Use **which** for clauses that are *nonrestrictive* (descriptive):

The house on the corner, **which** was built in the 1880s, will be restored to its original design.

Shakespeare's plays, **which** were written nearly 400 years ago, remain popular in theaters and movies as well as in English courses.

Use **who** for people. (**That** is sometimes used when the identification is distant or impersonal.) Do not use **which** for people:

Lady Macbeth is a character **that** (**who**) remains fascinating to many students.

Use **whom** when the pronoun is an object:

To **whom** should I give the information? (obj. of prep.)

Whom did you ask? (obj. of verb)

who/whom/whoever/whomever

When these *pronouns* introduce *clauses,* their form is determined *solely* by their function in the clause:

The new coach, **who** led the team to a county title, gave all the credit to her players.
(**Who** is the subject of the verb *led;* therefore, it is in the subject form.)

Please give the information to (**whoever** needs it.)
(**Whoever** is the subject in the clause; the *entire* clause is the object of *give to.*)

Please give the award to (**whomever** you choose.)
(**Whomever** is the object of the verb *choose;* the *entire* clause is the object of *give to.*)

Careful attention to the conventions of usage and style outlined in this chapter will enhance your ability to express ideas and discuss information clearly and persuasively. When you have command of the language you use, you have command of the relationship between thought and expression.

Chapter 9

PUNCTUATION: GUIDELINES AND REMINDERS

When is the semicolon or colon used? Are there any rules for commas? Do I underline titles of books and poems or put them in quotation marks? Where do I put the period when a sentence ends with quotation marks? Even experienced writers need to consult a usage handbook for the answers to some of these questions.

In conversation we use pauses, stresses, and tone of voice to make our meaning clear. The printed page, however, does not readily show what voice and gesture can reveal, so the writer uses punctuation to achieve absolute clarity. Below, you will find a review of the elements of punctuation high school students should know and use in their own writing. Featured are answers to those questions most often raised about how to punctuate. (Many of the examples from the writing of specific authors come from the passages reprinted elsewhere in the book.)

END PUNCTUATION

The period, exclamation mark, and question mark bring statements and expressions to a close; they signal a full stop.

The Period

Use a **period** to indicate the end of a sentence or of a group of words having the emphasis of a sentence.

Declarative sentences (make a statement):

Good writers are also good readers.

"The guns squatted in a row like savage chiefs." (Stephen Crane, *The Red Badge of Courage*)

Imperative sentences (give an order or direction):

Be sure to proofread.

Come to practice on time or leave the team.

Tell me how much I owe you.

Fragments for emphasis:

"No doubt my younger brother and sister were in the house and warm.
Eating cookies." (William Kittredge)

"Much of their [whales'] behavior seems to be recreational: they sing,
they play. *And so on.*" (Robert Finch)

The Exclamation Mark

Use an **exclamation mark** to show intensity and emphasis in sentences
or fragments.

Come to practice!

Be sure to proofread!

Look out!

Congratulations!

CAUTION: *Do not overuse the* **exclamation mark** *in expository writing;
use effective language and sentence structure to achieve emphasis.*

The Question Mark

Use a **question mark** to signal interrogative forms in complete sentences, fragments, or series.

Can you explain how to do this?

Do you understand what he said?

Can you recommend a good restaurant in the theater district?

What was that all about? a joke? a mistake?

Where should we meet? at home? at school?

Ask questions as you read an essay: What is the author's purpose?
tone? conclusion? Do you agree? disagree? feel convinced?

Question marks may also be used with single words or phrases as needed:

When?
Leave the team?
You did?
What homework?

SPECIAL CONSIDERATIONS

Periods are used in many abbreviations. For example:

U.S. government	Dipl.	B.A.	M.A.	Ph.D.
U.N. Security Council	D.D.S.	M.D.	Esq.	
N.Y.S. Board of Regents	A.M.	P.M.		

Some abbreviations take no periods:

CIA   mph
MTV   rpm
WCBS

A sentence may end with more than one kind of punctuation. If it ends with an abbreviation using a period, do not add a second period.

Please report to my office promptly at 10:00 a.m.

In order to apply for a teaching position, you must have completed your M.A.

If it ends with a quotation or expression in quotation marks, place the final period *inside* the quotation marks.

Most high school students have read Poe's short story "The Cask of Amontillado."

When told his wife is dead, Macbeth remarks, "She should have died hereafter."

If the **entire sentence** requires a question mark, place it outside the quotation marks:

Have you read Poe's story "The Cask of Amontillado"?

Why does Macbeth say, "She should have died hereafter"?

If the quotation at the end of a sentence requires a question mark, keep it within the quotes. (Do not add an additional period.)

The title of a recent editorial in *The New York Times* was "Where do we go from here?"

If a statement within the quotes is a question, the question mark within the quote is sufficient.

Did you read the editorial entitled "Where do we go from here?"

Similarly, if an exclamation point is part of a quoted expression, place it within the quote. An additional period is not required.

One of my favorite pieces by James Thurber is called "Excelsior!"

To make the above into a question, however:

Have you read Thurber's story "Excelsior!"?

If a sentence ends with a passage in parentheses, put the period outside the closing parenthesis:

We did not leave on time because Sally was late (as usual).

Even if the expression is a complete sentence, do not punctuate within the parentheses:

We did not leave on time because Sally was late (she always is).

If, however, the expression within the parentheses requires quotation marks, a question mark, or an exclamation point, include them:

We did not leave on time because Sally was late (isn't she always?).

In such cases, a better solution would be to separate the parenthetical statement:

We did not leave because Sally was late. (Isn't she always?)

What is the logic to all this? When sentences or passages are made up of a variety of elements, punctuation should make the structure of each element clear. If the end of a sentence becomes cluttered by the need to bring several individual pieces to a close at the same time, punctuate from the inside out—smaller pieces first, then larger. But do not double the end punctuation unless it is required for accuracy. If you have a question within a question, one question mark will do. If a closing quotation ends with a "strong" piece of punctuation, don't add a modest and redundant period to the whole sentence. Close with the strength of the quote.

INTERNAL PUNCTUATION

Internal punctuation includes the comma, the semicolon, the colon, and the dash. The single purpose of internal punctuation is to prevent confusion, to achieve clarity. The comma indicates brief pauses between separate elements in a sentence; the semicolon establishes a direct connection between two independent statements to form a single sentence; the colon serves to introduce things; and the dash permits you to digress or emphasize.

The Comma

Use the comma in compound sentences with coordinating conjunctions *and, but, yet, so, or, for.* A compound sentence joins two or more independent clauses that could be expressed separately as simple sentences. *Note that the comma precedes the conjunction:*

> "I walked slowly, *for* the detail on the beach was infinite." (Ernie Pyle)
>
> "The luncheon hour was long past; *and* the two had their end of the vast terrace to themselves." (Edith Wharton, "Roman Fever")
>
> "I was not going to talk about Whitewater today, *but* then I thought that if I didn't you'd think I know something about it, *and* the only way for me to prove that I don't is to talk about it at length, *so* I will." (Garrison Keillor)

In sentences where the clauses are short and the meaning is clear, you may omit a comma:

> The team tied the score in the last seconds of the game and the crowd cheered wildly.

If there is any possibility of misreading, you must use a comma:

> I went to the movies with Roger and Sally stayed home.
>
> I went to the movies with Roger, and Sally stayed home.

WHAT IS A COMMA SPLICE?

One of the most common errors in writing is the use of a comma alone to join independent clauses. This is the error familiar to students as the "run-on" sentence.

Run on: The crowd cheered wildly, the game was tied in the last few seconds.

I went to the movies with Roger, Sally stayed home.

The novel was riveting, I did not want it to end.

Correct: The crowd cheered wildly when the game was tied in the final seconds.

I went to the movies with Roger, and Sally stayed home.

The novel was riveting, so I did not want it to end.

DO I USE A COMMA BEFORE THE LAST ITEM IN A SERIES?

Some editors and instructors insist that all items in a series be set off by a comma; others prefer that you omit the last one, especially in a series of single words:

You can find models of style in books, newspapers, and magazines.

You can find models of style in books, newspapers and magazines.

SUGGESTION: For sentences like the one above, the second comma needlessly slows down the sentence and makes no contribution to clarity. In a series of longer expressions, however, or in a series without a conjunction, set off each with a comma.

For class you are expected to bring a notebook, a pen or pencil, and the text we are reading.

"He was white-headed as a mountain, bowed in the shoulders, and faded in general aspect." (Thomas Hardy)

Writing has many purposes: personal expression, persuasion, literary effect, information.

Use a Comma After Introductory Clauses

As the crowd cheered them on, the home team scored the winning touchdown.

If you are hungry, please help yourself to a sandwich.

"As the bell sounded the hour, there came a knocking at the street door." (Edgar Allan Poe)

Do not use a comma if the main clause is followed by a dependent clause:

Please help yourself to a sandwich whenever you get hungry.

The home team scored the winning touchdown as the crowd cheered them on.

Use a Comma After an Introductory Phrase Only When Needed

At last, the rain began to ease, and the sun came through breaks in the clouds.

The son of a tanner, Grant was everything Lee was not.

After the Labor Day recess, Congress will reconvene.

Feeling ill and confused, he left the dinner table without speaking.

These sentences require no comma:

On the desk you will find your final check and a letter of recommendation.

"For a long time they continued to sit side by side without speaking." (Edith Wharton)

Use Commas to Set off Descriptive and Nonessential Clauses or Phrases Within Sentences

"They were two strong men, these oddly different generals, and they represented the strengths of two conflicting currents that, through them, had come into final collision." (Bruce Catton)

The house on the corner, which was built in the 1880s, will be restored to its original design.

Shakespeare's plays, written nearly four hundred years ago, remain popular in theaters and movies as well as in English courses.

USE COMMAS WITH SOME SINGLE WORDS AND EXPRESSIONS

"Well, Jim's habits and his jokes didn't appeal to Julie . . ." (Ring Lardner, "Haircut")

"Now, I'll read the names—heads of families first." (Shirley Jackson, "The Lottery")

USE COMMAS WITH PARENTHETIC AND TRANSITIONAL EXPRESSIONS

Use commas to set off such expressions as *however, moreover, therefore, nevertheless, after all, by the way, of course, on the other hand, I think.*

"Yet it was not all contrast, after all . . . Furthermore, their fighting qualities were really very much alike." (Bruce Catton)

After all, what you learn is what really matters.

You must, of course, always proofread a paper before handing it in.

COMMAS IN DATES

For expressions of day, month, and year:

July 4, 1776, marks the beginning of the American Revolution.

Registration will take place on September 9, 1994, for the fall semester and on January 12, 1995, for the spring semester.

Do not use commas for expressions of month and year only.

Joan completed graduate school in June 1987, began her legal work in September 1987, and joined our firm in January 1993.

COMMAS WITH ADJECTIVES IN A SERIES

Use a comma when it means *and:*

The little room in Appomattox was "the scene of one of the poignant, dramatic contrasts in American history." (Bruce Catton)

The Regents examinations require you to write thoughtful, well-organized essays.

Do not use a comma if the adjective is part of the meaning of the noun:

She greeted her guests in the large sitting room.

USE COMMAS TO SET OFF QUOTES

"I always used to think," Mrs. Slade continued, "that our mothers had a much more difficult job than our grandmothers." (Edith Wharton, "Roman Fever")

"It isn't fair, it isn't right," Mrs. Hutchinson screamed, and then they were upon her. (Shirley Jackson, "The Lottery")

ADDITIONAL ILLUSTRATIONS OF COMMA USE

If you must sing, sing quietly.
These incidents took place a long, long time ago.

That's not what you meant, is it?
You have everything you need, don't you?

First come, first served.
Now you see it, now you don't.

Shakespeare's tragedy *Macbeth* is one of his best-known plays.
Verdi's only comic opera, *Falstaff,* is the last work he composed.

My sister Anne lives in Seattle; my sister Julia lives in New York.
My only sister, Anne, lives in Seattle.

COMMON ERRORS IN COMMA USE

Do not separate compound elements or isolate essential elements with commas.

Correct: "They greeted one another and exchanged bits of gossip as they went to join their husbands." (Shirley Jackson, "The Lottery")

Faulty: They greeted one another, and exchanged bits of gossip as they went to join their husbands.

Alternative:	*They greeted* one another, and *they exchanged* bits of gossip as they went to join their husbands.
Correct:	"Whales possess a highly complex language and have developed sophisticated communications systems that transmit over long distances." (Robert Finch)
Faulty:	Whales possess a highly complex language, and have developed sophisticated communications systems, that transmit over long distances.
Alternative:	*Whales possess* a highly complex language, *and they have developed* sophisticated communications systems that transmit over long distances.

In the faulty examples, the first comma may *look* necessary, but it improperly separates the subject from the second verb; the final clause in each case is essential description and should not be separated from the rest of the sentence. The alternative versions are accurately punctuated and show how the original, correct sentences could be revised into compound sentences.

SUGGESTION: In all the examples and explanations above, the commas serve one purpose: to make the expression clear on first reading. Insert commas in your own writing as you compose, as you hear the need for them. When you revise, do not be tempted to add commas simply because they look right—chances are, they do not belong.

The Semicolon

A comma indicates a brief pause between separate elements in a sentence, whereas a semicolon indicates a longer pause between independent statements that form a single sentence. The semicolon may replace *and* or *but* in compound sentences. Here are some of the examples used earlier now revised with semicolons.

> I walked slowly; the detail on the beach was infinite.

> The luncheon hour was long past; the two had their end of the vast terrace to themselves.

> I was not going to talk about Whitewater today; then I thought that if I didn't, you'd think I know something about it; the only way for me to prove that I don't is to talk about it at length; so I will.

In each of these revisions, you can see that the effect of the semicolon is to indicate a cause and effect relationship or to show consequence without stating it directly. This results in forceful and emphatic sentences. The semicolon also has a formal quality; it creates a feeling of balance and equivalence among statements.

> ". . . with a semicolon . . . you get a pleasant little feeling of expectancy; there is more to come; read on; it will get clearer." (Lewis Thomas)

The Colon

Use the colon to introduce something: a list, the body of a letter, a quotation, or an explanation.

> "Political courage stems from a number of sources: anger, pain, love, hate." (Madeleine Kunin)
>
> "Mrs. Slade began again: 'I suppose I did it as a sort of joke'—" (Edith Wharton)
>
> "The purpose of life is to be useful. It is, above all, to *matter:* to have it make some difference that you lived at all." (Leo Rosten)

The Dash

The dash permits you to pause without notice and insert an idea too interesting to delay and too important to put in parentheses—but don't overdo it!

> "At some gut level, the art of politics—combative, competitive, self-asserting—is sometimes difficult to integrate with our feminine selves." (Madeleine Kunin)
>
> "Different as they were—in background, in personality, in underlying aspiration—these two great soldiers had much in common." (Bruce Catton)
>
> "The wonder of ourselves, of each other, and of life—this is the true subject matter of all novels." (Sandy Asher)

The Ellipsis

The ellipsis is used in quoted passages to show that something has been omitted.

> "The purpose of life is to be useful . . . above all, to *matter*." (Rosten)

When an ellipsis comes at the end of a sentence, the final period must be retained; that is, you will use four periods, not three. The following example shows the use of three ellipses: one in the middle of a sentence and two, each with a fourth period added, at the ends of sentences:

> Mark Van Doren asserts that "Iago's cynicism consists of believing that . . . the passions of men are toys for him to play with . . . . He likes nothing better than to make plans which other men's emotions will execute . . . ."

The Bracket

Brackets indicate where the writer has added a word or phrase to a quoted passage. Such additions are sometimes necessary to make connections in extended quotes where you have used ellipsis.

> "The persons of the tale were long since types [to Hawthorne], as were their souls' predicaments. The broken law, the hidden guilt, the hunger for confession, the studious, cold heart that watches and does not feel . . ." (Mark Van Doren)

> Men's passions should lead them to "more and better feeling . . . ," but Iago's knowledge of men's hearts transforms those passions into destructive forces, into "toys . . . tools to use." Iago contrives malign "plans which other men's [benign] emotions will execute."

The Apostrophe

The apostrophe has many important uses: to form contractions, to show possession, and to form the plural of numbers, symbols, and letters. Apostrophes are also easily misused. Below are examples of the most common uses.

CONTRACTIONS

The apostrophe takes the place of a missing letter or letters in a contraction:

> It's very warm day. = It is very warm today.

> You don't have to return the book right now. = You do not . . .

Remember that contractions are characteristic of spoken language and are not generally used in formal writing.

The apostrophe is also used to abbreviate dates:

June '82

The Class of '98

POSSESSIVE FORMS OF NOUNS AND PROPER NAMES

You form the possessive of a singular noun or name by adding an apostrophe and an *s*:

The novel's major themes (= The major themes of the novel)

My neighbor's house

Charles's notebook

Dickens's novels

In general, you form the possessive of a plural noun by adding the apostrophe alone:

My neighbors' yards

the jurors' verdict

the witnesses' statements

The Smiths' house

the Davises' horse

NOTE: Be sure to avoid the common error of confusing the possessive form with the plural.

Mark Twain wrote several novels; he did not write "novel's."

The local nursery sells plants; it does not sell "plant's."

SOME PLURALS

Use the apostrophe to form the plurals of letters and some abbreviations:

There were sixteen A's on the last exam.

"Dot your *i*'s and cross your *t*'s."

Mark has earned two Ph.D.'s, each in a different discipline.

TITLES OF WORKS OF LITERATURE

Titles of books and other full-length, separately published works should be set in italics. If you are composing on a typewriter or writing by hand, *underline* such titles. Movies and plays are also set in italics.

The Great Gatsby	*Death of a Salesman*
Huckleberry Finn	*The Glass Menagerie*
To Kill a Mockingbird	*Macbeth*

The names of newspapers and magazines should also be in italics.

The New York Times   *Harper's*   *Newsweek*

Titles of poems, essays, and short stories are set off in quotes.

"The Tell-Tale Heart"	"The Sleeping Giant"
"Roman Fever"	"The Road Not Taken"
"The Lottery"	"Old Photograph of the Future"

A title should not be underlined *and* set in quotes; this is redundant and confusing.

Your own title for an essay or paper should not be underlined; use quotes only for names or phrases actually quoted within the title.

A FINAL NOTE ON PUNCTUATION

The topics reviewed here are meant to offer fundamental guidelines and to illustrate how accurate punctuation helps make writing clear. Review some of the prose passages in other parts of the book for vivid examples of how different authors use punctuation to make their meaning and tone clear.

Chapter 10

VOCABULARY

Formal vocabulary study may begin as early as kindergarten; associating meaning with different sounds begins virtually at birth. As all students have discovered, however, there always seem to be new words to learn. Every novel, essay, or newspaper article we read is likely to include some new expressions or unfamiliar words. Deliberately studying new words and preparing for tests on them is certainly one way to expand our vocabularies, and every serious student has developed a method for such study. But if you do not continue to use those new words—that is, read, speak, and write with them—they may be forgotten soon after the test.

The thousands of words you *know* were acquired through repeated use over time and through association with their contexts, that is, through reading and listening. As you review lists of words and actively work to expand your reading and writing vocabularies, try to learn every new word in a context: Associate it with a phrase, an experience, an object or person, an action or incident. Every word you study should create some kind of image for you; if you have no image, you do not truly know the word yet.

The words included on Regents and SAT vocabulary tests are those a high school student is likely to encounter in assigned texts and other works of literature. The English Regents exam assesses your vocabulary skills in the multiple-choice questions of Session One and Part A of Session Two, and by the degree to which you use language effectively in your essays; the exam does not have a separate section on vocabulary.

At the end of this chapter you will find three collections of words to review or learn. The first includes all the words that were tested on Regents exams from 1986 through 2003. The second is a list compiled by high school students from their reading of the Op-Ed pages of *The New York Times*. The third, from published book reviews, was also compiled by students. Each list offers the thoughtful reader and writer a rich source of vocabulary in current use.

STUDYING NEW WORDS

Learning in Context

Even the most diligent student cannot reasonably expect simply to memorize—out of context—the hundreds, even thousands, of words on Regents and SAT lists. Recent studies also confirm that vocabulary study confined to lists of words without a context or pattern of association—as with a particular work of literature, for example—does not result in long-term retention. Moreover, the practice of recording dictionary definitions alone gives only general and sometimes misleading information about the meaning and correct use of words. Learning words means learning their precise meanings, connotations, and appropriate context.

Unless you are working with an unabridged dictionary, which often includes illustrative examples in sentences or phrases, you are likely to find in a desk dictionary only brief definitions, general in nature, and possibly a list of synonyms. This limited information is valuable as a *reference,* especially if you are reading a passage and need to know a word's meaning in order to understand the passage. Learning the full meaning of unfamiliar words, however, requires more active study. In the sections below you will find recommendations for ways to prepare and organize your vocabulary study.

ROOTS AND PREFIXES FROM LATIN AND GREEK

Although English is certainly not derived from Greek and Latin only, familiarity with the Greek or Latin forms in English words is often useful to students taking vocabulary tests. Recognition of root meanings in particular may help you determine the correct answer for a word you may not be sure of. Even more important, however, is the value of knowing the Latin and Greek origins of English when you are first studying new words. When you are aware of the meanings of the individual parts of a word you often can form an image for it. Think of the Latin root *spect*, for example. This root means *look into, observe, behold* and, with variations in spelling *spec* and *spic,* is the base of many English words: *inspect, introspect, expect, respect, speculate, spectacle, spectacular, conspicuous*—and many others. Even the word *spy* is related to this Latin root.

When you are looking up words in the dictionary, do not skip over the etymology—the section that shows you in abbreviated form the origin and history of a word. Grouping words by related origin can be a very useful way to organize when you are studying large groups of new words; by using their common origin, you will learn to associate a new word with others you already know. It is the process of forming associations in meaning, forming images, and knowing contexts that permits you to learn efficiently—and to remember—the words you study. (Familiarity with roots and prefixes is also very helpful in understanding spelling patterns, as you will see in Chapter 11.)

Listed below, with examples, are many of the Latin and Greek roots found in English. (As you review the meanings of these roots, provide additional examples from your own knowledge; you should also guess about possible examples—then look them up in a dictionary to confirm your guess.) This process is a demonstration of what is meant by *active* vocabulary study. It means you are thinking about a word and associating it with others you know.

As you examine the list of Greek and Latin roots common in English, you should be struck by how familiar many of these forms are. You should also note that all these roots denote specific actions or ideas. Knowing the meanings of these elements as you study new words, or review familiar ones, will give you specific images or experiences to associate with them. This in turn will make the meaning of many words more vivid and easier to remember than will an abstract definition or list of synonyms alone.

LATIN ROOTS

Forms	Meaning	Examples
alter	other	altercation, alternative
ami (amicus)	friend	amiable, amicable, amity
amor	love	amorous, enamored
anima	breath, mind, spirit	animation, unanimous, inanimate, animosity
bell (bellum)	war	bellicose, belligerent, antebellum
cad (cadere), cid	to fall	decay, decadence, deciduous
cap, cip	contain	captivate, capacity, capable
capit (caput)	head	capital, capitol, recapitulate
cede, ceed, cess (cedere)	to move, yield	proceed, accede, exceed, precede, excess, success, procession
cept (capere)	to take, seize, hold	intercept, reception, accept
cid, cis (caedere)	to cut, kill	precise, incisive, homicide
clam, claim (clamare)	to cry, call out	exclaim, proclaim, clamor
clud, clus (claudere)	to shut, close	include, exclusion, recluse
cred (credere)	to believe, loan, trust	creditable, incredible, credulous
culp (culpa)	fault, guilt	culpable, exculpate
cur, curs (currere)	to run	course, cursor, current, incur, precursor, recur
dict (dicere)	to say, tell	dictator, diction, edict, predict
doc (docere)	to teach	doctor, docile, indoctrinate
duc, duct (ducere)	to lead	deduce, induction, conduct
err (errare)	to go, lead astray	error, erroneous, erratum
err (errer)	to travel, wander	errand, arrant, erratic
fac, fact, fect, fic (facere)	to make, do	affect, defect, effect, facsimile, factor, artificial, deficit
fer (ferre)	to bear, carry	inference, offer, reference
fid (fidelitas)	faith, loyalty	infidel, perfidious, diffident
flect, flex (flectere)	to bend	reflex, reflection, flexibility
flu, fluct, flux (fluere)	to flow	affluent, fluctuation, fluent, influence, influx
fund (fundare) (fundus)	to base, bottom	(to) found, fundamental, profundity
fus (fundere)	pour	effusive, foundry, fusion

gen (genus) *(genare)*	kind, sort, birth, to beget	genre, heterogenous, genetic, generate, progenitor, genocide
grad, gress (gradus)	to walk, go, stage or step	digress, graduate, progress, grade, gradient, retrograde
greg (gregis)	flock, herd, group	egregious, gregarious, integrate
her, hes (haerere)	to cling, stick	adhesive, coherence, inherently
ject, jet (jacere)	to throw	inject, projection, jettison
jud, jur, jus (jus)	to judge; to swear just, right; law	abjure, adjudicate, prejudge, jury, justification, perjury
lat (latus)	borne, carried	correlative, related, superlative
leg (legis, lex)	law	legality, legislative
locus	place	location, locale, locomotive
locu, loqu (loqui) *locutor*	to speak speaker	eloquent, loquacious, soliloquy, interlocutor, locution, obloquy
lude (ludere)	to play	interlude, ludicrous, prelude
mit, mitt, mis, miss (mittere)	to dispatch, send, to let go	emit, permit, remit, submissive, commission, missile, permission
mob, mot (movere)	to move	demote, motivate, promote, commotion, mobility
mor, mort (mortis)	death	immortal, mortality, mortified
ped (pedis)	foot	expeditious, impede, pedestrian
pel, puls (pellere)	to drive, push	compel, dispel, impulse, repel, compulsive, repellent
pend, pens (pendere)	to hang, weigh, pay	append, compensate, dependent, impending, pension, pensive
ple, plet (plere)	to fill	complete, complement, deplete
plen (plenus)	full	plentiful, replete
pon, pos, posit (ponere)	to place, put	component, depose, propose, juxtapostion, impose, opponent
port (portare)	to carry	comport, deportment, purport, portable, portfolio
pot, poten, poss (posse)	to be able	impossibility, omnipotent, potential
rad (radius)	root, spoke (wheel)	eradicate, radical, radiation
rect, reg (regula) *(regire)*	right, straight to guide, rule	direction, rectified, regal regimen, regime
rupt (rumpere)	to break, burst	disrupt, corrupt, interruption
sat (satis)	enough	dissatisfy, insatiable, saturated
sci (scire)	to know	conscience, omniscient, prescience, scientific
scrib, script (scribere)	to write	describe, inscription, scripture
sect (sectare)	to cut	dissect, intersection
secu, sequ (sequi)	to follow	consequence, obsequious, sectarian, sequel
sed, sid, sess (sedere)	to sit	dissidence, possess, residual, sedation, sedentary
sent, sens (sentire)	to feel	consensus, insensitive, sentient
son (sonus)	sound	consonant, dissonance, sonic, sonogram, sonority, unison
spec, spect, spic	to look at, observe	auspicious, conspicuous, expect,

(spectare)		inspect, respect, spectacular
spir, spirit	to breathe	inspiration, respiratory, spirit
sta, state, stit (stare)	to stand	constitute, instability, obstacle, stability, status
strict, string (stringere)	to draw tight	constrict, restriction, stringent
sume, sump (sumere)	to take	assume, consume, presumption
tact, tang, ting, tig (tangere)	to touch	contact, contiguous, intangible, tactile, tangential
ten, tain (tenere)	to hold, keep	abstain, pertain, restrain, tenacious, untenable
tend, tens (tendere)	to reach, stretch	contend, intensity, portent, pretentious, tendency
tort (torque)	to twist	contortion, extort, tortuous
tract (trahere)	to draw, pull	distract, intractible, protracted, retraction
ver (veritas)	truth	aver, veracity, verification
vers, vert (vertere)	to turn	adverse, aversion, diversity, inadvertent, reversion, subvert, version, versification
vid, vis (videre) (video)	to see	evident, improvident, supervise, revision, visage, visionary
vit, viv (vivere) (viva)	to live; life	revival, survive, vivacious, unviable
vinc, vict (vincere)	to conquer	conviction, eviction, invincible
voc, voke (vocare)	to call	advocate, equivocal, invocation, provocative, revoke, vocation
volv, volu (volvere)	to roll, turn	convoluted, evolution, revolving

GREEK ROOTS

Forms	Meaning	Examples
anthrop	man, humankind	anthropocentric, misanthropist, philanthropy
arch	rule, ruler	anarchy, patriarchal
astr, astron	star	astronomical, disastrous
bio	life, living things	biography, microbiology
chron	time	anachronistic, chronic
cosm (kosmos)	order, universe	cosmic, microcosm
demo	among the people	democratic, demography
gen	birth, race	genesis, progeny
gno, gnosis	know	agnostic, diagnosis, gnomic
gram, graph	write, writing	epigrammatic, biography
log, logue	word, reason	analogy, illogical, prologue
lect, lex	language, speak	dialect, lexical
lysis	dissolution, destruction	catalyst, paralysis

metr	measure	diametric, metrical
morph	form, shape	amorphous, metamorphose
mne, mnes	memory, remember	amnesty, mnemonic
onym	a name	eponymous, synonym
opti, optic	eye, sight	optical, synopsis
path (pathos)	feeling, suffering	apathy, empathetic, pathetic
ped	child	pediatrician, pedagogy, pedantic
phon	sound	euphony, phonetic, symphonic

Prefixes are units of one or two syllables that are not words in themselves but that have distinct meanings. The addition of a prefix to the beginning of an existing word (what is called a *stem* or *root)* creates a word with an additional meaning. The spelling variations for many of the prefixes listed below are reminders that in English the spelling of a prefix will be altered to match the root to which it is attached. For example, *ad,* which means *to* or *toward,* is attached to many words in English; the *d* often changes to the first letter of the word to which it is added, making the resulting new forms easier to pronounce. (See the examples below as well as those in Chapter 11, Spelling.)

LATIN PREFIXES

Forms	Meaning	Examples*
a, ab, abs	away, from	abdicate, absence, abstraction
a, ad (ac, af, al, etc.)	to, toward	absent, acclimate, adherent, alliteration, assign, attribution
ambi	both, around	ambiance, ambiguous, ambidextrous, ambivalent
ante	before	antebellum, antecedent
bene, ben	good, well	beneficial, beneficent, benign
circum	around	circumnavigate, circumstances, circumlocution
co (col, com, cor)	together	coincidence, collaboration, commiserate, correspondence
contra, contro, counter	against, opposite	contradiction, controversy, counterfeit, counteract
de	away, down, from	deduction, deterrence, deviate
dis (di, dif)	apart, away; not; separate	disavow, disdain, disappear, disregard, disperse, discern
en (var. of in)	make, put into	enable, enhance, encourage
equ, equi	equal, even	equable, equanimity, equivalence, equivocate
ex (e, ef)	away from, out	efface, effective, ejection, exodus, expiration
in (il, im, ir)	in, within	immersion, impending, innate
in (il, im, ir)	not, without	illegible, imprudent, incognito
inter	among, between	intercede, intermediary, interim

magn	great	magnificence, magnanimous
mal	bad, evil	malevolent, malice, malefactor, malign, malignant
ob (oc, of, op)	to, toward; against; over; totally	objection; obdurate, obnoxious; obfuscate; obsolete, obliterate
omni	all	omnipotent, omniscient
per	completely; through	perceive, perdurable, pervasive
post	after	posterity, posthumous
pre	before, in advance	pre-empt, preclude, premonition
pro	before, forward	proclivity, prodigy, profane
re	again	reiterate, reverberate, retort, revise, remember
retro	backward	retrogression, retroactive
se	apart, aside	secession, sedition, select
sub (suf, sup, sus)	from below, under	subsidize, substandard, suffuse, suppress, sustenance
super	above, over	supercilious, superfluous, supervise, supersede
tra, trans	across, beyond	transgression, transcend

GREEK PREFIXES

Forms	Meaning	Examples
a, an	not, without	agnostic, anarchy, apathetic
ana	back, backward according to; through	anagram, anachronistic, anapest analogy, analysis
ant, anti	against, opposite	antipathy, antithesis, antipodes
auto	self	autonomous, autocracy
cata	down	cataclysm, catalyst, catastrophe
dia	through, between	dialect, dialogue, diameter
dys	bad, ill, difficult	dysfunctional, dyspeptic
epi	upon	epicenter, epigram, epilogue
eu	good, well	euphemism, euphoria, eugenics
hetero	different	heterodox, heterogeneous
homo	alike, same	homogeneous, homonym
macro	large, long duration	macrocosm, macroscopic
meta, met	after, beyond; changed	metaphor, metaphysical, metamorphosis
micro	small	microscope, microbe
mon, mono	one, single	monotheism, monolith
pan	all, complete	panacea, pandemonium
pro	before; favorable	prophecy; propitiate
proto	first, primary	protagonist, prototype
sym, syn	together, with	symmetry, synergy, synopsis

* When you review the lists for study at the end of the chapter you will readily see how many words in English are formed with these prefixes. Use those lists to add to the examples offered here.

Here is the first group of vocabulary words from the Regents exams list on page 219. Note how many are formed from the Greek or Latin prefixes reviewed on the previous pages.

abdicate	**ab**errant	**ab**horrent	abridgment
absolve	**ac**claim	**ac**cost	**ac**credit
acme	**ac**quiesce	**ac**quittal	**ad**age
adhere	**ad**junct	**ad**monish	**ad**versity
afflict	agrarian	**al**lot	**al**lure
ally	**alter**cation	amass	**ambi**ance
ambidextrous	**ambi**guous	**ambi**valent	amnesty
amorphous	**ana**chronistic	**an**ecdotes	animation
appease	**ap**prehend	arbitrator	archaic
ardent	armistice	**ar**ray	**ar**rogantly
ascendancy	ashen	**a**spire	assay
astute	**a**sylum	atrocious	audacity
autonomous	avarice	**a**verse	**a**version
avidly	azure		

In many of these examples, the meaning of the original prefix has been absorbed into the meaning of the entire word, in **adage** and **allot**, for example. The highlighted prefixes illustrate, however, how extensively Greek and Latin forms are found in English.

PREPARING NOTE CARDS

Here are samples of detailed note cards for some of the listed words. They show origin, definition, context, and connotation.

---

aberrant, *adj.* [from L. *aberrare*, to go astray, *ab-* from + *errare,* to wander]

deviating from what is true, correct, normal, or typical. Used to describe human behavior, mental lapses; also describes behavior of physical phenomena, esp. in astronomy or physics

"We could not explain the child's *aberrant* behavior; she is normally polite and well-mannered."

"The low scores on last week's chemistry test were an *aberration*; normally the students in this class do very well."

Also, **aberrantly** (adv.) **aberration, aberrance, aberrancy** (n.)

---

adversity, *n.* [from L. *adversus*, turned against, *ad-* from + *versare* to turn]

misfortune, wretched state, poverty, calamity; a condition of extreme hardship

In history and literature, we often read of characters who have "overcome adversity" to lead fulfilling lives or to make notable achievements.

Also, **adverse** (adj.), hostile, harmful, contrary, opposed; conditions and reactions may be described as *adverse.* An **adversary** is an opponent.

---

acquiesce, *v.i.* [Fr. *acquiescer,* to yield to, from L. *ad-* to + *quiescere,* to be at rest]

To accept, agree to, consent *without protest;* assent *without enthusiasm*

Young people sometimes must *acquiesce* in the demands of their parents. On a committee, some may have to *acquiesce* in the decisions of the majority.

Also, **acquiescence** (n.), **acquiescent** (adj.)

Such comprehensive note cards are not required for all words you wish to study; they are most useful when you intend to make certain words part of your own speaking and writing vocabulary. Most students like to prepare flash cards with synonyms or brief definitions for quick review.

A NOTE ON SYNONYMS AND USING A THESAURUS

As thoughtful students and careful writers know, synonyms are rarely equivalents. Synonyms are words closely related in meaning to a given word, but they should not be considered equally interchangeable with it.

Here is a list of synonyms for **acquiesce** that you might gather from a thesaurus:

accede	accept	agree to	allow
assent	capitulate	come to terms with	comply with
concede	concur	conform	consent
give in	grant	permit	submit
surrender	yield		

This list is very helpful in enriching your understanding of the word, especially because it includes several terms that emphasize that there is a sense of giving in, of reluctance, in **acquiesce**. The closest synonyms in this list are *accede, come to terms with, conform, give in, yield. Capitulate, submit,* and *surrender* accurately reflect the connotation of the word, but they denote a more forceful sense of defeat than does *acquiesce.* The others, *accept, agree to, concur, consent, permit,* are less precise because they reflect only the general meaning and do not denote the sense of reluctance and the lack of enthusiasm inherent in **acquiesce**.

Learning to distinguish among variations in meaning and context is an important part of developing your vocabulary. It is also essential to the craft of good writing. In Chapter 5, Writing about Literature, and Chapter 9, Composition, you will find several *synonymies,* which are words grouped by general meaning or connotation. The purpose of the *synonymies* is to help you develop precision and variety in your own writing. You should review those as part of your vocabulary study as well.

ORGANIZING VOCABULARY STUDY

Another way to work with lists such as the ones at the end of this chapter is to *sort* them, much as you would sort playing cards. Depending on the card game you are playing, you might sort a hand by suit, by numerical sequence, or by kind. You can sort a group of words in various ways as well: by part of speech, by connotation, by human or abstract qualities, and so on. Many students create their own flash cards for the words they study, which makes sorting in various ways easy. (See page 211 for sample note cards.)

Here are some suggestions for how you might sort the first group of words from the Regents list (page 219). First, sort by part of speech. In the list below, the *verbs* are printed in bold type:

VERBS

abdicate	aberrant	abhorrent	abridgment
absolve	**acclaim**	**accost**	**accredit**
acme	**acquiesce**	acquittal	adage
adhere	adjunct	**admonish**	adversity
afflict	agrarian	**allot**	allure
ally	altercation	**amass**	ambiance
ambidextrous	ambiguous	ambivalent	amnesty
amorphous	anachronistic	anecdote	animation
appease	**apprehend**	arbitrator	archaic
ardent	armistice	**array**	arrogantly
ascendancy	ashen	**aspire**	**assay**
astute	asylum	atrocious	audacity
autonomous	avarice	averse	aversion
avidly	azure		

Then classify the group of verbs further as either *transitive* or *intransitive;* that is, according to the nature of the action they denote and the nature of the objects, if any, they take. When you look up these words in a dictionary, they will be identified as *v.i.* or *v.t. Transitive verbs (v.t.)* take a direct object; the action is directed from the subject to an object. For example, "She *admonished* (scolded, warned) the unruly child" and "King Midas *amassed* (accumulated) a fortune in gold." *Direct objects,* of course, may be persons and living creatures, or they may be things, even abstractions: "She quickly *apprehended* the danger she was in."

Intransitive verbs (v.i.) denote actions that are contained within the subject or that signify what we call states of being: "He *adhered* strictly to his ethical principles." *Adhere* connotes a state of mind, an attitude.

The distinction between transitive and intransitive action is not always easily made, but one way to demonstrate the difference is to make an active statement passive. For example, we can reverse the statement "She admonished the child" and turn it into "The child was admonished by her." The statement above about King Midas can be expressed in the passive as "A fortune in gold was amassed by King Midas." Although transitive actions may be reversed in this way, intransitive actions do not reverse. For example, the sentence "The principles were adhered by him" has no meaning. Some verbs may function both as transitive and intransitive. A simple example is the verb *to sink*: "The small sailboat sank during the heavy storm" (*v.i.*), but "The submarine fired a torpedo that sank the enemy battleship." (*v.t.*).

Most verbs in this first group are transitive, so it would be useful to sort them by the kinds of objects they take; that is, whether they denote actions directed at persons or at things and abstractions. You would, of course, note this information as you look up each unfamiliar word in a dictionary. Here is the list of verbs further sorted:

ACTIONS DIRECTED AT PERSONS

to **absolve** (free from, relieve) someone of guilt or responsibility

to **acclaim** (praise, honor) a person's performance, action, or work

to **accost** (approach, confront) someone

to **admonish** (caution, scold) someone for misbehavior or inaction

to **afflict** (burden, attack) someone with suffering or illness

to **appease** (conciliate) a person, a nation, or a government

to **apprehend** (catch, capture) a suspect or a criminal

ACTIONS DIRECTED AT THINGS OR ABSTRACTIONS

to **abdicate** (relinquish, abandon) a throne, a responsibility

to **accredit** (certify, recognize) a school or university, the value of an idea

to **allot** (distribute, assign) funds, resources

to **amass** (gather, accumulate) a fortune, an army

to **append** (add, match) a section, passage, body of information

to **apprehend** (understand, comprehend, capture) an idea, a concept

to **articulate** (verbalize, clarify, explain) ideas, feelings, understanding

to **array** (arrange) a display, a number of objects

to **assay** (measure, evaluate) a task, a situation

to **assert** (declare, claim, affirm, profess) ideas, an opinion, a judgment

INTRANSITIVE ACTIONS

to **acquiesce** (give in to, agree reluctantly) in demands of others

to **adhere** (hold, cling to, comply) to demands or to principles

to **ally** (join, support) with another person, group, or nation

to **aspire** (strive, seek) to a goal, an achievement

For purposes of study, these verbs could be shuffled, and then resorted, by *connotation.* Which are generally positive in feeling and association, and which are negative? There are many words for which this is not a useful distinction, but appreciation of connotation is often essential to fully understanding the meaning of a word.

POSITIVE

absolve	acclaim	accredit	adhere
ally	aspire		

NEGATIVE

abdicate	accost	acquiesce	admonish
afflict	appease		

215

As you make your notes or compose your flash cards, be sure to include connotation if it is relevant. A dictionary usually does not define a word by its connotation; you must infer it from the meanings and examples offered.

NOUNS

The *nouns* are in bold type:

abdicate	aberrant	abhorrent	**abridgment**
absolve	**acclaim**	accost	accredit
acme	acquiesce	**acquittal**	**adage**
adamant	adhere	adjunct	admonish
adversary	**adversity**	afflict	affluent
agrarian	allot	**allure**	**ally**
altercation	amass	**ambiance**	ambidextrous
ambiguous	ambivalent	**amnesty**	amorphous
anachronistic	**anecdote**	**animation**	appease
append	apprehend	apprehensive	**arbitrator**
archaic	ardent	**armistice**	**array**
arrogant	articulate	**ascendancy**	ashen
aspire	**assay**	assert	astute
asylum	atrocious	**audacity**	autonomous
avarice	averse	**aversion**	avidly
azure			

As you look at a collection of nouns, try to group them in various ways based on the kinds of things or persons they name. Note that in this group only two, **adversary** and **arbitrator,** name persons. This list, however, includes several political or legal terms that would form a useful group for study:

acquittal	**adversary** (adversarial)	**ally**
amnesty	**arbitrator** (arbitration)	**armistice**
ascendancy	**asylum**	

A small group of terms is related to literature:

abridgment   **adage**   **anecdote**

Other terms name attitudes or feelings. (Note the contrast in connotation here.)

POSITIVE

acclaim   **animation**

NEGATIVE

audacity   **aversion**   **avarice**

Finally, there are nouns that name forces, situations, conditions, and other concepts.

acme   **ambiance**   **allure**   **array**

ADJECTIVES

The *adjectives* are in bold type:

abdicate	**aberrant**	**abhorrent**	abridgment
absolve	acclaim	accost	accredit
acme	acquiesce	acquittal	adage
adamant	adhere	**adjunct**	admonish
adversary	adversity	afflict	**affluent**
agrarian	allot	allure	ally
altercation	amass	ambiance	**ambidextrous**
ambiguous	**ambivalent**	amnesty	**amorphous**
anachronistic	anecdote	animation	appease
append	apprehend	**apprehensive**	arbitrator
archaic	**ardent**	armistice	array
arrogant	articulate	ascendancy	**ashen**
aspire	assay	assert	**astute**
asylum	**atrocious**	audacity	autonomous
avarice	**averse**	aversion	avidly
azure			

Because adjectives modify—that is, qualify, limit, or describe—nouns, a useful way to group them is by the nature of what they describe. For example, some of the adjectives in the list above describe human behavior or *actions:*

aberrant   **abhorrent**   **atrocious**

(all strongly negative in connotation)

Several adjectives describe human *attitudes, feelings, aspects of character:*

NEGATIVE

adamant   **ambivalent**   **arrogant**

POSITIVE

ardent   **astute**   **avid**

Still others characterize *the way people appear or express themselves:*

ambiguous   **ambivalent**   **apprehensive**   **averse**

Language may be:

ambiguous   **anachronistic**   **archaic**

Two adjectives relate to color:

ashen   **azure**

One term, **ambidextrous,** describes a physical characteristic.

This particular group contains no adverb forms, but for many of the adjectives in the list, the adverb is formed by adding *-ly*. For example:

aberrantly   **adamantly**   **ambiguously**   **apprehensively**
astutely   **atrociously**   **avidly**

Reminder: When you prepare your own note cards for study, be sure to include all forms of the word. For example, your notes for **ambivalent** (adj.) would also include **ambivalence** (n.).

These groups overlap and should be combined in different ways as you work through larger numbers of words. The process of sorting, or reshuffling, as new categories and associations occur to you is a very effective way to learn new words. Each time you sort, you are actively thinking about a word in a particular context and are associating it with other words; this process is essential to making a word a permanent part of your reading and writing vocabulary.

VOCABULARY FOR STUDY

Below are lists of words that have been collected from Regents exams, Op-Ed pages, and book reviews.

Vocabulary from Regents Exams

abdicate	aberrant	abhorrent	abridgment
absolve	acclaim	accost	accredit
acme	acquiesce	acquittal	adage
adhere	adjunct	admonish	adversity
afflict	agrarian	allot	allure
ally	altercation	amass	ambiance
ambidextrous	ambiguous	ambivalent	amnesty
amorphous	anachronistic	anecdotes	animation
appease	apprehend	arbitrator	archaic
ardent	armistice	array	arrogantly
ascendancy	ashen	aspire	assay
astute	asylum	atrocious	audacity
autonomous	avarice	averse	aversion
avid	azure		

badger	barrage	bask	beguile
belied	bemused	benevolent	berate
blatant	bleary	boisterous	brazen
breach	brevity		

cache	carnage	celebrated	chafe
chagrin	charade	charisma	chasm
clandestine	clique	coalition	collate

commencement	commiserate	conception	congeal
consecrate	constrict	converse	convivial
craven	credence	crestfallen	cringe
dauntless	de facto	debonair	decrepit
deduce	deferred	deflect	defunct
deified	deluge	delve	demeaning
denizen	depict	deride	derogatory
desist	desolate	deter	detest
diffuse	dilemma	diminutive	discord
discreet	dissidence	dissuade	divulge
domain	dredge	dynamic	
eccentric	edify	eject	elicit
elude	elusive	embroil	eminence
encore	endorse	endow	enfeeble
enhance	ensnare	entail	entreaty
envoy	equanimity	equilibrium	equitable
equivocal	eradicate	erratic	escapade
euphoric	eviction	exemplary	exodus
exonerate	expedite	exploitation	exulted
facet	fallible	fanatic	fanfare
farcical	feasible	fiasco	fidelity
finesse	finite	flail	fleeting
forage	foreboding	formidable	fortitude
fortuitous	fracas	frugal	futility
garish	garrulous	gaudy	genial
genuine	geriatric	gesticulate	grapple
grate	gratuity	grievously	grisly
guise	guttural		
hallowed	harangue	harrowing	heinous
heretical	hinder	homage	humid

idiosyncrasies	ignoble	illuminate	immutable
impartial	impending	imperative	imperceptible
imperiled	imperious	impertinent	imprudent
inadvertent	inaugural	incensed	incessant
incognito	incompetent	incorrigible	indignant
indisputably	induce	infernal	infringe
ingenuity	inherent	inimitable	innocuous
insatiable	insolent	insomnia	insubordinate
insurgent	inundated	invoked	irate
irksome	irrational	itinerant	

jeer	jocular	jovial	juncture
jut			

lacerated	lackluster	lament	languorously
latent	lateral	lavish	laxity
lesion	lineage	liquidate	loquacious
lucrative	lugubrious	lull	

madcap	maim	malefactor	malice
malleable	marauding	martial	meager
mediate	melancholy	meticulous	militant
misconstrue	misgivings	mitigate	mollify
morose	mortify	mundane	muzzle

nefarious	negligible	nepotism	niche
nimble	nonentity	nostalgia	notorious
nullification	nuptial	nurture	

obliquely	obliterate	obstinate	oligarchy
omnipotent	omniscient	onslaught	opportune
optimum	oscillate	oust	ouster
override			

pacifism	palatable	pandemonium	parable
paraphrase	penchant	perjury	perpetual
perplexity	philanthropic	piety	pinnacle
placid	plague	plausible	plight
poise	precariously	precipice	precludes
prestige	prevail	procrastinate	prodigious
profoundly	proponent	protrude	prowess
proxy	putrid		

qualms	quandary

ramification	rampant	ramshackle	rancid
rant	rapport	ravenous	recalcitrant
reciprocal	recoil	recrimination	rectify
refute	reminiscent	reparation	repercussion
repress	resolute	retort	revamped
reverberate	revulsion	roster	rouse
rue	ruinous	russet	

sacrosanct	salve	sanction	sanctity
saunter	scandalous	scathing	scrupulous
scrutiny	seedy	sheen	shortcomings
shrewd	singularly	skeptical	skulk
sleek	slipshod	smolder	sporadic
squalor	stalwart	stark	stealthily
strew	strut	subliminal	submissive
subside	subsidize	substantiate	subtlety
sullen	sumptuous	superfluous	suppress
surcease	surreptitious	swagger	synopsis

tainted	tally	tawny	tenacity
throng	token	topple	transcend
transient	trauma	traverse	trifling
trudge	tumult		

unassuming	uncanny	unnerve	unobtrusive
unpalatable	unscrupulous	utilitarian	
vanquish	variance	vehement	verbatim
verbose	veritable	viable	vigilance
virtually			
waive	warily	weather (vb.)	whack
wield	wily	wrangle	wrath
writhe			
yield			
zenith			

Vocabulary from Op-Ed Pages

a priori	abdicate	aberration	abrogation
abysmal	abyss	accede	acclimate
accolade	accrue	acrimonious	actuary
acumen	ad hoc	adamant	addled
aegis	affidavit	affront	aggrieved
agnostics	albeit	alleviate	allude (to)
amalgamation	ambivalence	amiss	amorphous
androgyny	annals	annotate	anoint
antidote	antipathy	apathy	append
arbiter	arbitrage	arbitrary	arcane
archetype	archive	ardent	artifice
ascribe	assessment	assimilate	assuage
asylum	au courant	audit	autonomous
barrage	beguile	beleaguered	benighted
bereft	berth	besmirch	bias

bipartisan	blatant	blighted	blunder
brass (slang def.)	brute (vb.)	budgetary	bureaucrats
burgeoning			

cacophony	cajole	callous	canard
candor	canonical/canon	capitulate	cataclysmic
caveat	censure	chasm	chimera
circumspect	civics	clandestine	clerical
coda	coffer	collusion	compliant
complicit	compound (vb.)	compulsion	concede
conciliate	conciliatory	concubine	condone
confrere	conspiratorial	constituent	contemporaries
contend	contender	contingent	conundrum
convene	conversant	conversely	convocation
covet	crafty	craven	credibility
cul-de-sac	cupidity	curtail	cushy
cynical	cynicism		

daunting	debase	decadence	decibel
decree	decry	deferment	defrocked
defunct	deluded	demagogue	demise
demonize	demur	demystify	denounce
denuded	denunciation	deplorable	depredation
deprivation	derail	derangement	deregulation
deride	derisive	despot	deter
detract	didactic	disavow	discernible
discourse	discretion	discretionary	disenchantment
disingenuous	disjointed	dispel	dispirit
disposition	disquieting	dissemble	disseminate
dissident	dissipate	diversity	don (vb.)
doting	Draconian		

earmark	egregious	electorate	elixir
eminence	empathetic	empathy	encapsulate

enclave	enfranchise	enmesh	ennobling
ennui	envoy	epitomize	equanimity
equivocate	eradicate	erode	ethos
eugenics	eviscerate	exhort	exonerate
exorbitant	expenditure	expostulate	expunge
exude			

fallacious	farcical	fedora	feint
fiasco	finagle	firebrand	fiscal
flounder (vb.)	flummoxed	fodder (fig.)*	folly
forlorn	formidable	formulate	fray (n.)
frenetic	fritter (vb.)	frothing	furor
fusillade (fig.)	futility		

gaffe	gag rule	galvanize	garner
gaudy	gauge	gerrymander	glut
gouging	grapple	grim	grotesque
gubernatorial	guffaw		

habeus corpus	hackneyed	hamlet	hapless
harbor (vb.)	heckle	hectoring	heresy
hoosegow (slang)	hubris	hyperbole	

iconography	ideological	idiosyncratic	idyllic
ignominious	ilk	impede	imperil
implement (vb.)	implicit	importune	impunity
incendiary	incessant	incipient	incite
incontrovertible	incumbent	indefatigable	indigenous
indignity	ineptitude	infiltrate	infirmity
inflationary	infuse	inherent	innuendo
inquisitorial	insignia	insular	integrity

---

*In this case, consider the figurative meaning of the words.

interlocking	intransigence	inure	invaluable
inviolate	irk	irredentism	

lacerate	laconic	lambaste	languish
largess	latent	laureate	lebensraum
leery	leitmotif	levitate	litany
lout	lucid		

malady	malaise	malign	manifestation
mantra	martyr	maudlin	megalomaniac
meritorious	meticulous	milieu	mimesis
molder	monolith	morass	moratorium
moribund	morose	mortar	murky
myopic			

nadir	nascent	nexus	nomadic
nuance			

obfuscate	obsolescence	obstreperous	oddity
odious	ominous	omnipresent	oncology
oppression	outlay	overhaul	overt
overweening			

palliative	panacea	pandering	paradox
paramount	parochial	parsimonious	partisan (adj.)
passel	pathology	patrician	pedantic
peevish	pejorative	penchant	perennial
peripheral	pernicious	peroration	perpetuate
perquisite	perversion	pillage	pinnacle
pious	pique	placable/placate	plaudits
plight	plummet	plunder	pogrom
polarization	polemic	polyglot	portend
pragmatism	prattle	preeminent	preempt
preclude	presage	probity	profound

progeny
propensity
psyche
purvey/purveyor

prohibitive
protocol
pugnacity
pusillanimous

proliferate
provocation
pundit
pyrotechnics

proliferation
prurience
purport

quagmire
quintessential

qualm

quaver

quibble

rabid (fig.)
rapprochement
reconcile
reparations
restorative
revile
rudimentary

rakish
raucous
rectitude
replete
retributive
rhetoric
ruse

rancor
realpolitik
rejoinder
resolute
reverberate
rifle (vb.)

rapacious
recidivism
relegate
resonance
reverence
rogue

salve (vb.)
scoff
sham
siphon
sophomoric
spate
staid
stint
stymie
sullen
supersede
sword of
  Damocles

sartorial
scourge
shaman
snare
sordid
speculative
stark
stipend
subsidize
summarily
supplant
sycophant

sashay
seamy
shore up
snide
sorghum
staggering
staunch
strident
substantive
sumptuary
surfeit
synergy

scion
self-effacing
shudder
sobriquet
sovereignty
stagnation
steely eyed
stringent
subterfuge
sunder
swindle

temporal
throng
tout
troupe

temporize
thwart
transgression
tsunami

tenacity
torpor
transitory
turbulent

tendentious
totter
treacherous

undergird	undermine	undiluted	unduly
unencumbered	unfettered	unilateral	universality
unprecedented	unrelenting	unscrupulous	usurp

vagaries	venality	veracity	verdant
vestige	vexing	viable	victimize
vigilante	vilify	visceral	vituperation
volatile	voyeurs		

waffling	wallow	wastrels	welter
wheedling	winnow	writ	writhe
wrongheaded			

xenophobia

zeal	zeitgeist

Vocabulary from Book Reviews

accolade	accretion	accrue	acerbic
acolyte	acrimonious	acumen	adage
adduce	adherent	adumbrate	adversity
aesthetic	albeit	alluring	amatory
amiable	amok	anapest	ancillary
animus	annotate	antipodes	aphrodisiac
aplomb	apotheosis	arbiter	arbitrary
archaic	ardor	arduous	arsenal
ascetic	asinine	aspire	attenuate
austere	authorial		

banal	barren	bathetic	bedraggled
bemused	bestiality	bevy	bifurcation
blight	blithe	bohemian	boorish
boulevardier	bowdlerize	Byzantine	

cache	cadence	canny	catharsis
caveat	chafe	charisma	chastening
chastise	chic	clandestine	cleric
cloying	coffer	cohere	coherence
colloquial	compendious	compendium	complicity
congenial	consign	contend	contrivance
copious	counterpoise	covert	credo
cribbed	crotchety	cupidity	curmudgeon
cursory			
dash	daunting	debunk	deft
delineate	delude	demigod	denouement
deploy	despotic	detritus	devolve
dichotomy	didactic	discursive	dispense
dispossess	dither	divagation	divergence
droll	duplicity	dysfunctional	dystopia
eccentric	eclectic	edify	egregious
elegy	elocution	elucidate	enclave
encomium	ensconce	entreaty	envisage
epigraph	epitomize	equanimity	eradicate
Eros	eschew	esoteric	espouse
esthetic	ethereal	ethos	evangelical
evocative	exacerbate	exhort	exigency
existential	expansive	expatriate	expurgate
exultant			
fabulist	facsimile	faction	farce
fervid	florid	foray	forbearance
formulaic	fruition	furtive	
galvanize	gamut	gorgon	grapple
guile	gustatory		

hackneyed	hagiography	harrowing	hedonism
hewn (details)			

iconoclast	iconography	idiosyncratic	idyll/idyllic
ignite (fig.)	imminent	imperative	impetus
implacable	impresario	incoherent	incongruous
incur	indelible	indeterminate	indigenous
ineffable	ineffectual	inept	inextricably
insidious	insinuation	insouciance	intelligentsia
intercede	intractable	inured	invidious
irreverent	itinerant		

jarring	jettison	jostle	Joycean

kamikaze

lacuna	lament	languish	lapidary
largess	libertine	lilting	litigious
loquacious	Lothario	lucid	lucrative
lyricism			

macabre	malaise	malevolent	malign
manifold (adj.)	matrix	mawkish	melodrama
mendacious	mercurial	mien	milieu
minutiae	misogyny	mogul	moldering
mordant	moribund	mosaic	muddle
murky	musing	muster	myopia

naiveté	narcissistic	nascent	natter
nihilism	nimble	nonpareil	non sequitur
noxious	nuance		

obfuscation	opprobrium	ostensible	ostracize

palatable	pantheon	paradigm	pathos
paucity	pedagogical	pelt (vb.)	penchant
penumbra	perdurable	peregrination	perennial
petulance	piety	placebo	plodding
portent	portentous	practitioner	pragmatic
prattle	precocious	premonition	prescient
prevaricate	prodigious	prosaic	protean
punitive	purport		

querulous	query	quintessential	quixotic
quotidian			

rancor	rapacious	rapture	rancor
raucous	reap	recalcitrant	recapitulate
relegate	repatriation	replete	repository
reverence	revile	rhetorical	ricochet
riff	risible	riveting	rudimentary
ruminate			

sagacity	salacious	sally forth	sap (vb.)
savor	scatological	scourge	scuttlebutt
searing	sedentary	self-effacement	sepulchral
shaman	shenanigans	snippet	solicitous
spurn	squander	stanch	standoffish
staunch	stilted	stultifying	sublimate
sublime	subterfuge	succumb	sunder
supercilious	surreptitious	surrogate	symbiosis
symmetry	synoptic		

taut	teeter	temporal	thrall
throng	titillating	torpid	tortuous
traffic (vb.)	transcendent	transient	transitory
transmogrify	travail	treatise	trenchant
trilogy	truism	tweak	

unabashed	uncanny	unfathomable	unflinching
vacillate	valediction	vapid	venal
venality	verisimilitude	vernacular	vicissitude
vignette	vindictiveness	virtuosity	vis à vis
vitriol	voluminous	vortex	votary
waft	welter	wend	whimsy
withal			

Chapter 11

SPELLING

We know how to spell many words because we recognize them from our reading and because we have, from childhood or as English language learners, developed awareness of the conventions of English spelling. Even though English spelling may seem confusing at times, most of the troublesome sounds or patterns reflect the history of English pronunciation and the fact that the English language developed after the forces of William the Conqueror, a Frenchman from Normandy, had invaded and settled in what is now the island of Great Britain. The resulting language is a fusion of Anglo-Saxon, French, and Latin.

SPELLING ON WRITING EXAMS

Does spelling count? The rubric for each essay on the English Regents exam includes the "conventions" as a quality to be assessed. These are defined as ". . . conventional spelling, punctuation, paragraphing, capitalization, grammar and usage"; and on the SAT essay, frequent errors in grammar, usage, and mechanics are considered significant weaknesses in a student's writing.

If you know you have difficulties in spelling, use this chapter to review the common patterns of English spelling and to study the list of words commonly misspelled.

A word misspelled is a word misused, and egregious spelling errors may affect the scoring of your essays. You would also be expected to observe conventional spelling in preparing a college essay, a resume, or cover letter, and would avoid the spelling "shortcuts" we sometimes find useful in composing e-mail or text messages.

SPELLING RULES AND PATTERNS

As you review spelling rules and patterns, you need to be familiar with the following terms:

vowels The letters *a, e, i o, u,* and occasionally *y* signal the vowel, or sustained, sounds in English. The variations in these vowel sounds are spelled as combinations of more than one letter or as combinations with consonants.

consonants In English, the consonant letters and sounds are composed by the following: *b, c, d, f, g, h, j, k, l, m, n, p, q, r, s, t, v, w, x*. In contrast to vowels, consonant sounds do not sustain.

syllable A vowel sound or a combination of a vowel and consonant sounds that makes up a single impulse, or "beat," in a word. Words of one syllable: *think, read, act*. Words of two syllables: *reflect, insist, review*. We regularly use words of six or more syllables: *unintentionally, coincidentally*.

endings Single letters or syllables that indicate grammatical forms, such as noun plurals or verb conjugations. English, in contrast to other languages high school students may study, has relatively few "endings." Among them are *-s* or *-es* to form plural nouns or to indicate third-person *singular* verb forms, and the verb endings *-ing* and *-ed*.

suffixes Endings used to form new words and different parts of speech: *love, lovely, loveliness; occur, occurrence*. The addition of endings and suffixes to words often alters their spelling. (See next page.)

prefixes Units of one or two syllables that, like suffixes, are not "words" in themselves but have distinct meanings. They are placed at the beginning of existing words, or of what are called *stems* or *roots*. (See the section Roots and Prefixes from Latin and Greek, Chapter 10, for many examples in English of Latin and Greek roots.) Words formed in this way are spelled to show their meanings: *illogical, overreact, misspell*.

Although most spelling "rules" have exceptions, there are many common patterns for spelling in English. The first group (pages 234–239) involves adding endings or suffixes.

Words That End in Silent *e*

➤ Drop the *e* before adding a suffix or ending that begins with a vowel:

dare	+ -ing	➤	= daring	➤	+ -ed = dared
hope	+ -ing	➤	= hoping	➤	+ -ed = hoped
amuse	+ -ing	➤	= amusing	➤	+ -ed = amused
revise	+ -ion	➤	= revision	➤	+ -ed = revised
advise	+ -able	➤	= advisable,	➤	+ -ed = advised
reverse	+ -ible	➤	= reversible	➤	+ -ed = reversed

➤ When adding *s* or a suffix that begins with a consonant, retain the *e*:

amuse	➤	amuses	➤	amusement
arrange	➤	arranges	➤	arrangement
hope	➤	hopes	➤	hopeless
huge	➤	hugeness	➤	hugely
place	➤	places	➤	placement
spite	➤	spiteful		
sure	➤	surely		

➤ When the word ends in *ce* or in *ge,* retain the *e* when adding *able* or *ous:*

change	➤	changeable
peace	➤	peaceable
service	➤	serviceable
advantage	➤	advantageous
courage	➤	courageous
outrage	➤	outrageous

➤ But drop the silent *e* before adding *ing:*

change	➤	changing
rage	➤	raging
service	➤	servicing
trace	➤	tracing

➤ Note the following **exceptions:**

argue	➤	argument
true	➤	truly
judge	➤	judgment
nine	➤	ninety
whole	➤	wholly

Words That End in y

➤ For words preceded by a consonant, change the *y* to an *i* before adding a suffix:

accompany	➤	accompaniment		
busy	➤	business	➤	busily
easy	➤	easily		
funny	➤	funnier	➤	funniest
happy	➤	happiness	➤	happily
lonely	➤	loneliness		
silly	➤	silliness	➤	sillier	➤	silliest

➤ The same pattern applies when we add *s* to form plural nouns or third-person-singular verb forms:

army	➤	armies
baby	➤	babies
city	➤	cities
marry	➤	marries
try	➤	tries
worry	➤	worries

➤ But retain the *y* before adding *ing, ism, ish*:

baby	➤	babyish	➤ babying
copy	➤	copying	
crony	➤	cronyism	
marry	➤	marrying	
try	➤	trying	
worry	➤	worrying	

➤ For words that end in *y* preceded by a vowel, retain *y:*

annoy	➤	annoys	➤	annoyance	➤	annoyed	➤	annoying
boy	➤	boys	➤	boyish				
day	➤	days						
destroy	➤	destroys	➤	destroyed	➤	destroying		
monkey	➤	monkeys						
play	➤	plays	➤	played	➤	playing	➤	player ➤
playful								
valley	➤	valleys						

➤ However:

say	➤	says	➤	**said**
pay	➤	pays	➤	**paid**

Double Letters

In writing, we must often stop to think whether to double letters in adding suffixes to words. Here are guidelines to follow.

➤ For one-syllable words that end in a single consonant preceded by a single vowel, *double* the final consonant before a suffix beginning with a vowel:

bat	➤	batter	➤	batting		
big	➤	bigger	➤	biggest		
fit	➤	fitted	➤	fitting	➤	fittest
sit	➤	sitter	➤	sitting		
spot	➤	spotty	➤	spotted		

As you look at the examples, you will see that the effect of the double consonant is to retain the pronunciation of the base word.

➤ Words formed by adding prefixes to one-syllable words follow the same pattern:

outfit	➤	outfitted ➤	outfitter
unwrap	➤	unwrapped	

➤ For one-syllable words that have double vowels or that end in more than one consonant, do *not* double the final consonant:

beat	➤	beating	
neat	➤	neatest	
mail	➤	mailing ➤	mailed
read	➤	reading ➤	reader
fail	➤	failure	
list	➤	listed	
faint	➤	fainted	

➤ However:

quit ➤ quitting

Because *u* must follow the *q*, *-ui* is considered a single vowel.

➤ Do not double the final consonant for words ending in *w, x,* or *y:*

draw	➤	drawing	
mix	➤	mixing	
play	➤	playing ➤	player

It is when we add endings to words of more than one syllable that spelling errors commonly occur.

➤ For words of more than one syllable ending in one vowel and one consonant, double the final consonant before an ending that begins with a vowel *if the last syllable of the base word is accented*:

confer	➤	conferred
infer	➤	inferred
refer	➤	referred
begin	➤	beginning
deter	➤	deterrence
omit	➤	omitted
commit	➤	committed
occur	➤	occurrence
equip	➤	equipped

➤   If the accent is *not* on the syllable to which the ending is added, *do not* double the final consonant:

benefit	➤	benefited	
credit	➤	credited	
open	➤	opening	
happen	➤	happening	
develop	➤	developing ➤	developed
deliver	➤	delivered ➤	delivering

➤   Note how the shift in accent determines spelling:

confer	➤	conference
infer	➤	inference
prefer	➤	preference
refer	➤	reference

Note the following exceptions:

➤   The following words double the final consonant:

program	➤	programmed ➤	programmer
question	➤	questionnaire	
excel	➤	excellence ➤	excellent

➤   Either form is considered acceptable for the following, but the first form, with a single -*l*, is preferred:

canceled	➤	cancelled
traveled	➤	travelled
traveling	➤	travelling

Adding Prefixes and Suffixes

With the exception of the patterns reviewed on the previous pages, which reflect how we pronounce the words, most words formed by adding prefixes and suffixes retain the spelling of each separate part. As a result, the full meaning of the word is reflected in its spelling:

mis + spell + ed	➤	= misspelled (both *s*'s are required)
mis + understand + ing	➤	= misunderstanding
dis + agree + able	➤	= disagreeable
dis + taste + ful	➤	= distasteful
dis + appear + ance	➤	= disappearance
dis + satisfaction	➤	= dissatisfaction

un + necessary	➤	= unnecessary
un + ending	➤	= unending
cool + ly	➤	= coolly
moral + ly	➤	= morally
co + operate	➤	= cooperate
de + emphasize	➤	= de-emphasize
re + entry	➤	= reentry
mean + ness	➤	= meanness
amuse + ment	➤	= amusement

➤ Note that words ending in *c* add a *k* as follows:

panic, panics	➤	panicky, panicked, panicking
mimic, mimics	➤	mimicked, mimicking
picnic, picnics	➤	picnicking, picnickers

Words That Include *ie* or *ei*

➤ Is it *i* before *e* or *e* before *i*? This is the spelling pattern everyone remembers.

i before *e*:

chief	thief	relief	yield

➤ Except after *c*:

receive	ceiling	conceit

➤ Or, when *ei* sounds long *a*:

sleigh	neighbor	weigh	veil

There are, however, several **exceptions** to this pattern. They must be memorized:

caffeine	counterfeit	either	financier	foreign
forfeit	leisure	neither	plebeian	protein
seize	sheik	sovereign	surfeit	weird

Noun Plurals

➤ Noun *plurals* are generally formed by adding *s*:

cat	→	cats
house	→	houses
delay	→	delays
piano	→	pianos

➤ Nouns ending in *s, sh, ch, x,* and *z,* add *es* to form the plural:

watch	→	watches
brush	→	brushes
waltz	→	waltzes

➤ Nouns ending in the consonant *y*: add *es*:

spy	→	spies
lady	→	ladies
quantity	→	quantities

➤ However, do *not* alter the spelling of proper names:

There are two "Sallys" in the junior class.

Shakespeare wrote plays about the "Henrys" of England.

➤ Some words ending in *o* add *es* to form the plural:

echo	→	echoes
tomato	→	tomatoes
potato	→	potatoes
hero	→	heroes
veto	→	vetoes

➤ Some nouns ending in *f* or *fe* form the plural with *ves*:

calf	→	calves
elf	→	elves
knife	→	knives
life	→	lives
self	→	selves
thief	→	thieves
wife	→	wives

➤ Other nouns change their form internally:

man	→	men
woman	→	women
child	→	children
mouse	→	mice.

➤ In compound expressions, the principal noun is made plural:

sisters-in-law

passers-by

spoonsful

Homophones

Many spelling problems occur because words have syllables whose sounds are alike but could be spelled in more than one way: for example, *cede, ceed, sede*. These are called homophones.

➤ The most common form is *cede:*

precede   concede   antecede   intercede

➤ A few forms are spelled *ceed:*

exceed   proceed   succeed

➤ Only one form is spelled *sede:*

supersede

➤ For *able, ible,* the more common form is *able:*

curable   imaginable   lovable   movable   peaceable

➤ Though fewer in number, there are many common words ending in *ible*:

admissible   compatible   credible   eligible   horrible
intelligible   legible   perceptible   possible   visible

➤ There are also words ending in *ance, ant,* or *ence, ent:*

assistant   attendant   dominant   extravagant   fragrant
hesitance   ignorance   relevance   resistance

➤ Note, however:

adolescent   competent   correspondent   current   frequent

negligence   permanence   vehemence

➤ Many nouns end in -*er*:

consumer   defender   interpreter   organizer

philosopher

➤ Note, however:

actor   creator   counselor   governor   professor

tailor

NOTE: *The careful writer must memorize the most common spellings. We cannot always use a dictionary or a spellcheck program!*

On the following pages you will find a list of words often confused and an extensive list of words commonly misspelled.

WORDS COMMONLY CONFUSED

Many words in English sound or look very similar to one another. Such words are often "misspelled" as a result of the writer's confusion about them. Here are some of the most commonly confused words; *all are correctly spelled*. Be sure you know their respective meanings.

accept/except	access/excess
adapt/adopt	advice/advise
affect/effect	allusion/illusion
already/all ready	altogether/all together
breath/breathe	choose/chose/chosen
cite/sight/site	cloths/clothes
coarse/course	complement/compliment
desert/dessert	device/devise
discreet/discrete	dyeing/dying
elicit/illicit	elude/allude
envelop/envelope	formally/formerly
fourth/forth	hear/here

holy/wholly	hoping/hopping
idle/idol	imminent/eminent/emanate
its/it's	loath/loathe
local/locale	loose/lose
medal/meddle/metal/mettle	moral/morale
night/knight	principal/principle
quite/quiet	rain/reign/rein
right/rite	shone/shown
sight/site	stationary/stationery
than/then	their/there/they're
thorough/through	though/thought
threw/through	throne/thrown
to/too/two	vain/vane/vein
weather/whether	which/witch
who's/whose	your/you're

WORDS COMMONLY MISSPELLED

You will recognize the most familiar and the most notorious spelling demons in this list.

absence	absolutely	academic	accept
acceptance	accessory	accidentally	accommodate
accompanying	accomplish	accuracy	achievement
acknowledge	acquaintance	acquire	across
actually	address	adequately	adherence
adjournment	adjustment	admittance	adolescent
advantage	advantageous	advertisement	advising
against	aggravate	aggravation	aggressive
alleviate	alliance	ally	almanac
already	altitude	amateur	ambassador
amendment	among	analysis	analyze
ancient	angrily	announcement	annually
antagonist	antibiotic	anticipation	antique
anxious	apologetically	apologies	apologize

apology	apostrophe	apparently	appreciate
appropriate	approximate	aptitude	architecture
Arctic	argue	argument	arising
arrangement	article	artistically	ascend
ascent	assassin	assent	assistance
assumption	assurance	atheist	athlete
athletic	attempt	attendance	attractive
audience	authoritative	authority	auxiliary
availability	avalanche	average	awfully
awkward			

bachelor	baggage	banana	bankruptcy
bargain	barrel	basement	basically
beautify	becoming	before	beginning
belief	believing	beneficial	benefit
benefited	bibliography	bicycle	biscuit
boring	boundary	breakfast	breath
breathe	bribery	brief	brilliant
Britain	brittle	bruise	budget
buoy	buoyant	bureau	burglar
burglarize	business	businesslike	busy

cafeteria	caffeine	calculator	calendar
calorie	campaign	candidate	cannibal
canoe	capable	capacity	captain
career	carrying	cashier	catastrophe
category	caucus	carefully	cease
ceiling	cellar	cemetery	censor
censure	century	certainly	challenge
changeable	changing	channel	characterize
chauffeur	chief	chimney	chivalry
chloride	cholera	choose	choosing
choral	chose	chuckle	cite
client	closet	clustered	coalition
coherence	collar	college	colonel
column	combustible	comfortable	coming

commencement commercial commission commit
committee communal community companies
comparative comparison compatible compel
compelled competitive competitor comprehensible
conceivable conceive concentrate conception
condemn condescend conference conferred
confidence confidential connotation connote
conqueror conscience conscious consequence
consequently considerable considerably consistency
consistent conspicuous contemporary contempt
contemptible contemptuous continual continuous
contribution controlled controlling controversial
convenience convenient convertible convocation
cool coolly cooperate corollary
corps correlate corrode corrupt
counterfeit courteous courtesy cousin
credible creditor credulous crisis
critical criticism criticize cruel
cruelly cupola curiosity curious
current curriculum curtain customary
customer cyclical cylinder

dangerous debris debt debtor
deceit deceitful deceived decency
decent deception decide decision
default defendant defense defer
deference deferred define definitely
definition deity delegate deliberately
deodorant dependable dependent depth
deputy descend descendant descent
desert desirable despair despite
dessert destroy detriment devastate
developed development deviate device
devise dexterity diameter different
difficult dilemma diligent dining
disappearance disappointment disapprove disaster

disastrous	discern	disciple	disciplinary
discipline	discomfort	discriminate	discriminatory
disease	disillusion	dispatch	disposal
disregard	dissatisfied	dissent	dissimilar
dissipate	divinity	divisible	division
doesn't	dominant	dominate	dormitory
dough	dramatize	drunkenness	due
dully	duly	during	dye
dyeing	dying		

earnest	easily	economically	economy
ecstasy	edge	edgy	edition
editor	effect	efficiency	efficient
eight	eighth	eighty	electoral
elicit	eligible	eliminate	eloquent
elude	emanate	embarrass	embassy
emigrant	emigrate	emphasis	emphasize
emphatic	empirical	employee	encouragement
encouraging	endeavor	enough	entangle
enterprise	entertain	entirely	envelop
envelope	environment	equality	equally
equipment	equipped	equivalent	erroneous
escapade	especially	essential	everything
evidently	exaggerate	exaggeration	exceed
excellence	exceptional	excessive	excitable
excitement	exclusive	exclusively	excursion
exhibit	exhibition	existence	expedite
expedition	experience	experiment	explanation
explanatory	exploit	explore	extension
extraordinary	extravagant	extremely	

facility	fallacious	fallacy	familiar
fantasy	fascinate	fashion	fatality
faulty	favorable	favorite	February
felicity	feminine	feminist	feud
fictitious	fidelity	fiend	fiery

filial   finally   financial   financier
flair   fluent   forbidden   forehead
foreign   forewarn   forgetting   formally
formerly   forth   forty   fourth
fraternity   freight   frequency   frequently
fried   friendless   friendliness   friendly
friendship   fulfill   fulfillment   fundamental
furious   furthermore

gaiety   gallant   gardener   gaseous
gasoline   generally   generation   generic
genetics   genius   genuine   global
glorious   glossary   goddess   government
governor   gradually   grammar   grandeur
graphics   grief   grievance   grieve
grievous   grocery   guarantee   guidance
guilt   gymnasium

hammer   handkerchief   handsome   happiness
harassment   harpoon   headache   heard
heathen   heavily   height   heir
hereditary   heroes   heroic   heroine
hindrance   honorable   hopeful   hopeless
hoping   hopping   humidity   humor
humorous   hundredth   hungrily   hurrying
hybrid   hygiene   hypnosis   hypnotism
hypnotize   hypocrisy   hypocrite   hypothesis
hysteria

icicle   ignorant   illegal   illicit
illusion   illusory   imaginary   imagine
immaculate   immediately   immense   immigrant
immoderate   impressionable incidentally   incompetent
inconvenience   incredible   indebted   indecisive
indefinite   independence   indispensable   indivisible

indulge	interference	inertia	inevitable
infancy	inferiority	infinite	ingenious
ingenuity	ingenuous	inhabitant	initiative
innocence	inquiry	insistent	inspiration
intelligence	intentionally	interaction	intercede
interrelated	interrupt	intimate	introduce
invisible	ironic	irony	irrelevant
irresistible	irritable	island	isle
jealousy	jewelry	journal	journey
judge	judgment	junction	justifiable
justify			
kerosene	kindergarten	knight	knowledge
kowtow			
laboratory	laborer	launch	lawyer
league	legacy	legible	legislator
legitimate	leisure	leisurely	lenient
library	license	lighten	lightning
likelihood	likely	limb	literary
literature	liveliness	loathe	loneliness
lonely	loose	lose	losing
lottery	lovable	loveless	luncheon
luscious	luxurious	lying	
macaroni	machinery	magazine	magnificent
maintenance	malaria	manageable	management
managing	maneuver	marriage	massacre
mathematics	maximum	meanness	medical
medicinal	medicine	medieval	medley
melancholy	memorable	merchandise	merchant
merger	meteor	mettle	miniature
minimum	minister	miracle	mirror
mischief	mischievous	misdemeanor	misfit
missile	missionary	misspell	monarch

monogram	monopoly	moral	morale
mortgage	mortified	mosquitoes	mountain
movable	muffle	muscle	mysterious
naturally	necessary	necessity	negligent
neighborly	nickel	niece	ninety
ninth	noticeable	notorious	nuclear
nuisance			
obedience	oblige	obnoxious	obscure
observant	obstacle	obtuse	occasionally
occur	occurred	occurrence	official
omission	omitted	opinion	opportunity
opposite	optimism	orchard	ordinarily
organize	originally	outrageous	overrated
owing			
package	pageant	paid	pamphlet
parachute	paradox	paradoxical	paragraph
parallel	paralysis	parcel	parenthesis
parliament	partial	particle	particularly
pastime	patient	patriotic	patriotism
patron	peaceable	peasant	peculiar
pennant	perceive	percentage	perception
perilous	permanence	permanent	permissible
perplex	persistence	persistent	personally
personnel	persuade	persuasion	persuasive
pertinent	philosophy	physical	physician
pianos	picnic	picnicking	piece
pierce	pigeon	pillar	planned
plausible	playwright	pleasant	pledge
plentiful	politeness	politician	popularity
portable	possess	possession	possibility
possibly	potatoes	practicality	prairie
prayer	precede	precedent	precious
predominant	preference	preferred	prejudice

preoccupied	preparation	presence	presidency
prestige	prevail	prevalence	priest
primitive	principal	principles	priority
privilege	probability	probable	procedural
procedure	proceed	professional	professor
prohibitive	prologue	promenade	prominent
promising	pronunciation	propel	propeller
prophecy	proprietor	psychiatrist	psychoanalysis
psychologist	psychosomatic	publicity	punctuation
purchase	purchasing	purgatory	purity
pursue	pursuit		
qualified	qualitative	quandary	quantity
query	questionable	quiet	quite
radiant	ratify	realize	really
recede	receipt	receive	recessive
recognizable	recollect	recommend	recruit
recur	reference	referred	reign
rein	reliable	relieve	reluctance
remembrance	reminisce	repetitious	requirement
requisition	residence	resistance	resolving
resourceful	responsible	restaurant	reveille
rewrite	rhapsody	rhetoric	rheumatism
rhyme	rhythm	ridiculous	rigidity
routine			
sacrifice	safety	salary	satellite
satisfactory	savage	scandal	scarcely
scary	scenery	scent	schedule
schism	scissors	scold	sculptor
secede	secrecy	secretary	seize
seniority	senseless	sensible	sensitive
separate	sergeant	several	shadowy
shady	shepherd	sheriff	shield
shining	shoulder	siege	sieve

significant	simile	simultaneous	sincerely
singular	siphon	skillful	society
solemn	solicit	soliloquy	solos
sophomore	source	sovereign	spaghetti
specimen	spectacles	spectacular	spirited
sponsor	squirrel	statue	stifle
stomach	straight	strategy	strength
strenuous	stressful	studying	submission
subsidy	substantial	substitute	subtle
succeed	successful	successive	sufficient
suffix	summary	superb	surgeon
surprise	susceptible	suspense	suspicion
suspicious	sustained	syllable	syllabus
symbol	symmetrical	sympathize	symphonic
symptom	synonym		

tableau	tailor	technique	temperament
temperature	temporary	tendency	terrific
terrifying	territory	testimony	thematic
theoretical	therefore	thorough	tireless
tobacco	tolerance	tomato	tomatoes
tomorrow	tournament	traction	traffic
trafficked	tragedy	tragic	transfer
transferred	transistor	transitive	transparent
traveler	treachery	treason	treasury
truant	truly	turmoil	twelfth
twilight	typical	tyranny	tyrant

umbrella	unanimous	unconscious	undoubtedly
unison	unnecessary	unprecedented	unveil
urban	urgent	usually	utensil
utterance			

vacuum	valleys	valuable	variety
various	varying	vegetable	vehicle
vengeance	vengeful	vicinity	victim

| village | villain | villainous | vinegar |
| volcano | volunteer | | |

warrant	warrior	wary	weapon
weather	weird	whereabouts	whimsical
whistle	wholesome	wholly	woolen
wrangle	wrestle	write	writing
written			

| yacht | yield | | |

RECOMMENDED READING

The titles listed below, readily available in paperback, represent many of the classic and contemporary works most widely read and studied in comprehensive high school English courses; the emphasis is on works written in English, primarily by American writers. These titles are recommended to the student seeking to supplement regular course assignments or to prepare independently for the Regents exam. All would be suitable choices for the critical lens task on the New York State Regents exam or on the AP English exams. These works also represent valuable additions to a student's personal library.

NOVELS

1984	George Orwell
A Death in the Family	James Agee
A Farewell to Arms	Ernest Hemingway
A Separate Peace	John Knowles
A Star Called Henry	Roddy Doyle
A Tale of Two Cities	Charles Dickens
All the King's Men	Robert Penn Warren
Arrowsmith	Sinclair Lewis
Babbitt	Sinclair Lewis
Beloved	Toni Morrison
Billy Budd	Herman Melville
Brave New World	Aldous Huxley
Catch-22	Joseph Heller
Catcher in the Rye	J. D. Salinger
Cat's Eye	Margaret Atwood
Cold Mountain	Charles Frazier
Daisy Miller	Henry James
Deliverance	James Dickey
Ethan Frome	Edith Wharton
Farenheit 451	Ray Bradbury
Felicia's Journey	William Trevor
Great Expectations	Charles Dickens
Huckleberry Finn	Mark Twain
In Country	Bobbie Ann Mason
Invisible Man	Ralph Ellison
Light in August	William Faulkner

Lord of the Flies	William Golding
Main Street	Sinclair Lewis
Native Son	Richard Wright
Oliver Twist	Charles Dickens
One Hundred Years of Solitude	Gabriel Garcia Marquez
Ordinary People	Judith Guest
Rabbit, Run	John Updike
Ragtime	E. L. Doctorow
Rebecca	Daphne DuMaurier
Red Badge of Courage	Stephen Crane
Rumors of Peace	Ella Leffland
Sister Carrie	Theodore Dreiser
Slaughterhouse Five	Kurt Vonnegut
So Long, See You Tomorrow	William Maxwell
Song of Solomon	Toni Morrison
Summer	Edith Wharton
That Night	Alice McDermott
The Age of Innocence	Edith Wharton
The Assistant	Bernard Malamud
The Awakening	Kate Chopin
The Bean Trees	Barbara Kingsolver
The Bluest Eye	Toni Morrison
The Bonesetter's Daughter	Amy Tan
The Bonfire of the Vanities	Tom Wolfe
The Caine Mutiny	Herman Wouk
The Centaur	John Updike
The Color Purple	Alice Walker
The Crying of Lot 49	Thomas Pynchon
The Grapes of Wrath	John Steinbeck
The Great Gatsby	F. Scott Fitzgerald
The Heart Is a Lonely Hunter	Carson McCullers
The Human Stain	Philip Roth
The Joy Luck Club	Amy Tan
The Natural	Bernard Malamud
The Old Man and the Sea	Ernest Hemingway
The Secret Agent	Joseph Conrad
The Scarlet Letter	Nathaniel Hawthorne
The Shawl	Cynthia Ozick
The Time Machine	H. G. Wells
Things Fall Apart	Chinua Achebe
Things Invisible to See	Nancy Willard
Time and Again	Jack Finney
To Kill a Mockingbird	Harper Lee
Washington Square	Henry James
World's Fair	E. L. Doctorow

AUTOBIOGRAPHY, ESSAYS, AND OTHER NONFICTION

A Civil Action	Jonathan Harr
A Hole in the Sky	Robert Finch
An American Childhood	Annie Dillard
Angela's Ashes	Frank McCourt
Black Boy	Richard Wright
Cities on the Hill	Francis Fitzgerald
Dreams from My Father	Barack Obama
Growing Up	Russell Baker
Hiroshima	John Hersey
Hunger of Memory	Richard Rodriguez
I Know Why the Caged Bird Sings	Maya Angelou
In My Place	Charlayne Hunter-Gault
Into Thin Air	Jon Krakauer
Iron and Silk	Mark Salzman
Late Innings	Roger Angell
Nickled and Dimed	Barbara Ehrenreich
Night	Elie Wiesel
Notes of a Native Son	James Baldwin
Out of Africa	Isak Dinesen
Pilgrim at Tinker Creek	Annie Dillard
Stop-Time	Frank Conroy
Such, Such Were the Joys	George Orwell
The Art of Fiction	David Lodge
The Color of Water	James McBride
The Courage of Turtles	Edward Hoagland
The Crack-Up	F. Scott Fitzgerald
The Devils of Loudon	Aldous Huxley
The Duke of Deception	Geoffrey Wolff
The Last Cowboy	Jane Kramer
The Lives of a Cell	Lewis Thomas
The Mismeasure of Man	Stephen Jay Gould
The Solace of Open Spaces	Gretel Ehrlich
The Way to Rainy Mountain	N. Scott Momaday
The White Album	Joan Didion
This Boy's Life	Tobias Wolff
This House of Sky	Ivan Doig
Travels with Charley	John Steinbeck
Up from Slavery	Booker T. Washington
Walden	Henry David Thoreau

There are many excellent collections of essays and literary nonfiction available. Here are some recommended classic and contemporary authors whose works are available in paperback editions:

Ray Bradbury	Malcolm Cowley	Stanley Crouch
Joan Didion	Ralph Waldo Emerson	M. F. K. Fisher
Benjamin Franklin	Ian Frazier	Adam Gopnik
Stephen Jay Gould	Garrison Keillor	Verlyn Klinkenborg
Tracy Kidder	Jane Kramer	Walter Lippman
Peter Mathiesson	John McPhee	H. L. Mencken
Richard Rodriguez	Roger Rosenblatt	Brent Staples
Gore Vidal	Eudora Welty	E. B. White

Recommended anthologies include:

The Art of the Personal Essay, by Philip Lopate; Anchor Books
The Best American Essays of the Century, Joyce Carol Oates, ed.;
　　Houghton Mifflin Co.
The Best American Essays, compiled from essays written for magazines
　　and journals and published annually by Houghton Mifflin Co.

Other volumes in the Best American Series, also published annually, include:

The Best American Sports Writing
The Best American Travel Writing
The Best American Science and Nature Writing
The Best American Nonrequired Reading

POETRY

Readers are urged to seek out collections of work by poets whom they encounter in class readings and whom they especially admire. *Dover Publications* offers nicely produced and very inexpensive paperback collections of poetry, including works of Shakespeare and other major British poets, as well as major American poets of the nineteenth and twentieth centuries. They are available from Dover online and in bookstores. Among the many poets introduced to high school students and whose work is widely available in paperback collections are the following:

W. H. Auden	Elizabeth Bishop	Louise Bogan
Gwendolyn Brooks	Billy Collins	e. e. cummings

Emily Dickinson	*Rita Dove	T. S. Eliot
Carolyn Forché	Robert Frost	Louise Glück
Donald Hall	Langston Hughes	Denise Levertov
W. S. Merwin	Edna St. Vincent Millay	Marianne Moore
Howard Nemerov	*Sharon Olds	*Marge Piercy
Robert Pinsky	Sylvia Plath	Adrienne Rich
Theodore Roethke	Carl Sandburg	Charles Simic
*May Swenson	William Stafford	Richard Wilbur
Nancy Willard	William Carlos Williams	

* denotes a poet whose work has appeared on a New York State English Regents exam

Some currently available paperback anthologies of poetry include:

Poetry 180, An Anthology of Contemporary Poems, Billy Collins, ed.; Random House
Good Poems, selected and introduced by Garrison Keillor; Penguin Books
Poetry Daily, 366 Poems, selected from the Poetry Daily web site; Sourcebooks Inc.
The Best American Poetry, annual series, David Lehman, ed.; Scribner
Contemporary American Poetry, Donald Hall, ed.; Viking
The Mentor Book of Major American Poets, Oscar Williams and Edwin Honig, eds.; New American Library
The Vintage Book of Contemporary American Poetry, J. D. McClatchy, ed.

Web sites for the interested reader:

Poetry Daily: *www.poems.com*
Academy of American Poets: *www.poets.org*
Poet's House: *www.poetshouse.org*
www.poemhunter.com

SHORT STORIES

Some recommended authors whose stories are available in paperback:

Sherwood Anderson	John Barth	Ambrose Bierce
Willa Cather	Isak Dinesen	William Faulkner

F. Scott Fitzgerald	Nathaniel Hawthorne	Ernest Hemingway
Bernard Malamud	Bharati Mukherjee	Alice Munro
Joyce Carol Oates	Flannery O'Connor	Edgar Allan Poe
Isaac Bashevis Singer	William Trevor	John Updike
Kurt Vonnegut	Edith Wharton	Eudora Welty
John Edgar Wideman		

Collections available in paperback include:

Annual publications:
The O. Henry Prize Stories
The Best American Short Stories
The Pushcart Prize: Best of the Small Presses

Anthologies:
American Short Story Masterpieces, Raymond Carver and Tom Jenks, eds.
The Norton Anthology of Short Fiction, R. V. Cassill, ed.
The Oxford Book of American Short Stories, Joyce Carol Oates, ed.
The Oxford Book of Short Stories, V. S. Pritchett, ed.
　　(includes British and American writers)
The Vintage Book of Contemporary American Short Stories, Tobias Wolff, ed.

PLAYS

Shakespeare	*Macbeth, Julius Caesar, Othello, As You Like It, Hamlet, King Lear, Much Ado About Nothing, The Tempest, Henry V*
Paddy Chayevsky	*Marty*
Anton Chekov	*Three Sisters, The Cherry Orchard, Uncle Vanya*
Henrik Ibsen	*A Doll's House, The Master Builder*
Edward Albee	*Who's Afraid of Virginia Woolf?, Zoo Story*
David Auburn	*Proof*
Samuel Beckett	*Waiting for Godot*
Robert Bolt	*A Man for All Seasons*
Noel Coward	*Blithe Spirit, Private Lives*
Mart Crowley	*The Boys in the Band*
Horton Foote	*Dividing the Estate, The Trip to Bountiful, The Young Man from Atlanta*
William Gibson	*The Miracle Worker*

Susan Glaspell	*Trifles*
John Guare	*Six Degrees of Separation*
A. R. Gurney	*The Dining Room*
Lorraine Hansberry	*A Raisin in the Sun*
Lillian Hellman	*The Little Foxes*
Beth Henley	*Crimes of the Heart*
William Inge	*Come Back, Little Sheba; Picnic; Bus Stop*
Eugene Ionesco	*The Lesson, The Bald Soprano, Rhinoceros*
George S. Kaufman/Moss Hart	*You Can't Take It With You, The Man Who Came to Dinner*
Jerome Lawrence/ Robert Lee	*Inherit the Wind*
Terrence McNally	*Master Class*
Arthur Miller	*All My Sons, Death of a Salesman, The Crucible, The Price, A View From the Bridge*
Clifford Odets	*Waiting for Lefty, The Country Girl*
Eugene O'Neill	*Long Day's Journey into Night*
Harold Pinter	*The Caretaker*
Terrence Rattigan	*The Winslow Boy, The Browning Version*
Yasmina Reza	*Art*
Rod Serling	*Requiem for a Heavyweight*
Peter Shaffer	*Equus, Black Comedy, The Royal Hunt of the Sun, Amadeus*
George Bernard Shaw	*Pygmalion*
Neil Simon	*The Odd Couple, Brighton Beach Memoirs*
Tom Stoppard	*Rosenkrantz and Guildenstern Are Dead, Arcadia, The Real Thing, Jumpers, The Coast of Utopia*
Alfred Uhry	*Driving Miss Daisy*
Wendy Wasserstein	*The Heidi Chronicles*
Oscar Wilde	*The Importance of Being Earnest*
Thornton Wilder	*Our Town, The Matchmaker, The Skin of Our Teeth*
Tennesse Williams	*The Glass Menagerie, A Streetcar Named Desire, Cat on a Hot Tin Roof, Sweet Bird of Youth*
August Wilson	*Fences, The Piano Lesson, Ma Rainey's Black Bottom, Jitney, Joe Turner's Come and Gone*

APPENDIX A:
AN INTRODUCTION TO THE NEW YORK STATE ENGLISH LANGUAGE ARTS LEARNING STANDARDS

As part of its revision of New York State standards and graduation requirements, the Board of Regents adopted the Learning Standards in English Language Arts, and a new Regents Comprehensive English exam was developed to assess the expectations set forth in those standards. That exam has been administered since June 1999.

The content of the ELA Standards was not new; what was new was the way in which what students should learn was described. The ELA Standards are no longer expressed simply as a list of topics to be "covered"; rather, they are expressed in terms of what students must be able to do. These standards are given in Appendix C, followed by key performance indicators in Appendix D.

APPENDIX B:
A GLOSSARY OF TERMS

assessment   You may hear teachers and other educators using the term **assessment** instead of test or examination. An **assessment** is more than a simple test (in arithmetic, say) because it seeks to measure a number of skills at one time. Although we continue to refer to the English Regents as an exam or test, its goal is to be a valid **assessment** of a broad range of listening, reading, thinking, and writing skills outlined in the new Learning Standards

audience   In talking about writing, we use the term **audience** to mean the intended readers. Session One, Parts A and B of the new Regents exam require that you write an essay or report for a particular group of readers and for a particular purpose.

conventions   This term is found in the **rubrics** (see below) and refers to conventional standards for spelling, punctuation, paragraphing, capitalization, grammar, and usage. You are expected to follow the **conventions** of standard written English in all four parts of the examination.

critical lens   This term is used in Part B of Session Two of the revised exam; the critical lens is a quote about a particular way of "looking at" and evaluating works of literature. You will use your interpretation and response to the **critical lens** to compose a literary essay.

guidelines   The **Guidelines** follow the description of each **Task** (see below) and list the specific steps you must take to write a successful essay.

overview   The **Overview** at the beginning of Part A of Session One of the Regents exam outlines what is required in that part. Requirements may also be expressed as **Directions** in other parts.

performance indicators   This is the technical term educators use to identify what students should be able to do in order to demonstrate that they have the listening, reading, thinking, and writing skills outlined in the new **Standards.**

rubric   A **rubric** is a descriptive guide to scoring or evaluating an essay, examination, or other task. Many teachers now use **rubrics** in their own courses to show students how their work is assessed or evaluated. You will find the **rubrics** for each part of the Regents exam in Appendix F. Be sure to review these carefully.

situation Parts A and B of Session One of the Regents includes a **Situation,** a specific context, purpose, and **audience** for the essay, article, or report that you will write.

standards For students in New York State, The Learning Standards for English Language Arts establishes four broad categories of language skills, states general goals for each, and then outlines **performance indicators** for each. These are described in detail in Appendix D. The English Regents exam reflects the emphasis on performance—specific expectations for the intellectual habits you must develop and the skills you must exercise on a habitual basis. (The map in Appendix E outlines the relationship of the **standards** to the **performance indicators**.)

task The **Task** is what you must actually *do* on each part of the exam. The exam is composed of a series of **tasks** because the exam requires that you *demonstrate* how well you comprehend, analyze, and write.

APPENDIX C: THE ENGLISH LANGUAGE ARTS LEARNING STANDARDS

The standards are identified as four broad areas of language experience, each requiring reading, listening, speaking, and writing.

STANDARD 1: LANGUAGE FOR INFORMATION AND UNDERSTANDING

Students will listen, speak, read, and write for information and understanding. As listeners and readers, students will collect data, facts, and ideas; discover relationships, concepts, and generalizations; and use knowledge generated from oral, written, and electronically produced texts. As speakers and writers, they will use oral and written language that follows the accepted conventions of the English language to acquire, interpret, apply, and transmit information.

STANDARD 2: LANGUAGE FOR LITERARY RESPONSE AND EXPRESSION

Students will read and listen to oral, written, and electronically produced texts and performances from American and world literature; relate texts and performances to their own lives; and develop an understanding of the diverse social, historical, and cultural dimensions the texts and performances represent. As speakers and writers, students will use oral and written language that follows the accepted conventions of the English language for self-expression and artistic creation.

STANDARD 3: LANGUAGE FOR CRITICAL ANALYSIS AND EVALUATION

Students will listen, speak, read, and write for critical analysis and evaluation. As listeners and readers, students will analyze experiences, ideas, information, and issues presented by others using a variety of established criteria. As speakers and writers, they will use oral and written language that follows the accepted conventions of the English language to present, from a variety of perspectives, their opinions and judgments on experiences, ideas, information, and issues.

STANDARD 4: LANGUAGE FOR SOCIAL INTERACTION

Students will listen, speak, read, and write for social interaction. Students will use oral and written language that follows the accepted conventions of the English language for effective social communication with a wide variety of people. As readers and listeners, they will use the social communications of others to enrich their understanding of people and their views.

APPENDIX D: PERFORMANCE INDICATORS

For teachers, as well as students and parents, the English Language Arts Learning Standards are most meaningfully expressed in what are called **performance indicators,** descriptions of what students are required to do, do habitually, and do on demand. Below are some of the required performance indicators at commencement (Regents exam) level for each standard.

ELA STANDARD 1: LANGUAGE FOR INFORMATION AND UNDERSTANDING

Students are expected to:

Interpret and analyze complex informational texts and presentations, including technical manuals, professional journals, newspaper and broadcast editorials, electronic networks, political speeches and debates, and primary source material, in their subject courses.

Synthesize information from diverse sources and identify complexities and discrepancies in the information.

Use a combination of techniques to **extract salient information** from texts.

Make distinctions about the relative value and significance of specific data, facts, and ideas. **Make perceptive and well-developed connections** to prior knowledge. **Evaluate** writing strategies and presentational features that affect interpretation of the information.

Write research reports, feature articles, and thesis/support papers on a variety of topics. **Present a controlling idea** that conveys an individual perspective and insight into a topic. **Support** interpretations and decisions. **Use** a wide range of organizational patterns.

Revise and improve early drafts by restructuring, correcting errors, and revising for clarity and effect. **Use standard English skillfully,** applying established rules and conventions for presenting information and making use of a wide range of grammatical constructions and vocabulary to achieve an individual style that communicates effectively.

ELA STANDARD 2: LANGUAGE FOR LITERARY RESPONSE AND EXPRESSION

Students are expected to:

Read and view independently and fluently across many genres of literature from many cultures and historical periods. **Evaluate** literary merit based on an understanding of the genre, literary elements, and the literary period.

Identify the distinguishing features of different literary genres, periods, and traditions and use those features to interpret the work. **Read aloud** expressively to convey a clear interpretation of the work.

Recognize and understand the significance of a wide range of literary elements and techniques (including figurative language, imagery, allegory, irony, blank verse, symbolism, stream-of-consciousness), and use those elements to interpret the work.

Understand how multiple levels of meaning are conveyed in a text. Produce literary interpretations that **explicate** the multiple layers of meaning.

Write original pieces in a variety of literary forms, using the conventions of the genre and using structure and vocabulary to achieve an effect.

Use standard English skillfully and with an individual style.

ELA STANDARD 3: LANGUAGE FOR CRITICAL ANALYSIS AND EVALUATION

Students are expected to:

Analyze, interpret, and evaluate ideas, information, organization and language of a wide range of general and technical texts . . . across subject areas, including technical manuals, professional journals, political speeches, and literary criticism.

Evaluate the quality of the texts . . . from a variety of critical perspectives within the field of study. **Make precise determinations** about the perspective of a particular writer.

Present well-developed analyses of issues, ideas, and texts . . . . **Make effective use** of details, evidence, and arguments . . . to influence and persuade an audience.

Use standard English, a broad and precise vocabulary, and the formal conventions of formal oratory and debate.

ELA STANDARD 4: LANGUAGE FOR SOCIAL INTERACTION*

Students are expected to:

Engage in conversations and discussions on academic, technical, and community subjects, anticipating listeners' needs and skillfully addressing them.

Express their thoughts and views clearly with attention to the perspectives and voiced concerns of others in the conversation. **Use** appropriately the language conventions for a wide variety of social situations.

Use a variety of print and electronic forms for social communication with peers and adults. **Make effective use** of language and style to connect the message with the audience and context.

You will find a map to the standards and performance indicators in Appendix E and the scoring rubrics for each part of the exam in Appendix F.

---

*This standard is not formally assessed in the Comprehensive English Regents Exam.

APPENDIX E:
A MAP TO THE ENGLISH LANGUAGE ARTS STANDARDS AND PERFORMANCE INDICATORS

	Task	Standard	Performance Indicators
SESSION ONE, PART A	(a) Extended written response to a speech (b) Multiple-choice questions on key ideas (6)	Listening and writing for information and understanding	Interpret and analyze complex informational texts and presentations . . . Use a combination of techniques to extract salient information from texts . . . Make distinctions about the relative value and significance of specific data, facts, and ideas Write . . . research reports, feature articles, and thesis/support papers on a variety of topics . . . Present a controlling idea that conveys an individual perspective and insight into the topic Use a wide range of organizational patterns . . . Support interpretations and decisions . . . Use standard English skillfully . . .
SESSION ONE, PART B	(a) Extended written response to informational materials (text and visual) (b) Multiple-choice questions on basic comprehension (salient information, vocabulary, and interpretation) (10)	Reading and writing for information and understanding	Interpret and analyze complex informational texts and presentations . . . Use a combination of techniques to extract salient information from texts . . . Make distinctions about the relative value and significance of specific data, facts, and ideas Write . . . research reports, feature articles, and thesis/support papers on a variety of topics . . . Present a controlling idea that conveys an individual perspective and insight into the topic Use a wide range of organizational patterns . . . Support interpretations and decisions . . . Use standard English skillfully . . .
SESSION TWO, PART A	(a) Extended written response to two linked passages of different genres (b) Multiple-choice questions on key ideas, details, and vocabulary (10)	Reading and writing for literary response	Read . . . independently and fluently across many genres of literature Identify the distinguishing features of different literary genres . . . and use those features to interpret the work Recognize and understand the significance of a wide range of literary elements and techniques . . . and use those elements to interpret the work Produce literary interpretations that explicate the multiple layers of meaning Use standard English skillfully . . .
SESSION TWO, PART B	Extended written response to literature read for school	Reading and writing for critical analysis and evaluation	Analyze, interpret, and evaluate . . . a wide range of . . . texts . . . Evaluate the quality of texts . . . from a variety of critical perspectives Make precise determinations about the perspective of a particular writer . . . Present . . . well-developed analyses of issues, ideas, and texts . . . Make effective use of details, evidence, and arguments . . . Use standard English skillfully . . .

SESSION ONE, PART A: LISTENING AND WRITING FOR INFORMATION AND UNDERSTANDING

QUALITY	6 Responses at this level:	5 Responses at this level:	4 Responses at this level:	3 Responses at this level:	2 Responses at this level:	1 Responses at this level:
Meaning: the extent to which the response exhibits sound understanding, interpretation, and analysis of the task and text(s)	—reveal an in-depth analysis of the text —make insightful connections between information and ideas in the text and the assigned task	—convey a thorough understanding of the text —make clear and explicit connections between information and ideas in the text and the assigned task	—convey a basic understanding of the text —make implicit connections between information and ideas in the text and the assigned task	—convey a basic understanding of the text —make few or superficial connections between information and ideas in the text and the assigned task	—convey a confused or inaccurate understanding of the text —allude to the text but make unclear or unwarranted connections to the assigned task	—provide no evidence of textual understanding —make no connections between information in the text and the assigned task
Development: the extent to which ideas are elaborated using specific and relevant evidence from the text(s)	—develop ideas clearly and fully, making effective use of a wide range of relevant and specific details from the text	—develop ideas clearly and consistently, using relevant and specific details from the text	—develop some ideas more fully than others, using specific and relevant details from the text	—develop ideas briefly, using some details from the text	—are incomplete or largely undeveloped, hinting at ideas, but references to the text are vague, irrelevant, repetitive, or unjustified	—are minimal, with no evidence of development
Organization: the extent to which the response exhibits direction, shape, and coherence	—maintain a clear and appropriate focus —exhibit a logical and coherent structure through skillful use of appropriate devices and transitions	—maintain a clear and appropriate focus —exhibit a logical sequence of ideas through use of appropriate devices and transitions	—maintain a clear and appropriate focus —exhibit a logical sequence of ideas but may lack internal consistency	—establish, but fail to maintain, an appropriate focus —exhibit a rudimentary structure but may include some inconsistencies or irrelevancies	—lack an appropriate focus but suggest some organization, or suggest a focus but lack organization	—show no focus or organization
Language Use: the extent to which the response reveals an awareness of audience and purpose through effective use of words, sentence structure, and sentence variety	—are stylistically sophisticated, using language that is precise and engaging, with a notable sense of voice and awareness of audience and purpose —vary structure and length of sentences to enhance meaning	—use language that is fluent and original, with evident awareness of audience and purpose —vary structure and length of sentences to control rhythm and pacing	—use appropriate language, with some awareness of audience and purpose —occasionally make effective use of sentence structure or length	—rely on language from the text or basic vocabulary, with little awareness of audience or purpose —exhibit some attempt to vary sentence structure or length for effect, but with uneven success	—use language that is imprecise or unsuitable for the audience or purpose —reveal little awareness of how to use sentences to achieve an effect	—are minimal —use language that is incoherent or inappropriate
Conventions: the extent to which the response exhibits conventional spelling, punctuation, paragraphing, capitalization, grammar, and usage	—demonstrate control of the conventions with essentially no errors, even with sophisticated language	—demonstrate control of the conventions, exhibiting occasional errors only when using sophisticated language	—demonstrate partial control, exhibiting occasional errors that do not hinder comprehension	—demonstrate emerging control, exhibiting occasional errors that hinder comprehension	—demonstrate a lack of control, exhibiting frequent errors that make comprehension difficult	—are minimal, making assessment of conventions unreliable —may be illegible or not recognizable as English

SESSION ONE, PART B: READING AND WRITING FOR INFORMATION AND UNDERSTANDING

QUALITY	6 Responses at this level:	5 Responses at this level:	4 Responses at this level	3 Responses at this level:	2 Responses at this level:	1 Responses at this level:
Meaning: the extent to which the response exhibits sound understanding, interpretation, and analysis of the task and document(s)	—reveal an in-depth analysis of the documents —make insightful connections between information and ideas in the documents and the assigned task	—convey a thorough understanding of the documents —make clear and explicit connections between information and ideas in the documents and the assigned task	—convey a basic understanding of the documents —make implicit connections between information and ideas in the documents and the assigned task	—convey a basic understanding of the documents* —make few or superficial connections between information and ideas in the documents and the assigned task	—convey a confused or inaccurate understanding of the documents —allude to the documents but make unclear or unwarranted connections to the assigned task	—provide no evidence of understanding —make no connections between information in the documents and the assigned task
Development: the extent to which ideas are elaborated using specific and relevant evidence from the document(s)	—develop ideas clearly and fully, making effective use of a wide range of relevant and specific details from the documents	—develop ideas clearly and consistently, using relevant and specific details from the documents	—develop some ideas more fully than others, using specific and relevant details from the documents	—develop ideas briefly, using some details from the documents	—are incomplete or largely undeveloped, hinting at ideas, but references to the documents are vague, irrelevant, repetitive, or unjustified	—are minimal, with no evidence of development
Organization: the extent to which the response exhibits direction, shape, and coherence	—maintain a clear and appropriate focus —exhibit a logical and coherent structure through skillful use of appropriate devices and transitions	—maintain a clear and appropriate focus —exhibit a logical sequence of ideas through use of appropriate devices and transitions	—maintain a clear and appropriate focus —exhibit a logical sequence of ideas but may lack internal consistency	—establish, but fail to maintain, an appropriate focus —exhibit a rudimentary structure but may include some inconsistencies or irrelevancies	—lack an appropriate focus but suggest some organization, or suggest a focus but lack organization	—show no focus or organization
Language Use: the extent to which the response reveals an awareness of audience and purpose through effective use of words, sentence structure, and sentence variety	—are stylistically sophisticated, using language that is precise and engaging, with a notable sense of voice and awareness of audience and purpose —vary structure and length of sentences to enhance meaning	—use language that is fluent and original, with evident awareness of audience and purpose —vary structure and length of sentences to control rhythm and pacing	—use appropriate language, with some awareness of audience and purpose —occasionally make effective use of sentence structure or length	—rely on language from the documents or basic vocabulary, with little awareness of audience or purpose —exhibit some attempt to vary sentence structure or length for effect, but with uneven success	—use language that is imprecise or unsuitable for the audience or purpose —reveal little awareness of how to use sentences to achieve an effect	—are minimal —use language that is incoherent or inappropriate
Conventions: the extent to which the response exhibits conventional spelling, punctuation, paragraphing, capitalization, grammar, and usage	—demonstrate control of the conventions with essentially no errors, even with sophisticated language	—demonstrate control of the conventions, exhibiting occasional errors only when using sophisticated language	—demonstrate partial control, exhibiting occasional errors that do not hinder comprehension	—demonstrate emerging control, exhibiting occasional errors that hinder comprehension	—demonstrate a lack of control, exhibiting frequent errors that make comprehension difficult	—are minimal, making assessment of conventions unreliable —may be illegible or not recognizable as English

QUALITY	6 Responses at this level:	5 Responses at this level:	4 Responses at this level:	3 Responses at this level:	2 Responses at this level:	1 Responses at this level:
Meaning: the extent to which the response exhibits sound understanding, interpretation, and analysis of the task and text(s)	—establish a controlling idea that reveals an in-depth analysis of both texts; —make insightful connections between the controlling idea and the ideas in each text	—establish a controlling idea that reveals a thorough understanding of both texts; —make clear and explicit connections between the controlling idea and the ideas in each text	—establish a controlling idea that shows a basic understanding of both texts; —make implicit connections between the controlling idea and the ideas in each text	—establish a controlling idea that shows a basic understanding of the texts; —make few or superficial connections between the controlling idea and the ideas in the texts	—convey a confused or incomplete understanding of the texts; —make a few connections but fail to establish a controlling idea	—provide minimal or no evidence of textual understanding; —make no connections between the texts or among ideas in the texts
Development: the extent to which ideas are elaborated using specific and relevant evidence from the text(s)	—develop ideas clearly and fully, making effective use of a wide range of relevant and specific evidence and appropriate literary elements from both texts	—develop ideas clearly and consistently, with reference to relevant and specific evidence and appropriate literary elements from both texts	—develop some ideas more fully than others, with reference to specific and relevant evidence and appropriate literary elements from both texts	—develop ideas briefly, using some evidence from the texts; —may rely primarily on plot summary	—are incomplete or largely undeveloped, hinting at ideas, but references to the text are vague, irrelevant, repetitive, or unjustified	—are minimal, with no evidence of development
Organization: the extent to which the response exhibits direction, shape, and coherence	—maintain the focus established by the controlling idea; —exhibit a logical and coherent structure through skillful use of appropriate devices and transitions	—maintain the focus established by the controlling idea; —exhibit a logical sequence of ideas through use of appropriate devices and transitions	—maintain a clear and appropriate focus; —exhibit a logical sequence of ideas but may lack internal consistency	—establish, but fail to maintain, an appropriate focus; —exhibit a rudimentary structure but may include some inconsistencies or irrelevancies	—lack an appropriate focus but suggest some organization, or suggest a focus but lack organization	—show no focus or organization
Language Use: the extent to which the response reveals an awareness of audience and purpose through effective use of words, sentence structure, and sentence variety	—are stylistically sophisticated, using language that is precise and engaging, with a notable sense of voice and awareness of audience and purpose; —vary structure and length of sentences to enhance meaning	—use language that is fluent and original, with evident awareness of audience and purpose; —vary structure and length of sentences to control rhythm and pacing	—use appropriate language, with some awareness of audience and purpose; —occasionally make effective use of sentence structure or length	—rely on basic vocabulary, with little awareness of audience or purpose; —exhibit some attempt to vary sentence structure or length for effect, but with uneven success	—use language that is imprecise or unsuitable for the audience or purpose; —reveal little awareness of how to use sentences to achieve an effect	—are minimal; —use language that is incoherent or inappropriate
Conventions: the extent to which the response exhibits conventional spelling, punctuation, paragraphing, capitalization, grammar, and usage	—demonstrate control of the conventions with essentially no errors, even with sophisticated language	—demonstrate control of the conventions, exhibiting occasional errors only when using sophisticated language	—demonstrate partial control, exhibiting occasional errors that do not hinder comprehension	—demonstrate emerging control, exhibiting occasional errors that hinder comprehension	—demonstrate a lack of control, exhibiting frequent errors that make comprehension difficult	—are minimal, making assessment of conventions unreliable; —may be illegible or not recognizable as English

• If the response addresses only one text, the response can be scored no higher than a 3.

• Responses totally unrelated to the topic, illegible, incoherent, or blank should be given a 0.

• If the student writes only a personal response and makes no reference to the text(s), the response can be scored no higher than a 1.

• A response totally copied from the text(s) with no original student writing should be scored a 0.

271

SESSION TWO, PART B: READING AND WRITING FOR CRITICAL ANALYSIS

QUALITY	6 Responses at this level:	5 Responses at this level:	4 Responses at this level:	3 Responses at this level:	2 Responses at this level:	1 Responses at this level:
Meaning: the extent to which the response exhibits sound understanding, interpretation, and analysis of the task and text(s)	—provide an interpretation of the "critical lens" that is faithful to the complexity of the statement and clearly establishes the criteria for analysis —use the criteria to make an insightful analysis of the chosen texts	—provide a thoughtful interpretation of the "critical lens" that clearly establishes the criteria for analysis —use the criteria to make a clear and reasoned analysis of the chosen texts	—provide a reasonable interpretation of the "critical lens" that establishes the criteria for analysis —make implicit connections between the chosen texts and the chosen texts	—provide a simple interpretation of the "critical lens" that suggests some criteria for analysis —make superficial connections between the criteria and the chosen texts*	—provide a confused or incomplete interpretation of the "critical lens" —may allude to the "critical lens" but do not use it to analyze the chosen texts	—do not refer to the "critical lens" —reflect minimal analysis of the chosen texts or omit mention of texts
Development: the extent to which ideas are elaborated using specific and relevant evidence from the text(s)	—develop ideas clearly and fully, making effective use of a wide range of relevant and specific evidence and appropriate literary elements from both texts	—develop ideas clearly and consistently, with reference to relevant and specific evidence and appropriate literary elements from both texts	—develop some ideas more fully than others, with reference to specific and relevant evidence and appropriate literary elements from both texts	—develop ideas briefly, using some evidence from the texts	—are incomplete or largely undeveloped, hinting at ideas, but references to the text are vague, irrelevant, repetitive, or unjustified	—are minimal, with no evidence of development
Organization: the extent to which the response exhibits direction, shape, and coherence	—maintain the focus established by the critical lens —exhibit a logical and coherent structure through skillful use of appropriate devices and transitions	—maintain the focus established by the critical lens —exhibit a logical sequence of ideas through the use of appropriate devices and transitions	—maintain a clear and appropriate focus —exhibit a logical sequence of ideas but may lack internal consistency	—establish, but fail to maintain, an appropriate focus —exhibit a rudimentary structure but may include some inconsistencies or irrelevancies	—lack an appropriate focus but suggest some organization, or suggest a focus but lack organization	—show no focus or organization
Language Use: the extent to which the response reveals an awareness of audience and purpose through effective use of words, sentence structure, and sentence variety	—are stylistically sophisticated, using language that is precise and engaging, with a notable sense of voice and awareness of audience and purpose —vary structure and length of sentences to enhance meaning	—use language that is fluent and original, with evident awareness of audience and purpose —vary structure and length of sentences to control rhythm and pacing	—use appropriate language, with some awareness of audience and purpose —occasionally make effective use of sentence structure or length	—rely on basic vocabulary, with little awareness of audience or purpose —exhibit some attempt to vary sentence structure or length for effect, but with uneven success	—use language that is imprecise or unsuitable for the audience or purpose —reveal little awareness of how to use sentences to achieve an effect	—are minimal —use language that is incoherent or inappropriate
Conventions: the extent to which the response exhibits conventional spelling, punctuation, paragraphing, capitalization, grammar, and usage	—demonstrate control of the conventions with essentially no errors, even with sophisticated language	—demonstrate control of the conventions, exhibiting occasional errors only when using sophisticated language	—demonstrate partial control, exhibiting occasional errors that do not hinder comprehension	—demonstrate emerging control, exhibiting occasional errors that hinder comprehension	—demonstrate a lack of control, exhibiting frequent errors that make comprehension difficult	—are minimal, making assessment of conventions unreliable —may be illegible or not recognizable as English

Examination June 2008

English

Session One

Part A

Overview: For this part of the test, you will listen to an account about Madame Marie Curie, answer some multiple-choice questions, and write a response based on the situation described below. You will hear the account twice. You may take notes on the page alloted anytime you wish during the readings.

> **The Situation:** Your science class is exploring qualities that make scientists successful. You have decided to make a presentation to your class on the qualities that made Madame Marie Curie a successful scientist. In preparation for writing your presentation, listen to an account by writer and historian Barbara Goldsmith about Madame Marie Curie. Then use relevant information from the account to write your presentation.

Your Task: Write a presentation for your science class in which you describe the qualities that made Madame Marie Curie a successful scientist.

Guidelines:

Be sure to

- Tell your audience what they need to know about Madame Marie Curie and the qualities that made her a successful scientist
- Use specific, accurate, and relevant information from the account to support your description
- Use a tone and level of language appropriate for a presentation to a science class
- Organize your ideas in a logical and coherent manner
- Indicate any words taken directly from the account by using quotation marks or referring to the speaker
- Follow the conventions of standard written English

Note: For this portion of the examination, the teacher will read a passage aloud. You will not actually see the passage reprinted below. Therefore, you are encouraged to have someone read the passage to you, in order to simulate the examination as closely as possible.

Listening Passage

When I was a teenager, a class assignment was to find a hero or heroine, someone who inspires you to be the best person you can be. Perhaps because she seemed exotic, I chose Madame Curie. I cut a photograph of her out of a newspaper and tacked it up on my bulletin board. Underneath, I put her quotation, "Nothing in life is to be feared, it is only to be understood."

Good advice, I thought. In truth, I didn't know much about her—just a few facts and, I found out later, a lot of misconceptions. I knew that in 1893 Madame Curie became the first woman to secure a degree in physics at the Sorbonne in Paris—one of only two women in a science program of more than 1000 men. She was first in her class. She was the first woman to be appointed a professor at that institution. She was the first woman to win not one but two Nobel Prizes: the first in 1903 for her contribution to the discovery of radioactivity and the second in 1911 for her isolation of the elements polonium and radium.

At the beginning of the 20th century, the luminous element radium was hailed as an almost magical substance. Its discovery was thought to be Marie Curie's greatest accomplishment. Radium destroyed cancers and other deep-seated tumors, but it also became a world-class fad when it was added to cosmetics, toothpaste, tea and tonics. Since it glowed in the dark, it was used for paint, watch dials, costumes and toys, among other products. Radium was widely utilized until people began to die from overexposure to it—as did Madame Curie, her daughter Irène and countless others.

In fact, Marie Curie's great discovery was not the element radium but the uses of radioactivity, the fierce invisible energy released by atoms that could be used for the good of humanity or for its destruction. Her discovery paved the path to the atom bomb but also to harnessing the energy we now use to improve our daily lives. Her insight that radioactivity was an atomic property led to scientific discoveries that are being made right now. . . .

As I began to research Marie Curie's papers, I discovered not the idol of my youth but a real woman who was forced to cope with many of the same problems we have today: trying to balance a career with family life, raising children as a single mother, fighting the prejudice that often follows successful professional women, and having to prove again and again her worth to others and to herself.

The Marie Curie I found was not what I'd expected. She wasn't French; she wasn't even Marie. She was born Marya Salomee Sklodowska in 1867 in Warsaw, Poland (a country that, at that time, technically did not exist, having been taken over by three other countries after Napoleon's defeat at Waterloo in 1815). In school she was forced to speak and write only in Russian. Her father, once a respected physics professor, was dismissed for trying to teach Polish pride. When Marya was 7, her sister died of typhus; four years later, her mother succumbed to tuberculosis. But this brave child later wrote, "Never let one be beaten down by persons or by events."

Her family was desperately poor—poor in a way that a stamp, or a skuttle of coal or an occasional apple, was a treat. But Marya had dreams—big dreams. She worked for eight years as a governess to earn enough money to come to Paris, where she lived in an unheated fifth-floor garret on a measly diet of bread, tea and an occasional egg. Yet, she wrote, this was "the happiest time of my life. All I saw and learned was a new delight to me . . . a new world opened to me . . . which I was at last permitted to know in all liberty." While she was determined to make her dream of becoming a scientist come true, she was well aware, she wrote, that "the way to progress is never swift or easy." Marie believed that if you pursue your dream, things that seem like sacrifices don't really matter.

Being a woman scientist was difficult in those days. Dr. Hélène Langevin-Joliot, Marie's physicist granddaughter, points out that at the 1911 Solvay Conference of eminent scientists there were 23 male scientists to one woman—Marie Curie. (She adds that the ratio is about the same today.)

Marie's husband, Pierre Curie, also was remarkable for his time. He treated his wife as an equal, championed her accomplishments and supported her work. I'd read that they had fallen in love at first sight. Their letters tell a different story. At first, Marie sought Pierre's technical assistance; neither of them was looking for love. Pierre wrote that he found women a distraction, and she had wanted to return to Poland to help others. They became best friends. It was only after they married that they fell deeply in love—a love that ended only when Pierre died in a horrible accident, struck down by a horse and wagon. Marie— who was only 38 when Pierre died—told her daughters that it's always good to marry your best friend.

The woman who emerged from the Curie papers was someone who lived a self- less life. "Our special duty is to aid those to whom we think we can be most useful," she wrote. The Curies, never wealthy, gave much of their money to the pursuit of science. They refused to patent radium because that "was not in the scientific spirit," even though they knew it could bring a fortune. They gained little profit from Marie's discovery, while others became multimillionaires.

After Pierre died, Marie bravely carried on, raising her two daughters and working steadily until her death at 67. As I came to know her, I realized that heroes and heroines can be all too human. Marie worried that her daughter Eve wore too much makeup and that daughter Irène had married a playboy who traded on the Curie name—until he proved her wrong by becoming a Nobel Prize-winning scientist (as did Irène, for chemistry).

Here was a woman who triumphed in a world where men made the rules but who also was shy and vulnerable and suffered periods of depression in which she was unable to function. Yet she always bounced back. In short, Madame Curie was not the frozen symbol of perfection I had picked as a young girl but a woman who displayed courage, dedication and a sense of values to guide other lives. Albert Einstein said of her that she was the only person he knew who "was not corrupted by fame."

These days, heroes and heroines are in scarce supply. We live in an age of image, where people are famous for being famous. Our celebrity culture often glorifies those who are notorious, not noteworthy. An image can be easily altered: It can go from good to bad in an instant. Today's heroine becomes tomorrow's villain, and we become cynical when these synthetic idols disappoint us. Not so with Marie Curie, who believed that "you cannot build a better society without improving individuals." She thought of the good of humanity before her own good. She blazed a trail for others to follow. By the time I completed my book, I'd found my heroine.

—excerpted from "I Found My Heroine"
Parade, November 28, 2004

Notes

Multiple-Choice Questions

Directions (1–6): Use your notes to answer the following questions about the passage read to you. Select the best suggested answer and write its number in the space provided. The questions may help you think about ideas and information you might use in your writing. You may return to these questions anytime you wish.

1 According to the speaker, Marie Curie advanced the cause of

  (1) religious freedom   (3) women's rights
  (2) universal literacy   (4) voting rights   1____

2 According to the speaker, scientific discoveries continue today based on Marie Curie's understanding of

  (1) radioactivity   (3) relativity
  (2) magnetism   (4) propulsion   2____

3 While first living in Paris, Marie Curie was happy despite her

  (1) failing health
  (2) harsh living conditions
  (3) limited academic success
  (4) mounting debt   3____

4 Madame Curie's claim that "the way to progress is never swift or easy" reflects an attitude of

  (1) pride   (3) perseverance
  (2) frustration   (4) skepticism   4____

5 As a team, Pierre and Marie Curie used their financial profits to

(1) patent chemical elements
(2) further scientific study
(3) sponsor Nobel prizes
(4) promote economic stability   5____

6 According to the speaker, Madame Curie could best
be described as

(1) a politician   (3) an industrialist
(2) an economist   (4) a humanitarian   6____

After you have finished these questions, review **The
Situation** and read **Your Task** and the **Guidelines.**
Use scrap paper to plan your response. Then write
your response on separate sheets of paper. After you
finish your response for Part A, complete Part B.

Part B

Directions: Read the text and study the table on the following pages, answer the multiple-choice questions, and write a response based on the situation described below. You may use the margins to take notes as you read and scrap paper to plan your response.

> **The Situation:** The students in your health class have been asked to produce a monthly newspaper for the school community that will provide information about health threats and suggest how to avoid them by adopting a healthier lifestyle. You have been asked to write an article about the threat of sun exposure and to suggest ways that people can protect themselves from this threat.

Your Task: Using relevant information from **both** documents, write an article for a monthly school newspaper in which you discuss the threat of sun exposure and suggest ways that people can protect themselves from this threat.

Guidelines:
Be sure to
- Tell your audience what they need to know about the threat of sun exposure
- Suggest ways that people can protect themselves from this threat
- Use specific, accurate, and relevant information from the text **and** the table to support your discussion
- Use a tone and level of language appropriate for an article for a school newspaper
- Organize your ideas in a logical and coherent manner
- Indicate any words taken directly from the text by using quotation marks or referring to the author
- Follow the conventions of standard written English

Text

Erin Elovecky loves to feel the warmth of the sun on her body. Growing up, she spent many summer days on Long Island Sound, cruising around in her parents' boat and soaking up rays. Elovecky admired her mother, who could quickly develop a rich, brown tan, thanks to her Lebanese heritage. But Elovecky
(5) took after the Irish side of the family, with fair skin and green eyes, and got burned by the sun more often than not.

Hoping to give her skin a year-round sun-kissed glow, Elovecky started visiting a tanning salon near her Southbury, Conn., home a few times a week in her early 20s. She went for a couple of years. "It made me feel like I didn't need
(10) to wear a lot of makeup, and I thought I looked so much healthier with a tan," she remembers.

Two years ago, at the age of 27, Elovecky noticed a small red spot at the edge of her eyebrow. It itched, and the skin kept peeling off. She didn't do anything about it until her hairdresser said, "You have to get that checked out right away."
(15) One very painful biopsy later, Elovecky got the bad news: She had basal cell skin cancer.

Cases like Elovecky's are becoming increasingly common. A recent study published in the *Journal of the American Medical Association* found that the incidence of basal cell carcinoma (a slow-growing tumor of the basal cells at the
(20) bottom of the epidermis) among women under the age of 40 more than doubled between 1976 and 2003, to 31.6 per 100,000. The rate for men increased only slightly during that time. The study also found that both women and men showed significant increases in squamous cell cancer, which occurs in the middle layer of the epidermis. Like basal cell cancer, squamous cell cancer typically doesn't
(25) metastasize[1] and is rarely ever fatal. The reasons for the rise in skin cancer are clear, say doctors. "Either they're getting lots of chronic sun exposure because they're out all the time or using tanning beds, or it's these intense burns that they're getting," says Leslie Christenson, a dermatologic surgeon at the Mayo Clinic and one of the study's authors. Stepped-up screening for skin cancer and
(30) the thinning ozone layer, which allows more of the sun's ultraviolet rays in, may also play a role. The Indoor Tanning Association notes that the study didn't address whether the women tanned indoors or outdoors.

Basal cell carcinoma is the most common cancer in humans, with 800,000 new cases each year. Squamous cell cancer is the second most common skin
(35) cancer, with 200,000 new cases. Next in line is melanoma, a tumor that begins in the cells that produce the skin's pigment, which accounts for only about 100,000

---

[1]metastasize — to change form and spread

new cases annually. But melanoma is much more lethal, killing 1 in 4 people who develop it. Ultraviolet radiation from the sun is a principal cause of all types of skin cancer, either from damaging sunburns or the cumulative effect of long-term

(40) exposure. Family history also plays a role, especially in melanoma. The typical sufferer used to be an older man who had either worked outdoors all his life or was an avid golfer or boat owner who spent long hours in the sun. But as the new study shows, that profile is changing.

Dermatologists who treat skin cancer aren't surprised. "A week doesn't go by

(45) that I don't see a woman in her 20s or early 30s with skin cancer," says David Leffell, a professor of dermatology and surgery at the Yale School of Medicine. And although basal cell and squamous cell cancers hardly ever kill, those who develop them are at higher risk for melanoma. Among 25-to-29-year-old women, melanoma is more common than any non-skin cancer, including breast and

(50) colon cancer.

When you're young, though, health concerns often take a back seat to more pressing worries, like having a tan for prom. That's how Erika Smith felt. Her grandmother died of melanoma, so Smith knew she was at higher risk for the disease, but that didn't stop her from sunbathing in the backyard of her family's

(55) home north of Seattle or going to the tanning parlor regularly. "I felt invincible," says Smith.

But then melanoma struck her family again. Her uncle's wife died of the disease last year at age 35, and Smith, then 19, was devastated. Because she wasn't a blood relative her risk didn't change, but her perspective did. She went

(60) to the dermatologist, who biopsied a mole on her calf that looked normal but for a tiny black speck on it. Diagnosis: melanoma, at a very early stage. Now she goes to the dermatologist every six months for a full-body skin exam and avoids the sun.

Leffell and other skin cancer experts believe tanning parlors are one of the

(65) major culprits in the rise of skin cancer among young women. A study published in the journal *Pediatrics* in 2002 found that 40 percent of 17- and 18-year-old girls reported visiting a tanning parlor in the past year (compared with just 11 percent of boys in the same age group). Twenty-three states now restrict minors' use of tanning beds in some way, according to the American Academy of Dermatology.

(70) Many states either require parental consent or restrict use to certain age groups. . . .

Even though most sun worshipers no longer aim for the deep, nut-brown tan that was popular in the 1970s, it's still fashionable to get a "healthy" tan in the summer. But there is no such thing, say dermatologists. People tan when the

(75) melanin in their skin darkens to protect it from the sun's rays. "The fact that you're making a tan is a sign that you've had an injury to your skin," says John

Carucci, director of Mohs micrographic and dermatologic surgery for Weill Medical College at Cornell University.

(80) Self-tanners are a safe alternative for people who want a golden glow that doesn't depend on radiation. These products contain a colorless sugar that stains the skin's surface cells darker, although most do not offer any protection from the sun's rays. Self-tanners were the fastest-growing sun care product between 1999 and 2004, according to Euromonitor International, a market research company....

(85) Since most skin cancers, even melanoma, are curable if caught soon enough, early detection is key. Check your own body for new or changing moles, lesions, or other spots on your skin once a month, and visit a dermatologist for a professional skin check annually. Any lesion that changes size, shape, or color, or that begins to itch, doesn't heal, bleeds intermittently, or becomes worse over the (90) course of a month should be examined right away. Shonda Schilling, 38, who has had five melanoma surgeries since 2001 and who founded the Shade Foundation to educate people about skin cancer, says some of her skin lesions didn't look bad at all. "It doesn't have to look nasty to be skin cancer," says Schilling. "If you wait until it's as nasty looking as the pictures in books, it's probably going to kill you."

—Michelle Andrews
excerpted from "Not So Sunny Spots"
U.S. News & World Report, November 14, 2005

TABLE

UV Index Sun Protection

UV (ultraviolet) rays can cause sunburns, eye cataracts, skin aging, and skin cancer. The higher the UV Index number, the stronger the sun's rays, and the greater the need to take precautions. The table below outlines the sun protection actions recommended at different levels of the UV Index.

UV Index	Description	Sun Protection Actions
0–2	Low	• Minimal sun protection required for normal activity • Wear sunglasses on bright days. If outside for more than one hour, cover up and use sunscreen • Reflection off snow can nearly double UV strength. Wear sunglasses and apply sunscreen
3–5	Moderate	• Take precautions – cover up, wear a hat, sunglasses and sunscreen especially if you will be outside for 30 minutes or more • Look for shade near midday when the sun is strongest
6–7	High	• Protection required – UV radiation damages the skin and can cause sunburn • Reduce time in the sun between 11 a.m. and 4 p.m. and take full precautions – seek shade, cover up, wear a hat, sunglasses and sunscreen
8–10	Very High	• Extra precautions required – unprotected skin will be damaged and can burn quickly • Avoid the sun between 11 a.m. and 4 p.m. and take full precautions – seek shade, cover up, wear a hat, sunglasses and sunscreen
11+	Extreme	• Values of 11 or more are very rare in Canada. However, the UV Index can reach 14 or more in the tropics and southern U.S. • Take full precautions. Unprotected skin will be damaged and can burn in minutes. Avoid the sun between 11 a.m. and 4 p.m., cover up, wear a hat, sunglasses and sunscreen • White sand and other bright surfaces reflect UV radiation and increase UV exposure

Source: (adapted) UV Index Program, Environment Canada
www.msc.ec.ca

Multiple-Choice Questions

Directions (7–16): Select the best suggested answer to each question and write its number in the space provided. The questions may help you think about ideas and information you might want to use in your writing. You may return to these questions anytime you wish.

7 According to the article, between 1976 and 2003 the population that experienced a large increase in cases of basal cell skin cancer was

(1) women under 40   (3) women over 40
(2) men under 40   (4) men over 40   7 _____

8 The sun's rays have become more dangerous because of the

(1) ineffective performance of modern sunscreens
(2) rapid increase in ocean temperatures
(3) unpredicted loss of cooling air currents
(4) continued depletion of the ozone layer   8 _____

9 A factor which contributes to an increased risk of people like Erika Smith developing skin cancer is

(1) geographic location   (3) family history
(2) population density   (4) education level   9 _____

10 According to Erika Smith, she engaged in risky behavior following her grandmother's death because she felt

(1) angry   (3) bewildered
(2) untouchable   (4) sad   10 _____

11 According to dermatologists, a tan that is labeled "healthy" (line 73) is actually

(1) preventing cancers   (3) increasing burns
(2) blocking radiation   (4) damaging skin   11 _____

12 According to the article, market researchers have observed a rapid increase in the use of

(1) sunscreens   (3) self-tanners
(2) tanning beds   (4) sunglasses   12 _____

13 According to the article, the cure rate for skin cancers is greatly increased by

(1) early detection
(2) modern medicine
(3) health insurance
(4) educational foundations   13 _____

14 According to the table, besides the skin, ultraviolet rays can cause damage to

(1) nerves   (3) muscles
(2) eyes   (4) bones   14 _____

15 According to the table, the strength of UV radiation can be greatly increased by

(1) wind   (3) mud
(2) rain   (4) snow   15 _____

16 According to the table, when is UV radiation from the sun the strongest?

(1) 9 a.m.   (3) 12 p.m.
(2) 10 a.m.   (4) 5 p.m.   16 _____

After you have finished these questions, review **The Situation** and read **Your Task** and the **Guidelines**. Use scrap paper to plan your response. Then write your response to Part B on separate sheets of paper.

Session Two

Part A

Directions: Read the passages on the following pages (a poem and an excerpt from an autobiography). Write the number of the answer to each multiple-choice question in the space provided. Then write the essay on a separate sheet of paper as described in **Your Task**. You may use the margins to take notes as you read and scrap paper to plan your response.

Your Task:

After you have read the passages and answered the multiple-choice questions, write a unified essay about attitudes toward nature as revealed in the passages. In your essay, use ideas from **both** passages to establish a controlling idea about attitudes toward nature. Using evidence from **each** passage, develop your controlling idea and show how the author uses specific literary elements or techniques to convey that idea.

Guidelines:
Be sure to
- Use ideas from **both** passages to establish a controlling idea about attitudes toward nature
- Use specific and relevant evidence from **each** passage to develop your controlling idea
- Show how each author uses specific literary elements (for example: theme, characterization, structure, point of view) or techniques (for example: symbolism, irony, figurative language) to convey the controlling idea
- Organize your ideas in a logical and coherent manner
- Use language that communicates ideas effectively
- Follow the conventions of standard written English

Passage I

The Trees are Gone

Rebecca Avenue has lost its trees:
the willow that would brush against my window,
and the spruce that cooled our porch out back,
the ginko I would rake in mid-October,
(5) with its matted leaves like Oriental fans.
Even the beech has been cut down,
that iron pillar of my mother's garden,
with its trunk so smooth against one's cheek.

The dirt I dug in has been spread
(10) with blacktop: tar and oil. They've rolled it
blithely over sidewalk slate
where cracks once splintered into island tufts.
Even leafy hills beyond the town
have been developed, as they like to say:
(15) those tinsel woods where I would rinse myself
in drizzle, in the pinwheel fall.

You can stand all day here without knowing
that it once knew trees: green over green
but gamely turning violet at dusk,
(20) then black to blue-vermillion in the dawn.
It's sentimental, but I miss those trees.
I'd like to slip back through the decades
into deep, lush days and lose myself again
in leaves like hands, wet thrash of leaves.

—Jay Parini
from *The Art of Subtraction*, 2005
George Braziller, Inc.

Passage II

The Serengetti Plains spread from Lake Nyaraza, in Tanganyika, northward beyond the lower boundaries of Kenya Colony. They are the great sanctuary of the Masai People and they harbour more wild game than any similar territory in all of East Africa. In the season of drought they are as dry and tawny[1] as the coats
(5) of the lion that prowl them, and during the rains they provide the benison[2] of soft grass to all the animals in a child's picture book.

They are endless and they are empty, but they are as warm with life as the waters of a tropic sea. They are webbed with the paths of eland[3] and wildebeest and Thompson's gazelle and their hollows and valleys are trampled by thousands
(10) of zebra. I have seen a herd of buffalo invade the pastures under the occasional thorn tree groves and, now and then, the whimsically fashioned figure of a plodding rhino has moved along the horizon like a grey boulder come to life and adventure bound. There are no roads. There are no villages, no towns, no telegraph. There is nothing, as far as you can see, or walk, or ride, except grass
(15) and rocks and a few trees and the animals that live there. . . .

From the open cockpit I could see straight ahead, or peer backward and down, past the silver wings. The Serengetti lay beneath me like a bowl whose edges were the ends of the earth. It was a bowl full of hot vapours that rose upward in visible waves and exerted physical pressure against the Avian, lifting
(20) her, as heat from a smouldering fire lifts a flake of ash. . . .

About noon I reached Rothschild's Camp[4] and circled over it. But there was no activity, no life—not even the compact, slow-moving silhouette of a lion. There was nothing but the distinguishing formation of high, grey rocks piled against each other, jutting from the earth like the weather-worn ruins of a desert
(25) cathedral. . . .

But, if there was no smoke to mark the site of a hearthstone or a camp, there were at least other signs of life, not human, but scarcely less welcome for that.

In a hundred places, as far as I could see and in all directions, little puffs of dust sprang suddenly into being, rolled across the plain and disappeared again.
(30) From the air they were like so many jinni[5], each bursting from the confines of his fabulous and bewitched jar to rush off with the wind on the urgent accomplishment of a long-plotted evil deed, or maybe a good one.

---

[1]tawny — a warm sandy color
[2]benison — a blessing
[3]eland — an African antelope
[4]Rothschild's Camp — a camping site for hunters
[5]jinni — genie

But when the dust puffs cleared, I could see that small bands of animals were running this way and that, looking everywhere but upward, trying to escape the
(35) sound of the plane.

Between Magadi and Narok I watched a yellow cloud take shape beneath me and just ahead. The cloud clung close to the earth and grew as I approached it into a swaying billow that blunted the sunlight and obscured the grass and mimosa trees in its path.

(40) Out of its farthest edge the forerunners of a huge herd of impala, wildebeest, and zebra plunged in flight before the shadow of my wings. I circled, throttled down and lost height until my propeller cut into the fringe of the dust, and particles of it burned in my nostrils.

As the herd moved it became a carpet of rust-brown and grey and dull red. It
(45) was not like a herd of cattle or of sheep, because it was wild, and it carried with it the stamp of wilderness and the freedom of a land still more a possession of Nature than of men. To see ten thousand animals untamed and not branded with the symbols of human commerce is like scaling an unconquered mountain for the first time, or like finding a forest without roads or footpaths, or the blemish of an
(50) axe. You know then what you had always been told — that the world once lived and grew without adding machines and newsprint and brick-walled streets and the tyranny of clocks.

In the forefront of the herd I could see impala leaping as they ran, and wildebeest flaunting their brittle horns, or flinging themselves on the ground with
(55) the abandon of mad dervishes. I do not know why they do this, but whether it is a faulty sense of balance or merely a shameless recourse to the melodramatic, the wildebeest, if frightened by a plane, will always react in the manner of the circus clown in his frantic attempts to escape the trained spotted dog around and around the sawdust arena. . . .

—Beryl Markham
excerpted from *West with the Night*, 1942
The Riverside Press

Multiple-Choice Questions

Directions (1–10): Select the best suggested answer to each question and write its number in the space provided. The questions may help you think about the ideas and information you might want to use in your essay. You may return to these questions anytime you wish.

Passage I (the poem) — Questions 1–5 refer to Passage I.

1 The purpose of the poem's first line is to introduce

    (1) an allegory   (3) an allusion

    (2) a setting   (4) a symbol   1 _____

2 In line 5, the leaf shape is described through the use of

    (1) a metaphor   (3) a simile

    (2) apostrophe   (4) onomatopoeia   2 _____

3 The beginning of stanza two suggests that trees have been replaced by

    (1) lawns   (3) water

    (2) flowers   (4) pavement   3 _____

4 The reference to "They've" in line 10 most probably refers to

    (1) construction workers

    (2) neighborhood children

    (3) street cleaners

    (4) town officials   4 _____

5 The description in line 12 suggests an image of

    (1) broken glass   (3) growing grass

    (2) children's games   (4) lonely parks   5 _____

Passage II (the autobiographical excerpt) — Questions 6–10 refer to Passage II.

6 In the first paragraph, the narrator reveals that the Serengetti Plains are dry, but also

(1) settled   (3) solid

(2) abundant   (4) windy   6 _____

7 The phrase "all the animals in a child's picture book" (line 6) emphasizes that these African animals are

(1) familiar   (3) domesticated

(2) young   (4) miniature   7 _____

8 As used in the passage, "the Avian" (line 19) refers to the narrator's location

(1) in a balloon   (3) in a plane

(2) on a hilltop   (4) on a roof   8 _____

9 The appearance of "little puffs of dust" (lines 28 and 29) is the narrator's first glimpse of

(1) fleeing animals   (3) nesting birds

(2) camping hunters   (4) traveling nomads   9 _____

10 According to the narrator, the charging animal that looks the most comical is the

(1) eland   (3) impala

(2) zebra   (4) wildebeest   10 _____

After you have finished these questions, review **Your Task** and the **Guidelines.** Use scrap paper to plan your response. Then write your response to Part A on separate sheets of paper. After you finish your response for Part A, complete Part B.

Part B

Your Task:
Write a critical essay in which you discuss *two* works of literature you have read from the particular perspective of the statement that is provided for you in the **Critical Lens**. In your essay, provide a valid interpretation of the statement, agree *or* disagree with the statement as you have interpreted it, and support your opinion using specific references to appropriate literary elements from the two works. You may use scrap paper to plan your response. Write your essay in Part B on separate sheets of paper.

Critical Lens:

> ". . . it is the human lot to try and fail . . ."
>
> —David Mamet
> "Attention Must Be Paid"
> *The New York Times*, February 13, 2005

Guidelines:
Be sure to
- Provide a valid interpretation of the critical lens that clearly establishes the criteria for analysis
- Indicate whether you agree *or* disagree with the statement as you have interpreted it
- Choose *two* works you have read that you believe best support your opinion
- Use the criteria suggested by the critical lens to analyze the works you have chosen
- Avoid plot summary. Instead, use specific references to appropriate literary elements (for example: theme, characterization, setting, point of view) to develop your analysis
- Organize your ideas in a unified and coherent manner
- Specify the titles and authors of the literature you choose
- Follow the conventions of standard written English

Regents Comprehensive Examination in English—June 2008
Chart for Determining the Final Examination Score (Use for June 2008 examination only.)

To determine the student's final examination score, locate the student's total essay score across the top of the chart and the student's total multiple-choice score down the side of the chart. The point where those two scores intersect is the student's final examination score. For example, a student receiving a total essay score of 16 and a total multiple-choice score of 19 would receive a final examination score of 70.

Total Multiple-Choice Score \ Total Essay Score	0	1	2	3	4	5	6	7	8	9	10	11	12	13	14	15	16	17	18	19	20	21	22	23	24
0	0	1	1	2	2	3	4	6	8	10	13	16	19	23	26	30	33	38	41	45	49	53	57	60	65
1	1	1	2	2	3	3	5	7	9	12	14	18	21	24	28	31	35	39	43	47	51	55	59	62	66
2	1	2	2	3	3	4	6	8	10	13	16	19	23	26	30	33	38	41	45	49	53	57	60	65	66
3	1	2	3	3	4	5	7	9	12	14	18	21	24	28	31	35	39	43	47	51	55	57	60	66	69
4	1	2	3	4	5	6	8	10	13	16	18	21	24	28	31	35	39	43	47	51	55	59	62	69	70
5	2	2	3	5	6	7	9	12	14	18	19	23	26	30	33	38	41	45	49	53	57	60	65	70	72
6	2	3	4	6	7	8	10	13	16	18	21	24	28	31	35	39	43	47	51	55	59	62	66	72	74
7	2	3	5	7	8	9	12	14	18	19	23	26	31	33	38	41	45	49	53	57	60	65	69	74	76
8	2	3	6	7	8	10	13	16	18	21	24	28	31	35	39	43	47	51	55	57	62	66	70	76	77
9	3	3	6	9	10	12	14	18	19	23	26	30	33	38	43	47	49	53	57	60	65	69	74	76	79
10	3	4	8	10	11	13	16	19	23	26	30	33	38	41	45	49	51	57	60	62	66	70	74	79	80
11	3	5	9	11	14	16	18	21	24	28	30	33	38	41	47	51	53	57	60	65	69	72	76	80	82
12	4	6	10	12	13	18	19	23	26	30	33	38	41	45	49	53	57	59	62	66	70	74	77	82	84
13	5	7	12	14	16	19	21	24	28	31	35	38	45	47	51	55	57	60	65	69	72	76	79	84	85
14	6	8	13	16	18	21	23	26	30	33	38	41	45	49	53	57	60	62	66	70	74	77	80	85	86
15	7	9	14	18	19	23	26	30	33	35	41	45	47	51	55	57	60	65	69	72	76	79	82	86	88
16	8	10	16	19	21	24	28	31	35	38	41	45	49	53	55	59	62	66	70	74	77	80	82	88	89
17	9	12	18	21	23	26	30	33	38	41	43	47	51	55	57	60	65	69	72	76	79	82	85	89	90
18	10	13	19	23	26	28	31	35	38	41	45	49	53	57	59	62	66	70	74	77	80	84	86	90	92
19	12	14	21	24	28	30	33	38	41	43	47	51	53	57	60	65	70	72	76	79	82	85	88	92	93
20	13	16	23	26	28	31	35	39	41	45	49	53	57	60	65	66	70	74	77	80	84	86	89	93	94
21	14	18	24	28	31	35	39	43	47	49	53	57	59	62	66	70	74	76	80	84	86	89	92	94	95
22	16	19	26	30	33	38	41	45	49	53	55	59	62	65	69	72	76	79	82	85	88	90	93	95	96
23	18	21	28	31	35	39	43	47	51	53	57	60	65	66	70	74	77	80	84	86	89	92	94	96	97
24	19	23	30	33	38	41	45	49	51	55	59	62	66	69	72	76	79	82	85	88	90	93	95	97	98
25	21	24	31	35	39	43	47	51	53	57	60	65	66	70	74	77	80	84	86	89	92	94	96	98	99
26	23	26	33	38	41	45	49	53	57	60	65	69	72	76	79	82	85	88	90	93	95	97	99	99	100

Answers
June 2008
English

Answer Key

Session One, Part A	Session One, Part B	Session Two, Part A
1. 3	7. 1	1. 2
2. 1	8. 4	2. 3
3. 2	9. 3	3. 4
4. 3	10. 2	4. 1
5. 2	11. 4	5. 3
6. 4	12. 3	6. 2
	13. 1	7. 1
	14. 2	8. 3
	15. 4	9. 1
	16. 3	10. 4

Examination June 2009
English

Session One

Part A

Overview: For this part of the test, you will listen to an account about therapy dogs, answer some multiple-choice questions, and write a response based on the situation described below. You will hear the account twice. You may take notes on the page alloted anytime you wish during the readings.

> **The Situation:** Your health class is exploring community needs. For a class project, you have decided to write a letter to the director of a local long-term care facility to persuade the agency that therapy dogs can be used to benefit the elderly. In preparation for writing your letter, listen to an account by Steve Reiman about therapy dogs in long-term care facilities. Then use relevant information from the account to write your letter.

Your Task: Write a letter to the director of a local long-term care facility in which you persuade the agency that therapy dogs can be used to benefit the elderly. *Write only the body of the letter.*

Guidelines:
Be sure to

- Tell your audience what they need to know about the use of therapy dogs in long-term care facilities and how they can benefit the elderly
- Use specific, accurate, and relevant information from the account to support your argument
- Use a tone and level of language appropriate for a letter to the director of a local long-term health care facility
- Organize your ideas in a logical and coherent manner
- Indicate any words taken directly from the account by using quotation marks or referring to the speaker
- Follow the conventions of standard written English

Note: For this portion of the examination, the teacher will read a passage aloud. You will not actually see the passage reprinted below. Therefore, you are encouraged to have someone read the passage to you, in order to simulate the examination as closely as possible.

Listening Passage

"There is no greater therapy than the love of a dog," the sign above my desk proclaims. This animal/human love bond is demonstrated every day in millions of homes around the world. It is also the basis for what is becoming a powerful, common mode of therapy in many long-term health care facilities.

Animals have long been recognized as being a positive force in the healing process. Dogs have a calming and therapeutic effect. They help people cope with the emotional issues related to their illness. They also offer physical contact with another living creature, something that is often missing in an elder's life. They always invoke pleasant memories of past pets. Best of all, they divert a person's attention from the pressing problems of the day. For long-term elders, it is not so much the stress of daily problems, but the boredom, loneliness, and lack of control. . . .

Dr. Michael McCulloch, a Portland, Oregon, psychiatrist, and Dr. Samuel Corson, of Ohio State University, are two active researchers and experts on why pets excel as therapeutic agents. The primary reasons McCulloch and Corson cite are an individual's "need to be needed," and "to touch and be touched." Further, Dr. McCulloch states, "Touch is one of our primary needs when we're born and one of our last needs to go." In long-term facilities, residents are often sorely lacking the feeling that they are needed. Pets allow them, even if for a short time, to be nurturers once again. Also, in a very real physical sense, residents can stroke their warm, furry visitors, facilitating social behavior and encouraging physical movement.

Dogs love almost everyone without prejudice and they eliminate the language barrier. One nurse made this comment about a resident after a visit with a Therapy Dog, "She is the calmest I have seen her today. The dogs have tremendously reduced her high anxiety level." Dogs, because of their social natures, often genuinely like people and choose to be around them in addition to their owners/handlers. Often, they are aware of illness and sadness and WANT to provide companionship and comfort; they are both intuitive and compassionate. It is always a joy to see them detect sorrow and watch them lick tears away.

Dogs are an antidote to depression—and an easy pill to take. Life in a long-term care facility can be lonely and boring. A visit from a Therapy Dog can break the daily routine and stimulate the mind in dramatic ways. The most serious problem for older adults is not of disease; it's loneliness. Therapy Dogs and their handlers can make a resident come alive, ultimately, inviting residents back to the world outside the facility in which they live. . . .

Therapy Dogs are highly trained working dogs. They must be tested, observed, and certified by a national Therapy Dogs Registry which provides insurance and identification dog tags. I am aware of three registries in the US; Therapy Dogs, Inc., Therapy Dogs International, and the Delta Society. Local registries also exist. All of the registries require a dog to pass a test that verifies it is neither human nor animal aggressive and that the handler is firmly in control. Dogs are screened to make sure they are suitable for the volunteer work that they will perform. The testers are usually certified by letters of recommendation from dog trainers or others who are similarly qualified. Following certification, the handler/canine candidate accompanies an existing team including a certified evaluator to a hospital or nursing home for three to five observed visits. After the tester and observers sign the proper paperwork, the handler can submit an application for membership in a therapy dog organization. . . .

Another way to utilize Therapy Dogs at a facility, a way that is not mutually exclusive from the above method, is to invite members of a Therapy Dog organization to make scheduled visits. I bring my two German Shepherds in to interact with the residents one-on-one in their rooms. I also bring them to the recreation center or living room as a scheduled event. Since some people are afraid of guard dog breeds, I always have mine in costumes. They dress as clowns, or cows, or in outfits related to the season. In hospitals, they dress in hospital scrubs with stethoscopes, masks, and beepers. That alone is enough to get the attention of even those people who aren't fond of dogs. Sadly, my dogs are the only visitors that some people get and they hug and pat and play with them just as if they are family members. . . .

While it may be difficult to quantify the benefits of dog therapy with hard scientific, empirical fact, the magical interaction possible between animal and human can be unmistakable. Tears dry. Frowns transform to smiles. Inactive hands caress soft fur. Silence becomes a conversation of coos whispered in a dog's ear.

Dogs offer themselves to patients with joy, unconditional love, great affection, and boundless patience. They can have a profound ability to touch residents not engaged by other kinds of therapies. Perhaps this is because they offer themselves in a nonthreatening, wordless way that speaks love and attention.

Indeed, there is no greater therapy than the love of a dog.

—excerpted and adapted from "Therapy Dogs in the
Long-Term Health Care Environment"
www.therapydogs.org

NOTES

Multiple-Choice Questions

Directions (1–6): Use your notes to answer the following questions about the passage read to you. Select the best suggested answer and write its number in the space provide. The questions may help you think about ideas and information you might use in your writing. You may return to these questions anytime you wish.

1 According to the speaker, the "work" of therapy dogs involves

(1) detecting illnesses
(2) calming anxious patients
(3) passing out snacks
(4) finding missing medications   1 _____

2 That therapy dogs are "both intuitive and compassionate" explains how they

(1) sense suffering
(2) answer commands
(3) exhibit intelligence
(4) enjoy entertaining   2 _____

3 To qualify as a therapy dog, the animal must be

(1) young and healthy
(2) cute and quiet
(3) non-aggressive and obedient
(4) large and athletic   3 _____

4 Part of the process to become a therapy dog includes

(1) observation at a site
(2) schooling in a kennel
(3) winning of show prizes
(4) certification of a breed   4 _____

5 When on a scheduled visit to a facility, the speaker dresses his German Shepherds in costumes in order to

(1) offer germ protection
(2) relieve the dog's boredom
(3) participate in games
(4) overcome patients' fears   5 ____

6 The account is primarily developed through the use of

(1) chronological order
(2) personal narrative
(3) order of importance
(4) compare and contrast   6 ____

After you have finished these questions, review **The Situation** and read **Your Task** and the **Guidelines**. Use scrap paper to plan your response. Then write your response on separate sheets of paper. After you finish your response for Part A, complete Part B.

PART B

Directions: Read the text and study the table on the following pages, answer the multiple-choice questions, and write a response based on the situation described below. You may use the margins to take notes as you read and scrap paper to plan your response.

> **The Situation:** Your local newspaper is publishing a special edition in honor of Word Environment Day. You have decided to write an article for the publication describing the benefits of using bicycles for commuting and what community leaders need to do to encourage more commuting by bicycle.

Your Task: Using relevant information from **both** documents, write an article for your local newspaper's World Environment Day special edition in which you describe the benefits of using bicycles for commuting and what community leaders need to do to encourage more commuting by bicycle.

Guidelines:
Be sure to
- Tell your audience what they need to know about the benefits of using bicycles for commuting
- Describe what community leaders need to do to encourage more commuting by bicycle
- Use specific, accurate, and relevant information from the text *and* the table to support your description
- Use a tone and level of language appropriate for an article for a local newspaper
- Organize your ideas in a logical and coherent manner
- Indicate any words taken directly from the text by using quotation marks or referring to the author
- Follow the conventions of standard written English

Text

Early in the 20th century, bicycling to do errands or to work was common in the United States, and seeing bikes on racks on the back of streetcars was not unusual. Commuters often used a combination of walking, cycling and taking mass transit. Even in the 1940s, bicycling was still a major means of
(5) transportation for not-too-distant trips. . . .

But that began to change in the 1950s and 60s, when car use rapidly accelerated, fueled by the building of the high-speed Interstate highway system, heavily subsidized through federal funding. Ultimately crisscrossing over 40,000 miles, the new freeways chiseled through cities and towns, sometimes splitting
(10) neighborhoods in two, and created new pathways for development and sprawl far away from urban centers.

Bicycling and walking increasingly took a back seat to driving or riding in cars. By 1990, the Federal Highway Administration called bicycling and walking "the forgotten modes" of transportation.

Rising population has worsened traffic snarls and pollution

(15) But bicycling was not forgotten for long. Over the last five decades, as the U.S. population nearly doubled and development pushed farther and farther from town centers, commutes grew longer, and pollution and traffic congestion worsened. Increasingly, city leaders and urban planners began to see that building more and more roads did little to solve traffic congestion and only
(20) seemed to add to the problems. But offering commuters 'carrots'—more travel choices including 'non-motorized' transportation like bicycling—did prod motorists out of their cars and help alleviate gridlock and traffic jams.

As the merits of bike- and pedestrian-friendly cities began to emerge, federal policies shifted, too. Also in 1990, the Department of Transportation adopted a
(25) new national transportation policy aimed at increasing bicycle use and spurring transportation planners to accommodate cyclists and pedestrians. Federal funding for bicycling and walking projects shot up from $6 million in 1990 to $422 million by 2003. And the 2005 federal transportation bill dedicated $1 billion to bicycling alone.

(30) Today, bicycling as a workhorse means of travel is experiencing a resurgence, thanks in part to our [Environmental Defense] transportation expert Michael Replogle, who has long advocated for more livable cities and increased federal funding for bicycling and walking. People are once again taking bicycling seriously as a welcome transportation alternative. And they are finding more
(35) commuter-friendly bikes. Today's are lightweight and faster than ever and, like best-loved cars, come in a variety of models, styles and colors.

Bicycling to work is healthy for cyclists and the planet

For those who bike to work the payoffs are many: saving money on gas, avoiding traffic, getting exercise, helping curb global warming pollution and often saving time, too. . . .

(40) "Getting more physical activity is key to better health whether or not you're overweight," says Dr. John Balbus, Environmental Defense health program director, medical doctor and an avid bicyclist himself. "Not enough exercise is associated with heart disease and diabetes, as well as depression and certain types of cancer. Pedaling to work 30 minutes a day or even twice a week is a great way

(45) to get more exercise while also helping reduce air pollution."

Physical inactivity is a main culprit for higher rates of cardiovascular disease in developed countries, according to a recent study from the World Health Organization. The study implicates road design and inadequate pedestrian and cycling infrastructure for significant injuries from traffic accidents. The upshot is

(50) that better transportation design and more options for walkers and bikers is a double health benefit.

Moreover, cars in the U.S. contribute a staggering amount of global warming pollution. The U.S. has 30 percent of the world's cars, but they account for 45 percent of automotive carbon dioxide (the main gas that contributes to global

(55) warming). Consider this: If everyone who lives within 5 miles of their workplace were to cycle to work just one day a week and left the car at home, nearly 5 million tons of global warming pollution would be saved every year, the equivalent of taking about a million cars off the road.

Bike paths and secure storage entice people out of their cars

In 2001 and 2002, nearly 2 million Americans cycled to work or used a bike

(60) as part of their job (compared with nearly 10 million who walked to work), according to the Bureau of Transportation. Bicycling trips have doubled since 1990, reported the 2004 [N]ational Bicycling and Walking Study. But in spite of rising numbers of Americans who cycle to work, national polls and surveys indicate that significantly more adults would bike to work if they had safe routes

(65) and secure workplace parking and changing facilities. . . .

Cities and states around the country are making biking safer

As both numbers of bicyclists and bike stations swell, cities and states across the country are devoting more resources to creating more bicycle- and pedestrian-friendly roadways. In mega-states California and Texas—where it's not unusual to hop in your car and drive a few blocks—and in large dense cities

(70) anchored by mass transit networks, planners are working more bike paths, greenways and bike lanes into development blueprints.

For example, in Austin, downtown neighborhoods have long had a network of hike-and-bike trails. There, a new commuter rail line connecting the northern exurbs[1] to the urban center is on track, feasibility studies are underway for biking
(75) and walking trails alongside the route and for parking and locked facilities for bicycles at some stations. Also, statewide plans are afoot to create 200 new miles of scenic and historic bicycle routes.

New York's Mayor Michael Bloomberg has spearheaded an ambitious plan, unveiled in 2002, to ring Manhattan with recreational multiuse paths and
(80) greenways to make the entire waterfront accessible to walkers and cyclists. City Hall recently pledged to improve safety and to add 200 more miles of bicycle lanes throughout the five boroughs. And Chicago's Mayor Daley recently announced his Bike 2015 Plan, which outlines a bevy of projects and policies to promote bicycling in the Windy City over the next decade.

If bicyclists can make it [in] Houston, they can make it anywhere

(85) Even notoriously spread-out Houston, tied with Atlanta as the worst cycling city in North America in Bicycling magazine, has gotten into the act. Mayor Bill White, an avid bicyclist himself, was key in creating the new annual bicycling event Tour de Houston through historic neighborhoods.

"Houston is a big car city, but there is a current [trend] to make it very bike
(90) friendly," says Robin Stallings, the executive director of the Texas Bicycle Coalition. The city now has 277 miles of on-street bikeways (bike lanes, bike routes and shared lanes) and another 13 miles totally off-limits to vehicles. Federal funding to the city has also enabled it to install 100 bike racks at locations such as schools, libraries and parks.

(95) Some cities plagued by poor air quality that falls short of federal health air quality standards, like Houston and Dallas, have tapped federal funds for walking and bicycling projects as one tool to curb air pollution.

Bad news: Even as bike trips grew, car trips grew more

But despite great strides since the 1990s, the picture is not all rosy. Although the number of bicycling trips has increased dramatically in recent years (nearly
(100) doubling from 1.7 billion trips in 1990), the number of driving trips has also exploded (from 249 billion in 1990 to 407 billion in 2001), according to the 2004 National Bicycling and Walking Study. That means that the percentage of bicycle trips of all trips counted by the study, has edged up only slightly, to 0.8, from 0.7. (Counting both biking and walking together, the percentage went up to
(105) 9.5 percent, from 7.9 percent.)

---

[1]exurbs — regions lying beyond the suburbs of a city

"It's not surprising that the share of walking and cycling trips has barely budged in relation to driving," says Replogle. "As a nation, we've designed most communities with unwalkable roads and with little thought to land use patterns and connectivity between jobs and homes. The good news is that the progress
(110) we've made on the funding front has begun to address the lack of cycling and walking options in communities.

"For a half a century, the Department of Transportation was throwing huge amounts of money to subsidizing roadways and sprawl while underfunding walking, cycling and public transportation—and it's going to take us many years
(115) to restore transportation choices and provide safe walking and cycling routes to schools and employment."

—Environmental Defense Fund
excerpted from "Bicycle Commuting Enjoys a Rebirth"
www.environmentaldefense.org, September 14, 2006

TABLE

Comparison of Characteristics and Impact of Modes of Urban Transportation*

Mode of Transportation	Bicycle	Subway or elevated rail	Bus on regular road lane	Private car
Characteristics of Mode of Transportation				
Range of distances traveled	2–5 km**	5–25 km	5–15 km	6–30 km
Average speeds per hour	8–15 km/h***	30–45 km/h	12–20 km/h	15–35 km/h
Access to city centers of activity	very high	very high	medium	very low
Availability to people of diverse ages, physical conditions and economic levels	very high	low to medium	medium	very low
Compatible with livable city streets used for business, socialization and recreation	very high	medium	low to medium	very low
Compatible with diverse transport modes sharing use of streets, rails, bridges, etc.	very high	low	medium to high	very low
Impacts of Mode of Transportation				
Cost for users, public and private sectors	very low	very high	medium	very high
Space consumed for motion and parking	low	low	medium	very high
Impact on local environment: air, noise, water pollution and nuisance	very low	low	high	very high
Impact on global environment: resource use, contribution to climate change	very low	low	medium	very high
Danger imposed on vulnerable road users	very low	low	medium	very high

*Data based on analysis of Asian city transportation.
**km — kilometer .62 mile
***km/h — kilometers per hour

Source (adapted) Paul Barter and Tamin Raad,
*Taking Steps: A Community Action Guide to People—
Centered, Equitable and Sustainable Urban Transport*,
www.geocities.com/March 2000

Multiple-Choice Questions

Directions (7–16): Select the best suggested answer to each question and write its number in the space provided. The questions may help you think about ideas and information you might want to use in your writing. You may return to these questions anytime you wish.

7 According to the article, bicycles were a major mode of transportation in the United States until about

(1) 1900   (3) 1950

(2) 1940   (4) 1990   7 _____

8 The decline in bicycle use for commuting was largely due to the development of

(1) highways   (3) skyscrapers

(2) subways   (4) teleconferencing   8 _____

9 In line 20, the phrase "offering commuters 'carrots'" most nearly implies

(1) continuing construction
(2) using incentives
(3) collecting opinions
(4) funding legislation   9 _____

10 According to the article, in 2005, federal funding for development of bike paths increased to

(1) $1 billion   (3) $6 million

(2) $5 billion   (4) $422 million   10 _____

11 In lines 37 through 45, the article implies that an increased use of bicycles for commuting would lead to

(1) more traffic accidents
(2) lessened job productivity
(3) increased global warming
(4) fewer heart attacks   11 ____

12 According to the article, the United States is responsible for nearly half of the world's

(1) traffic accidents
(2) automotive pollution
(3) bicycle manufacture
(4) oil depletion   12 ____

13 According to the article, Austin, Houston, and New York City have allocated funding for and begun to

(1) construct car-free zones
(2) repair roadways
(3) improve housing
(4) develop subway systems   13 ____

14 The table specifies that one way to create livable city streets is to

(1) build wider roads
(2) encourage street vendors
(3) limit automobile access
(4) provide better parking   14 ____

15 According to the table, the mode of transport causing the most urban pollution is the

(1) bicycle   (3) subway
(2) car   (4) bus   15 ____

16 Compared with other modes of transportation presented in the table, bicycling is more

(1) dangerous for other commuters
(2) practical for long distances
(3) harmful for the environment
(4) available for all people   16 _____

After you have finished these questions, review **The
Situation** and read **Your Task** and the **Guidelines.**
Use scrap paper to plan your response. Then write
your response to Part B on separate sheets of paper.

Session Two

Part A

Directions: Read the passages on the following pages (an excerpt from a novel and a poem). Write the number of the answer to each multiple-choice question in the space provided. Then write the essay on a separate sheet of paper as described in **Your Task**. You may use the margins to take notes as you read and scrap paper to plan your response.

Your Task:

> After you have read the passages and answered the multiple-choice questions, write a unified essay about childhood memories as revealed in the passages. In your essay, use ideas from **both** passages to establish a controlling idea about childhood memories. Using evidence from **each** passage, develop your controlling idea and show how the author uses specific literary elements or techniques to convey that idea.

Guidelines:

Be sure to

- Use ideas from **both** passages to establish a controlling idea about childhood memories
- Use specific and relevant evidence from **each** passage to develop your controlling idea
- Show how each author uses specific literary elements (for example: theme, characterization, structure, point of view) or techniques (for example: symbolism, irony, figurative language) to convey the controlling idea
- Organize your ideas in a logical and coherent manner
- Use language that communicates ideas effectively
- Follow the conventions of standard written English

Passage I

At first I used to dream of Mai Ling every night. I know that I dreamed about her and that it was her, it was Mai Ling, with her almond eyes in her pale face, her plait[1] hanging before her as she bent over me, and her smile. Above all it was her smile that I used to see, and her bending over me and talking to me. I
(5) would try to answer her; I would search for the right words, flounder about in the dream and yearn to speak but, try as I might, no sound would come from my throat. It was as though something prevented me from speaking. Then she would disappear, her eyes would disappear little by little, and so too would the half-loosened plait hanging before her as she leant forwards, until in the end only
(10) her smile remained, just that, a smile without those almond eyes and that pale face bent over me. Then that too dissolved into the darkness. And I would wake up.

It took me a while to realize where I was. My eyes searched instinctively for the brazier[2] in the centre of the yurt,[3] where the dried dung[4] had become a dark
(15) powder. During the winter nights, when the cold threatened our warmth, Mai Ling would get up from time to time to add more dung; as she did so the brazier would emit a startling flash of light, the wooden lattice of the yurt seemed to come alive and the crimson of the carpets ignited for an instant, then fell swiftly into shadow again as the flame died down into the bottom of the pan. Then the
(20) air filled with that sharp smell I knew well, a mixture of burnt hay and earth, and with the thin smoke which caught in the throats of guests who weren't used to living as we did and made them cough. I looked for the gleam of the little oil lamp in front of the image of the Padma Sambhava,[5] a glimmer which barely lit the lotus petals of the pedestal, the crossed legs and the fingers brushing the
(25) ground, while the torso, arms and ears down to the shoulders could dimly be made out through the darkness, as could the gilt which covered them. The lacquered cabinet in which the women kept their jewels and the few documents we had was itself red and gold, while the rugs draped on the rush walls and the fringed door were a glowing crimson, so that even the shadow inside the yurt
(30) seemed to have absorbed the reddish hues. And in the morning, when the first rays settled on the ceremonial saddle hanging on the wall, reflecting off its trim, its brass stirrups and its silk, the whole yurt seemed to fill with gold. In the

---

[1]plait—braid
[2]brazier—a pan for holding burning fuel/coals
[3]yurt—a circular domed tent used by Mongol nomads
[4]dung—dried manure used for fuel
[5]Padma Sambhava—a religious icon

evenings, lying in the place reserved for the youngest children, my eyes followed the winding of the carpets, the curve of deer horns and the course of a stream

(35) woven in a brighter thread. All around, everybody slept on their felt mattresses in their assigned place, the men on the right, on the left my cousins Haysce, Yesügen and Yesü, and my aunt Qada'an with her youngest son, Temüjin, who had not yet been weaned. In the winter, we put a small pen near the entrance of the yurt; the new-born animals slept with us, safe from the cold and the wolves.

(40) From time to time I would reach out an arm, slip it between the bars of the pen and touch the soft, silken coat of a new-born lamb. I would stroke the animal's warm body, feel it rise and fall, uncertain whether or not to trust the hand which fondled it. I was reassured by the breathing of all those bodies. Even though outside the wind blew and the dogs howled restlessly, the shadowy yurt was full

(45) of familiar presences and I soon closed my eyes. . . .

—Silvia Di Natale
excerpted from *Kuraj*, 2000
Bloomsbury Publishing

Passage II

Ironing Their Clothes

With a hot glide up, then down, his shirts,
I ironed out my father's back, cramped
and worried with work. I stroked the yoke,
and breast pocket, collar and cuffs,
(5) until the rumpled heap relaxed into the shape
of my father's broad chest, the shoulders shrugged off
the world, the collapsed arms spread for a hug.
And if there'd been a face above the buttondown neck,
I would have pressed the forehead out, I would
(10) have made a boy again out of that tired man!

If I clung to her skirt as she sorted the wash
or put out a line, my mother frowned,
a crease down each side of her mouth.
This is no time for love! But here
(15) I could linger over her wrinkled bedjacket,
kiss at the damp puckers of her wrists
with the hot tip. Here I caressed complications
of darts, scallops, ties, pleats which made
her outfits test of the patience of my passion.
(20) Here I could lay my dreaming iron on her lap

The smell of baked cotton rose from the board
and blew with a breeze out the window
to a family wardrobe drying on the clothesline,
all needing a touch of my iron. Here I could tickle
(25) the underarms of my big sister's petticoat
or secretly pat backside of her pyjamas.
For she too would have warned me not to muss
her fresh blouses, starched jumpers, and smocks,
All that my careful hand had ironed out,
(30) forced to express my excess love on cloth.

—Julia Alvarez
from *The Renewal of The Vision:*
Voices of Latin American
Women Poets 1940–80, 1987
Spectacular Diseases

Multiple-Choice Questions

Directions (1–10): Select the best suggested answer to each question and write its number in the space provide. The questions may help you think about the ideas and information you might want to use in your essay. You may return to these questions anytime you wish.

Passage I (the novel excerpt)—Questions 1–7 refer to Passage I.

1 According to the narrator, Mai Ling's responsibility was to

  (1) keep the yurt warm
  (2) attend to guests' needs
  (3) teach the children manners
  (4) protect the family's valuables   1 _____

2 The narrator most probably views Mai Ling as a

  (1) teacher   (3) playmate
  (2) tribal leader   (4) mother figure   2 _____

3 The narrator's memories of the yurt are strengthened through

  (1) youthful games   (3) old pictures
  (2) sensory impressions   (4) family stories   3 _____

4 According to the text, one feature of the narrator's culture was

  (1) land ownership   (3) extended families
  (2) vegetarian foods   (4) sign language   4 _____

5 The "new-born lamb" (line 41) and the narrator are similar in that both need

  (1) solitude   (3) exercise
  (2) grooming   (4) protection   5 _____

6 The narrator viewed the atmosphere in the yurt as

   (1) educational   (3) comforting

   (2) unhealthy   (4) crowded   6 _____

7 The narrator's story is told primarily through

   (1) contrast   (3) simile

   (2) flashback   (4) analogy   7 _____

Passage II (the poem)—Questions 8–10 refer to Passage II.

8 Lines 8 through 10 suggest that the narrator

   (1) sympathizes with the father

   (2) respects the father's work

   (3) resents ironing the father's shirts

   (4) believes the father is sick   8 _____

9 The ironing of the "wrinkled bedjacket" (line 15) represents the narrator's

   (1) desire to grow up

   (2) love for the mother

   (3) search for friendship

   (4) frustration with the task   9 _____

10 The narrator recalls that her big sister was concerned about the

   (1) smells of baking

   (2) amount of laundry

   (3) obedience of her siblings

   (4) looks of her clothes   10 _____

After you have finished these questions, review **Your Task** and the **Guidelines**. Use scrap paper to plan your response. Then write your response to Part A on separate sheets of paper. After you finish your response for Part A, complete Part B.

Part B

Your Task:

Write a critical essay in which you discuss **two** works of literature you have read from the particular perspective of the statement that is provided for you in the **Critical Lens**. In your essay, provide a valid interpretation of the statement, agree **or** disagree with the statement as you have interpreted it, and support your opinion using specific references to appropriate literary elements from the two works. Your may use scrap paper to plan your response. Write your essay in Part B on separate sheets of paper.

Critical Lens:

> ". . . the strongest man upon earth is he who stands most alone."
>
> —Henrik Ibsen
> "An Enemy of the People"
> from *Ghosts: An Enemy of the People: The Wild Duck*, 1890

Guidelines:
Be sure to
- Provide a valid interpretation of the critical lens that clearly establishes the criteria for analysis
- Indicate whether you agree **or** disagree with the statement as you have interpreted it
- Choose **two** works you have read that you believe best support your opinion
- Use the criteria suggested by the critical lens so analyze the works you have chosen
- Avoid plot summary. Instead, use specific references to appropriate literary elements (for example: theme, characterization, setting, point of view) to develop your analysis
- Organize your ideas in a unified and coherent manner
- Specify the titles and authors of the literature you choose
- Follow the conventions of standard written English

Regents Comprehensive Examination in English—June 2009

Chart for Determining the Final Examination Score (Use for June 2009 examination only.)

To determine the student's final examination score, locate the student's total essay score across the top of the chart and the student's total multiple-choice score down the side of the chart. The point where those two scores intersect is the student's final examination score. For example, a student receiving a total essay score of 16 and a total multiple-choice score of 19 would receive a final examination score of 70.

Total Essay Score →

Total Multiple-Choice Score ↓	0	1	2	3	4	5	6	7	8	9	10	11	12	13	14	15	16	17	18	19	20	21	22	23	24
0	0	1	2	2	3	4	5	7	9	11	14	17	20	23	27	30	34	38	41	45	49	53	57	61	65
1	1	1	2	3	3	4	6	8	10	13	15	18	21	24	29	32	36	40	43	47	51	55	59	63	67
2	1	2	2	3	4	5	7	9	11	14	17	20	23	27	30	34	38	41	45	49	53	57	61	65	69
3	1	2	3	3	4	6	8	10	13	15	18	21	24	29	32	36	40	43	47	51	55	59	63	67	70
4	2	2	3	4	5	7	9	11	14	17	20	23	27	30	34	38	41	45	49	53	57	61	65	69	72
5	2	3	3	4	6	8	10	13	15	18	21	24	29	32	36	40	43	47	51	55	59	63	67	70	74
6	2	3	4	5	7	9	11	14	17	20	23	27	30	34	38	41	45	49	53	57	61	65	69	72	76
7	3	3	4	6	8	10	13	15	18	21	24	29	32	36	40	43	47	51	55	59	63	67	70	74	77
8	3	4	5	7	9	11	14	17	20	23	27	30	34	38	41	45	49	53	57	61	65	69	72	76	79
9	3	4	6	8	10	13	15	18	21	24	29	32	36	40	43	47	51	55	59	63	67	70	74	77	80
10	4	5	7	9	11	14	17	20	23	27	30	34	38	41	45	49	53	57	61	65	69	72	76	79	82
11	4	6	8	10	13	15	18	21	24	29	32	36	40	43	47	51	55	59	63	67	70	74	77	80	84
12	5	7	9	11	14	17	20	23	27	30	34	38	41	45	49	53	57	61	65	69	72	76	79	82	85
13	6	8	10	13	15	18	21	24	29	32	36	40	43	47	51	55	59	63	67	70	74	77	80	84	86
14	7	9	11	14	17	20	23	27	30	34	38	41	45	49	53	57	61	65	69	72	76	79	82	85	88
15	8	10	13	15	18	21	24	29	32	36	40	43	47	51	55	59	63	67	70	74	77	80	84	86	89
16	9	11	14	17	20	23	27	30	34	38	41	45	49	53	57	61	65	69	72	76	79	82	85	88	90
17	10	13	15	18	21	24	29	32	36	40	43	47	51	55	59	63	67	70	74	77	80	84	86	89	92
18	11	14	17	20	23	27	30	34	38	41	45	49	53	57	61	65	69	72	76	79	82	85	88	90	93
19	13	15	18	21	24	29	32	36	40	43	47	51	55	59	63	67	70	74	77	80	84	86	89	92	94
20	14	17	20	23	27	30	34	38	41	45	49	53	57	61	65	69	72	76	79	82	85	88	90	93	95
21	15	18	21	24	29	32	36	40	43	47	51	55	59	63	67	70	74	77	80	84	86	89	92	94	96
22	17	20	23	27	30	34	38	41	45	49	53	57	61	65	69	72	76	79	82	85	88	90	93	95	97
23	18	21	24	29	32	36	40	43	47	51	55	59	63	67	70	74	77	80	84	86	89	92	94	96	98
24	20	23	27	30	34	38	41	45	49	53	57	61	65	69	72	76	79	82	85	88	90	93	95	97	99
25	21	24	29	32	36	40	43	47	51	55	59	63	67	70	74	77	80	84	86	89	92	94	96	98	99
26	23	27	30	34	38	41	45	49	53	57	61	65	69	72	76	79	82	85	88	90	93	95	97	99	100

Answers
June 2009
English

Answer Key

Session One, Part A	Session One, Part B	Session Two, Part A
1. **2**	7. **3**	1. **1**
2. **1**	8. **1**	2. **4**
3. **3**	9. **2**	3. **2**
4. **1**	10. **1**	4. **3**
5. **4**	11. **4**	5. **4**
6. **2**	12. **2**	6. **3**
	13. **1**	7. **2**
	14. **3**	8. **1**
	15. **2**	9. **2**
	16. **4**	10. **4**

INDEX